COOKING IN
# AMERICA, 1840–1945

# COOKING IN
# AMERICA,
# 1840–1945

### Alice L. McLean

*The Greenwood Press "Daily Life Through History" Series*

*Cooking Up History*
*Ken Albala, Series Editor*

Greenwood Press
Westport, Connecticut • London

**Library of Congress Cataloging-in-Publication Data**

McLean, Alice L.
  Cooking in America, 1840–1945/Alice L. McLean.
      p. cm.—(The Greenwood Press "Daily life through history" series. Cooking up history,
ISSN 1080–4749)
  Includes bibliographical references and index.
  ISBN 0–313–33574–5
  1. Cookery, American—History. 2. Food habits—United States—History. I. Title.
  II. Series.
  TX715.M47445 2006
  394.1'2097309034—dc22      2006015691

British Library Cataloguing in Publication Data is available.

Library of Congress Catalog Card Number: 2006015691
ISBN: 0–313–33574–5
ISSN: 1080–4749

First published in 2006

Greenwood Press, 88 Post Road West, Westport, CT 06881
An imprint of Greenwood Publishing Group, Inc.
www.greenwood.com

Printed in the United States of America

The paper used in this book complies with the
Permanent Paper Standard issued by the National
Information Standards Organization (Z39.48–1984).

10  9  8  7  6  5  4  3  2  1

**Copyright Acknowledgments**

The author and publisher gratefully acknowledge permission for use of the following material:

Illustrations by Lisa Cooperman.

The publisher has done its best to make sure the instructions and/or recipes in this book are
correct. However, users should apply judgment and experience when preparing recipes, especially parents and teachers working with young people. The publisher accepts no responsibility
for the outcome of any recipe included in this volume.

# ✍ CONTENTS

# 🦅 LIST OF RECIPES

## Bread and Biscuits

## Pastry, Pies, Puddings, Dumplings, and Fritters

### Savory Pastry

### Savory Pies

### Sweet Pastry

### Puddings

### Dumplings and Fritters

## Cakes, Cookies, Custards, and Creams

*Cakes and Cookies*

*Custards and Creams*

## Preserves

## 2. 1876–1910

## Soups, Chowders, and Stews

## Meat

## Seafood

## Gravies, Sauces, Catsups, and Pickles

## Vegetables, Salads, and Salad Dressings

### *Vegetables*

### *Salads*

### *Salad Dressings*

## Eggs, Rice, Pasta, and Sundry Other Dishes

## Bread and Biscuits

## Pies and Puddings

## Cakes, Cookies, Custards, and Creams

### Cakes and Cookies

### Custards and Creams

## 3. 1911–1945

### Soups, Chowders, and Stews

### Meat

## Eggs, Rice, Pasta, and Sundry Other Dishes

## Bread and Biscuits

## Pies and Puddings

## Cakes, Cookies, Custards, and Creams

## Preserves

# ꙮ GLOSSARY

**BAIN-MARIE:** A French term for a "water bath." The ingredients to be cooked are placed in a container, which, in turn, is placed in a larger container filled with water. This contraption is then heated in the oven or directly on the stove, and the heated water gently cooks the ingredients. A double boiler is, in effect, a stovetop bain-marie. Delicate custards and sauces are cooked in a bain-marie to keep them from curdling or separating, which happens far more frequently with direct heat.

**CAPON:** A castrated, fattened, young rooster.

**CLARET:** Red wine.

**COCHINEAL:** A red dye made from the dried, ground bodies of the female cochineal insect.

**COLLOP:** A small slice or piece of meat.

**CYMLINGS:** Summer squash. Also known as pattypan or scalloped squash.

**DREDGE:** To lightly coat food with flour, meal, or breadcrumbs before frying.

**DRIPPINGS:** The melted fat and juice that drip during the cooking of meat.

**FILÉ:** A powder made from the dried, ground leaves of the sassafras tree, which is used as a thickener.

**FORCEMEAT:** Finely ground meat, poultry, fish or vegetables mixed with breadcrumbs and seasonings. Forcemeat can be mixed with egg, shaped into ovals or balls, and fried in oil or poached in liquid; forcemeat balls are often poached in soups. Forcemeat is also frequently stuffed into other foods, such as a turkey or other fowl, before they are cooked.

**GRAHAM FLOUR:** Whole wheat flour, so named because the health reformer Sylvester Graham fought so hard to educate the American public about the benefits of eating whole, as opposed to refined, wheat.

**ISINGLASS:** A form of gelatin that comes from the air bladders of fish.

**LAWN SIEVE:** A fine sieve made of lawn (a sheer linen or cotton fabric) or silk.

**MACE:** The outer membrane of the nutmeg seed, which is dried, ground, and used to flavor sweet and savory dishes.

**MAÎTRE d'HÔTEL SAUCE:** Made from butter, lemon or vinegar, and parsley, this sauce is served with fish.

**MULLIGAN:** A catch-all stew, often containing meat, potatoes, and a combination of other vegetables.

**PAPILLOTE:** A dish cooked en papillote is baked in parchment paper. The paper seals in the moisture.

**PARCHMENT PAPER:** Moisture-resistant cooking paper used to line baking molds and tins and to enclose savory dishes when baked, a method known as en papillote. The moisture expelled during baking cannot escape through the parchment if properly sealed.

**PATTYPANS:** Small tin pans in which pies, cakes, or pastries are baked.

**PLANK COOKERY:** A method of cooking passed down from the Native Americans in which meat, fish, or vegetables are broiled or baked on a fragrant piece of wood. The heated wood, in turn, imparts flavor.

**QUEEN'S-WARE:** A type of stone or ceramic ware.

**RICER:** A large metal gadget through which potatoes are pressed. As they pass through tiny holes, they come out the other side in a form resembling rice. A ricer produces a smoother end product than a fork or a potato masher.

**ROUX:** A mixture of flour cooked in fat, which is used to thicken soups and sauces.

**SAGO:** A starch thickener extracted from palms. It is available in flour, meal, and pearl form. The latter resembles tapioca.

**SALAMANDER:** An instrument used to brown the top of foods, a salamander consists of a long handle with an iron disc on the end. The disc is heated in the flames of a hearth or stovetop burner and then placed a hair's breadth above the food to be browned.

**SALERATUS:** Soda bicarbonate, a leavening agent used to make baked goods rise. During the mid-nineteenth century it might refer to leavening agents such as potassium bicarbonate or sodium bicarbonate (now known as baking soda).

**SALTPETER:** Sodium nitrate, a crystallized salt used in curing meat.

**SANDERS:** Red dye made from sandalwood.

**SAVORY [SAVOURY]:** An herb related to the mint family, having a strong aroma and flavor.

**SCALLOP:** A thin, boneless slice of meat.

**SCUM:** The extraneous matter that rises to the surface of a cooking liquid to form a film. It is usually skimmed, or removed, from the surface.

**SPATCHCOCK:** To split a bird down the back, spread it flat, and grill it.

**STANDING PASTE:** A pastry sturdy enough to retain a heavy, juicy filling.

**SUET:** Fat that surrounds the kidneys and loins of beef and mutton.

**SWEETBREADS:** The thymus glands of veal, beef, lamb, or pork.

**TAMARIND:** A fruit with a pulp, which when dried gives off a sour flavor. An essential ingredient in much Indian and Middle Eastern cuisine, it is often used like lemon. Tamarind is a standard ingredient in Worcestershire sauce and chutney.

**TAMMY:** A cloth used as a strainer.

# ℐ SERIES FOREWORD

*The beasts have memory, judgment and all the faculties and passions of our mind, in a certain degree; but no beast is a cook.*

This quip by the eighteenth-century Scottish biographer James Boswell defines the essence of humanity in a way his contemporaries would have found humorous but also thought provoking. It is neither an immortal soul, reason, nor powers of abstraction that separate us from animals but the simple ability to use fire to transform our daily fare into something more palatable and nutritious. We are nothing more than cooking animals. Archaeological evidence bears this out; it is our distant Neanderthal relatives, whose sites offer the earliest incontrovertible evidence of cooking. From those distant times down to the present, the food we eat and how it is prepared have become the decisive factors in the survival of both individuals and whole civilizations, so what better way to approach the subject of history than through the bubbling cauldron?

Growing and preparing food has also been the occupation of the vast majority of men and women who ever lived. To understand ourselves, we should naturally begin with the food that constitutes the fabric of our existence. Yet every culture arrives at different solutions, uses different crops and cooking methods, and invents what amount to unique cuisines. These are to some extent predetermined by geography, technology, and a certain amount of luck. Nonetheless every cuisine is a practical and artistic expression of the culture that created it. It embodies the values and aspirations of each society, its world outlook as well as its history.

This series examines cooking as an integral part of important epochs in history, both as a way to examine daily life for women and men who cooked, and as a way to explore the experiences of people who ate what was served. Cookbooks are thus treated here as primary source documents that students can interpret just as they might a legal text, literary or artistic work, or any other historical evidence. Through them we are afforded a glimpse, sometimes of what transpired in the great halls of the powerful, but also of what took place in more modest households. Unlike most forms of material culture, we can also re-create these dishes today to get an immediate and firsthand experience of the food that people in the past relished. I heartily encourage you to taste the past in these recipes, keeping in mind good taste is not universal and some things are simply impossible to make today. But a good number of dishes, I assure you, will both surprise and delight.

We begin the series with six volumes stretching from ancient times to the twentieth century, including European and American regions, written by experts in culinary history who have done a superb job of interpreting the historical texts while remaining faithful to their integrity. Each volume is designed to appeal to the novice cook, with technical and historical terms amply defined, and timely advice proffered for the adventurous time traveler in the kitchen. I hope your foray into the foods of the past is nothing less than an absolute delight.

*Ken Albala*
*University of the Pacific*

# ✐ INTRODUCTION

This cookbook covers the years 1840 through 1945, a time during which American cookery underwent a full-scale revolution. Gas and electric stoves replaced hearth cookery. The time of year and location became decreasingly connected to the ingredients used in home cooking; canned, bottled, and eventually frozen products flooded the market, and trains began to transport produce and meat from one end of the country to the other. During two World Wars and the Great Depression women entered the workforce in unprecedented numbers, and household servants abandoned low-paying domestic jobs to work in factories. As a result of these monumental changes, American home cooking became irrevocably simplified, and cookery skills geared more toward juggling time to comb grocery store shelves for the best and most economical products than toward butchering and preserving an entire animal carcass or pickling fruits and vegetables.

The following collection of recipes reflects these changes, with each of the three chapters capturing the home cooking that typified the era. The first chapter covers the preindustrial period 1840 to 1875. During this time, home cooks knew how to broil, roast, grill, fry, and boil on an open hearth flame. They also handled whole sheep carcasses, made gelatin from boiled pigs trotters, grew their own yeast, and prepared their own preserves. Visitors to the United States frequently commented on the abundance and variety of available foods. They also commented on the enormous quantities served to and eaten by Americans. The flesh of game and domestic animals and birds abounded, as did many spices that virtually disappeared from the mainstream mid-twentieth-century kitchen. Because of the large amount of meat eaten in relation to vegetables, dyspepsia (a general term used for a range of gastrointestinal disorders) became a national curse. In response, nutritional experts, much like their contemporaries today, encouraged Americans to eat less meat and consume more vegetables and whole grains. Beginning as far back as the 1830s, American health reformers, such as Sylvester Graham, advocated vegetarianism. His message became so widespread that recipes for Graham (also known as dyspepsia) bread abounded; these loaves are still common today, although they are better known as whole grain or whole wheat.

The second chapter covers 1876 through 1910, a time when rapid urbanization transformed the United States from an agrarian society into an industrial giant, giving rise to food corporations such as Armour, Swift, Campbell's, Heinz, and Pillsbury. The mass production and mass marketing of commercial foods began to transform home cooking; meat could be purchased from a local butcher or grocery store and commercial gelatin became widely available. Although many cooks still made their own pickles and preserves, commercial varieties multiplied. Crops grown on one side of the country could now be shipped across the nation, leading to the development of new types of produce, such as iceberg lettuce, that could withstand rougher treatment than traditional varieties. As a result, home cooks became less dependent on the season and the region where they lived. East Coast cooks could buy West Coast vegetables and vice versa, and in landlocked regions one could enjoy fish caught in the Atlantic and the Pacific Oceans.

From 1910 to 1945, the period covered by Chapter 3, the home cook became a full-fledged consumer and the national food supply became standardized to a large extent. A select number of brands and cultivars began to dominate the nation's grocery store aisles and produce stands. The consumption of dairy almost doubled during this period. This increase resulted from the boom in commercial production and also from the growing accessibility of refrigeration. As the industrialization of the American food supply progressed, commercially produced breads, pastries, sauces, pickles, and preserves began to take over kitchen cupboards. Twentieth-century recipes increasingly relied on commercial products, such as canned soups, vegetables, and fruits. Meals also became far more simple and the number of courses declined, as servants began to disappear from middle-class homes. By the 1930s a soup, casserole, and fruit pie could serve as dinner instead of the elaborate array of soup, fish, roast meat, vegetable, side, and dessert dishes that typified the nineteenth-century middle-class table. Simultaneously, ethnic influences expanded the flavors of the mainstream American melting pot to include such ingredients as bean sprouts, avocados, paprika, spaghetti, olives, and olive oil.

## RECIPE SELECTION

The recipes have been culled from some of the most popular commercial and community cookbooks of the nineteenth and early twentieth centuries; a modest number of recipes have been collected from popular ladies' magazines, city newspapers, and unpublished family recipe collections. Taken together, the recipes reflect the major cookbook trends of the era. The first section includes recipes from three of the earliest American cookbooks: Mary Randolph's *The Virginia Housewife*; Eliza Leslie's *Directions for Cookery*; and Lydia Maria Child's *Frugal Housewife*. Chapter 2 reflects the rise of community cookbooks, including recipes from such classic regional collections as *The Buckeye, The Settlement,* and *The First Texas* cookbooks. It also includes recipes from the first known cookbook written by an African American, *What Mrs. Fisher Knows About Old Southern Cooking,* and the first cookbook written by an Hispanic in the United States *Encarnacion's Kitchen: Mexican Recipes from Nineteenth-Century California*. Reflecting the increase in male-authored home cookbooks, Chapter 3 includes recipes from such classics as Frank Shay's *The Best Men Are Cooks* and John MacPherson's *The Mystery Chef's Own Cook Book*. Chapter 3 also bears witness to the deprivations exacted by two World Wars and the Great Depression, including recipes from *Thrifty Cooking for Wartime*.

These collected recipes also reflect U.S. immigration, migration, and settlement patterns. The nineteenth-century American table was predominantly influenced by British and Western European cuisines along with West African culinary techniques, ingredients, and dishes. These latter not only influenced the slave diet but also that of the slave owners, whose food was gathered and prepared by African slave cooks. A vast number of immigrants arrived in the mid to late 1800s from Eastern and Southern Europe, Scandinavia, and China. The assimilation of the culinary influence of these immigrant groups varied. For example, the majority of the Chinese who immigrated to the West to work on the Transcontinental railroad arrived in the late 1840s and 1850s; however, Chinese American dishes did not make their way into cookbooks until the twentieth century. The culinary impact of many groups, however, was disseminated more quickly; the large wave of Italian immigration in the early 1900s had affected mainstream American cooking by the 1930s, in part, because Italians gravitated toward food industry jobs, often becoming waiters or cooks.

In addition to reflecting ethnic influences, these recipes also illustrate the lifestyle changes that accompanied industrialization. In particular, the shift of working classes from domestic service into factory jobs left many middle-class housewives in charge of meal preparation for the first time; previously they had been responsible for deciding the daily menu, overseeing the kitchen labor, and managing the particulars of dinner service. Now they were in charge of the hands-on cooking, a task many had little experience performing. To aid the novice cook, recipe authors began to provide the sort of detail previously unnecessary. By the 1930s, some recipe authors went as far as to specify that the reader should open a can before pouring its contents into a pot.

Not only does the detail included in recipes change over the course of the century, but so too do the types of recipes included in cookbooks. As a result, some of the recipe categories included here would not be found in most contemporary cookbooks. For example, the inclusion of sections on game, pickles, and ketchups are unusual by today's standards, although they were commonly found in most nineteenth-century cookbooks. The number of recipes included in each section also roughly reflects the emphasis cookbooks of a given time period typically devote to a category. For example, nineteenth-century cookbooks often include a large section on pickling and might devote over half their pages to breads and sweets. The emphasis placed on these categories decreases in the twentieth-century because home cooks have less time and skill to devote to time-consuming or elaborate recipes. As a result, these sections will be considerably shorter in the last chapter.

As time-consuming and elaborate recipes declined, the precision of recipes rose sharply. This shift in recipe writing not only reflects a decline in cookery knowledge, but also the rise of the domestic science movement, which worked to educate housewives, hired cooks, and immigrants about the nutritional properties of food and "balanced" meal preparation. Promoting the use of exact measurements in recipe directions and home cooking, the movement endorsed a scientific approach to cooking. This approach was taught in the college departments of domestic science, 30 of which had sprung up throughout the United States by 1900. Not only concerned with calories and nutrition, domestic scientists were also intent on creating recipes that would produce consistent, fail-proof results. To achieve this end, they left no step, no matter how minute, to the imagination, a trend that still prevails in today's recipe writing. As a result, recipes collected from domestic science instructors, such as Fannie Farmer and Sarah Tyson Rorer, read almost like scientific formulas, with a mind toward economy of language, as well as economy at the table; they can be followed by someone stepping up to the stove for the first time.

Interspersed with these highly detailed recipes are those from community cookbooks, which typically follow a less standardized format and are often addressed to readers with some level of culinary experience. Whereas domestic science cookbooks were written as educational texts and worked to standardize American cookery, community cookbooks were written to benefit local causes and often showcased regional cookery. As their name implies, these cookbooks include recipes contributed by members of a group, often a charitable organization such as a church congregation. The first community cookbooks were created to raise money for those left destitute or injured by the Civil War.

In addition to the variation in precision and detail, the following recipes also differ in style and tone, depending on the author's personality and general purpose. Some cookbooks can be enjoyed as much for their literary quality as for their culinary content. Just a few of the authors included here who wrote in a remarkably eloquent style include Eliza Leslie and Marion Harland, both writers who penned novels, as well as cookery books, and Countess Marcella Morphy, about whose life little is known. Each of these authors approach cookery as an artistic medium through which personal taste and creativity can be expressed.

A comparison of the recipes in Chapter 1 with those in Chapter 3 illustrates the enormous changes in American life that occurred from the Civil War era through World War II. Whereas a home cook in the early 1800s would have known how to handle whole animal carcasses, carve a calf's head, and cure meat, home cooks in the 1930s were learning how to distinguish the best commercial food brands and to concoct entire meals from boxes, jars, and cans. This increasing reliance on the food industry to supply our daily meals freed many women from the labor- and time-intensive cooking chores required of their forebears. As a result, the time spent preparing the average American meal declined. Nonetheless, women—even those who entered the workforce—still remained responsible for feeding the family. Although many home cooks still took great pride in cooking meals for their family from scratch, the American dining table became ever more weighted with commercially prepared foods, including bread, snack foods, soups and stews, instant cake mixes, and frozen dinners. Alongside this trend, however, competing movements were beginning to bud in the American culinary scene—a craving for gourmet foods, a curiosity about ethnic cuisines, and a longing for sustainable agriculture; each of these movements would blossom in the 1960s.

# 1

## 🪶 1840–1875

## MAJOR FOODSTUFFS

- Meat: beef and veal; pork; mutton and lamb primarily in the Northeast and Southwest
- Game: bear, buffalo, hare, rabbit, squirrel, venison
- Poultry and Fowl: chicken, duck, goose, grouse, guinea fowl, pigeon, quail, turkey
- Fish: bass, catfish, cod, eel, flounder, haddock, mackerel, perch, salmon, sea turtle, shad, snapper, sturgeon, trout, whitefish
- Shellfish: clam, crab, lobster, oyster, shrimp
- Vegetables: asparagus, beans, beets, cabbage, carrots, celery, corn, cucumbers, Jerusalem artichokes, okra, parsnips, peas, radishes, squash, tomatoes, turnips
- Fruits: apples, cherries, grapes, peaches, pears, rhubarb, strawberries
- Grains: corn; rice, common in the South; wheat, common in the upper Mississippi Valley
- Dairy: cow's milk and cheese, common in the North, but less so in the South because of the heat

## COOKING METHODS

### Heat Sources

- Hearth cooking
- Wood and coal cookstoves

### Preservation Methods

- Smoke-curing
- Salt-curing
- Corning
- Pickling and home canning

### Preparation

- Savory main dish, and increasingly sweet dessert, puddings were boiled in pudding bags made of animal intestines or cloth.
- The hearth remained the favored way of roasting meats.
- Lack of refrigeration meant that preserved cuts of beef, lamb, and pork featured far more regularly in the daily menu than fresh meat, which, for many, was served as an expensive seasonal treat or to mark a special occasion.
- Vegetables were often boiled for long periods of time or pickled; fresh vegetables played a minor role in the average American diet relative to today.
- Fruits were most often cooked in sugar syrup and preserved or turned into pies.

## PREVALENT CULTURAL INFLUENCES

- British
- French
- Spanish
- Dutch
- Native American
- African
- German
- Scandinavian
- Mexican

## BASIC COOKING EQUIPMENT

Iron fork, spoon, dipper, ladle, skimmer, butcher knife, chopping knife, skewers, colander, grater, pepper box, coffee mill and pot, pudding bag, earthenware mixing bowls and baking dishes; sieves, pie plates; dishpans.

## SPECIAL GADGETS

Rolling pin, egg beater, apple corer, potato masher, cleaver, jelly molds, jelly-cake pans, bread board, bread box, cake box, biscuit cutter, dessert molds.

## FOOD PRESERVATION

Because ice boxes were not common until the 1880s, rural households obtained fresh eggs, milk, and cream directly from their own or a neighbor's chickens and cows. As pasture space close to urban centers began to dwindle or disappear altogether, milk sold to urban dwellers was either shipped from nearby farms or came from cows kept in city dairies, which were often attached to breweries and

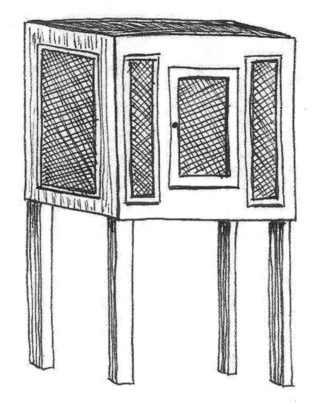

*Meat safe.*

distilleries. By the end of the century, city dairies had all but disappeared owing, in part, to sanitation issues. Eggs and meat were either eaten fresh or preserved by a variety of methods. Eggs were often kept in lime water or greased and packed in charcoal or wheat bran. Meat that was not consumed soon after slaughter was preserved by smoke-curing, salt-curing, corning (soaking in a mixture of salt, water, and spices), or pickling (soaking in vinegar or other acid-based liquids). Meat was often kept in a meat safe to keep insects and rodents at bay.

Highly perishable and difficult to transport, fresh fish was a larger part of the diet along the coast where it could be eaten within hours of being brought to shore. Cookbooks inevitably provided tips on judging the freshness of a fish. Even with careful selection, however, it needed to be eaten the same day of purchase. As a result, a great deal of salt fish, fish salted as a preservative method, was consumed.

In 1858, the safety and ease of home canning vastly improved when John L. Mason patented a glass jar with a screw-on lid and a rubber gasket; by 1860 mason jars were available throughout the United States. Home canning continued to remain a part of home cooking up through the mid-twentieth century, but the commercial mass production of bottled and canned goods, which skyrocketed after the Civil War, spread the availability of ready-prepared foods throughout the nation.

Although many home cooks made their sauces, catsups, and pickles from scratch, a range of bottled versions were available at grocery stores; so, too, were a growing number of canned goods. As early as the 1840s, fish was canned along the coast and shipped inland. Canned vegetables and meat also grew in popularity, although they were rarely mentioned in commercial cookbooks.

## COOKING METHODS

During this time, the cast-iron stove slowly began to replace the hearth as the primary heat source. Although many wealthy households used stoves by the late 1830s, it was not until the 1850s that they became widespread among the urban middle class and not until after the Civil War that they became common in rural areas. During the transition period, many kitchens newly equipped with a cookstove continued to rely on the hearth for roasting and baking. Reflective of this transitional period, the recipes below contain a mix of hearth cookery and stove cookery instruction.

### Hearth Cooking

Food could be boiled, simmered, and stewed in an iron pot, which was suspended directly above the flame or to the side, depending on the desired temperature. Foods that require a lower temperature to bake were often placed in the ashes, perhaps mixed with still-glowing embers for greater heat. Fireplaces had a long-handled shovel specifically designed to move the ashes and embers. An iron kettle with three short legs, the early American Dutch oven, could be placed directly above the embers, which heated it from below. The oven also contained a heavy, rimmed lid on which embers could be placed to heat its contents from above. When surrounded by embers, the Dutch

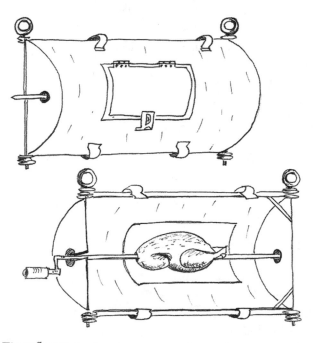

*Tin reflector oven.*

oven could be used to bake; when suspended directly over the flame it could be used to stew. And when hung above the flame and filled with fat, it could be used to fry foods. Grilling took place on a gridiron, which was placed over a bed of hot coals. Foods were roasted on a spit or with the aid of a tin kitchen, or reflector oven, which was placed in front of the fire to direct the heat back into the hearth.

## Wood and Coal Cookstoves

Closed stoves used far less wood than the open hearth, yet they still required lighting the fire and managing its temperature with drafts and dampers, skills long lost to the contemporary home cook. The stove, however, was less labor intensive and heated more quickly than the fireplace, enabling the cook to prepare more dishes for a single meal. By mid-century, manufacturers had begun to make flat-bottomed Dutch ovens for use in the cookstove. The high-rimmed lids, which held embers in place in hearth cooking, gave way to the dome-shaped lids still common in today's Dutch ovens, which are used for braising and stewing.

## DINING

Although enough Americans still ate with their knives in the 1840s to prompt comments of disgust from English visitors, the use of the fork at the dinner table was spreading and would become prevalent by the late nineteenth century. The two-pronged fork, which was common in the eighteenth century, gradually gave way to the three- and eventually four-tined variants. Whereas Europeans cut with the knife in their right hand and ate off the fork in their left, Americans, who were accustomed to eating from a knife in their right hand, learned to lay down the knife in order to transfer the fork to their right hand to eat.

## MEALS

Aided by servants, wealthy families often prepared complicated European fare with many courses, whereas working-class Americans ate cheap and easily prepared foods, relying on one to four dish meals.

Breakfast, which usually contained a healthy portion of meat or fish, was the second largest meal of the day and was eaten together with the family.

Traditionally dinner, the largest meal of the day, was served anywhere from noon to three o'clock, depending on the region. Over the course of the nineteenth century, however, city-dwelling men began to dine out more and more for the mid-day meal rather than returning home from work for lunch. As a result, the main meal of the day began to shift to the early evening, when everyone in the family was present, a trend that became ubiquitous by the late nineteenth century. In middle-class homes the main meal often consisted of two courses, composed of several dishes, followed by dessert. Most of the dishes would be laid on the table in advance and would be eaten in the following order: soup and fish, if included; meat with one or two starches and one or two vegetables; dessert of sweet pudding, custard, ice cream, or cake. At dinner parties a cold soup might be added to the first course, several more side dishes and game might be added to the second, and the dessert course might include pudding, custard, ice cream, and cake followed by coffee and cheese. By mid-century, upper class homes began to serve dinner *à la russe*, or Russian style, when entertaining special guests. This method of service, which is prevalent in restaurants and many homes today, is one in which dinner is served in a succession of courses, each of which servants brought around to the individual diners.

Tea was either taken in the afternoon or the evening. In the 1840s, middle-class women adopted the eighteenth-century, upper-class tradition of serving tea around 4 PM. The afternoon tea, taken only by women, usually lasted about two hours. For many families, evening tea (often referred to as high tea or 6 o'clock supper) served as a full meal taken by the entire family or, less often, served as a light meal between dinner and a late supper, taken around 8 or 9 PM.

When the mid-day meal was served as the main one, supper consisted of a light meal, which was served a few hours after tea if the family was staying up late.

## POPULAR RECIPES

Many types of foods, namely pickles, ketchups, and preserves, are not commonly prepared by today's home cooks, who buy them ready-prepared. Store-bought tomato ketchup[1] and dill pickles are almost all that remains of the enormous range of ketchups and pickles so prevalent in the nineteenth century.

Savory puddings and pies were also a far more regular part of the American table than they are today and speak to our English heritage. Alongside this inheritance, trends that differentiate the American palate from that of England began to emerge during the nineteenth century. For example, Americans began to develop an acute taste for sweets. As a result, many of the savory pies and puddings began to include increasing amounts of sugar, eventually becoming desserts served at the end of the meal. A taste for ice cream also spread throughout the country, fueled by the increasing availability of ice and the prevalence of ice boxes, which could be found in most homes by the 1850s.

## SOUPS, CHOWDERS, AND STEWS

Just as they are today, soups were often served as a first course, or the heartier ones were eaten as informal one-dish meals. The following soups were commonly prepared in the nineteenth century and, with the exception of turtle soup and Seminole soup (made with squirrel), can still be found frequently on American dinner tables. Turtle meat, which was popular and widely available until after the Civil War, has become a rare and expensive commodity in today's market. As a result, turtle soup, when served at all, is most commonly found today at high-end American restaurants. The consumption of squirrel has declined precipitously, although it is still cooked in the rural South.

### ❧ 1. DRIED BEAN SOUP ❧

*(Harland, 1871)*

A version of the following soup remains popular throughout the United States. It is most often made today from the black bean, also known as the turtle bean, or what the following recipe refers to as the mock-turtle soup bean. To obtain the consistency of a purée (what we'd accomplish today in a food processor), the beans are passed through a colander. In addition to the lemon slice called for below, black bean soup is often dressed up with a splash of sherry.

> *The beans used for this purpose may be the ordinary kidney, the rice or field bean, or, best of all, the French mock-turtle soup bean. Soak a quart of these over night in soft lukewarm water; put them over the fire next morning, with one gallon of cold water and about two pounds of salt pork. Boil slowly for three hours, keeping the pot well covered; shred into it a head of celery, add pepper—cayenne, if preferred—simmer half an hour longer, strain through a cullender [colander], and serve, with slices of lemon passed to each guest.*

### ❧ 2. BRUNSWICK STEW ❧

*(Harland, 1871)*

Brunswick stew, a dish still popular throughout the South where it originated, is fundamentally an economical one, often including squirrel, chicken, corn, tomatoes, and lima beans as its primary ingredients; some argue that the only meat added should be squirrel, others argue that squirrel and chicken should be used, and still others prepare it using either chicken or beef. Previous Brunswick stew recipes exist, but the following was the first-known printed recipe to call it by name.

*2 squirrels—3, if small*
*1 quart of tomatoes—peeled and sliced*
*1 pint butter-beans, or Lima*
*6 potatoes, parboiled and sliced*
*6 ears of green corn cut from the cob*
*1/2 lb. butter*
*1/2 lb. fat salt pork*
*1 teaspoonful ground black pepper*
*Half a teaspoonful cayenne*
*1 gallon water*
*1 tablespoonful salt*
*2 teaspoonfuls white sugar*
*1 onion, minced small*

*Put on the water with the salt in it, and boil five minutes. Put in the onion, beans, corn, pork or bacon cut into shreds, potatoes, pepper, and the squirrels, which must be cut into joints and laid in cold salt and water to draw out the blood. Cover closely and stew two and a half hours very slowly, stirring frequently from the bottom. Then add the tomatoes and sugar, and stew an hour longer. Ten minutes before you take it from the fire add the butter, cut into bits the size of a walnut, rolled in flour. Give a final boil, taste to see that it is seasoned to your liking, and turn into a soup-tureen. It is eaten from soup-plates. Chickens may be substituted for squirrels.*

### ‍3. GERMAN CHICKEN STEW ‍

*(Levy, 1871)*

The wave of German immigrants that came to the United States in the 1870s solidified the considerable influence of German cuisine on the American table. Whereas aspects of French cuisine filtered into the upper-middle and upper-class kitchens, German cookery most impacted the meals eaten by the middle and lower classes. In particular, the German delis that flourished in major American cities during the later half of the nineteenth century helped Americanize such foods as potato and cabbage salads, sauerbraten and bratwurst sausages, pastrami, pumpernickel and sour rye breads, and noodle soup.

*Cut up a good sized chicken in small pieces, and put them in a saucepan, with a quart of water. Let it stew till tender; season with pepper, ginger, salt, chopped parsley, sweet herbs, and a little garlic; thicken with a tablespoonful of flour. Dish up and garnish with lemon, parsley, and boiled carrots.*

## ⇥ 4. CORN SOUP ⇤

*(Ladies of the First Presbyterian Church, Dayton, Ohio, 1873)*

In addition to featuring in soups and stews or being paired with lima beans for succotash, corn kernels were frequently fashioned into puddings and fritters. Corn was such a prevalent part of nineteenth-century cooking that many kitchens housed an implement specifically designed to scrape the kernels from the cob. This procedure can be performed easily with a knife

*Clean and scrape twelve ears of corn. Boil the cobs for fifteen or twenty minutes in one quart of water; remove them and put in the corn. Let it boil a short time, then add two quarts of rich milk. Season with pepper, salt, and butter that has been melted enough to rub flour into it (two tablespoonsful of flour). Let the whole boil ten minutes, and then turn the soup into a tureen into which the yolks of three eggs have been beaten.*

## ⇥ 5. FISH CHOWDER ⇤

*(Howland, 1845)*

Traditionally a stew made from fish, shellfish, and vegetables, chowder has long been a favorite dish of New England. Like many fish recipes from the early to mid-nineteenth century, the following recipe does not specify a type of fish; white and firm-fleshed fish such as cod and haddock were commonly included. The chowder, often served for dinner, was prepared in a large iron pot known as the chowder kettle.

*Cut some slices of pork very thin, and fry it out in the dinner-pot; then put in a layer of fish cut in slices, on the pork and fat, then a layer of onion, and then potatoes, all cut in thin slices; then fish, onions, and potatoes again, till your materials are all in, putting some salt and pepper on each layer of onions; split some crackers, and dip them in water, and put them around the sides and over the top; put in water enough to come up in sight; boil about half an hour, till the potatoes are done; add half a pint of milk or a tea-cup of sweet cream, five minutes before you take it up.*

## ⇥ 6. GUMBO ⇤

*(Leslie, 1851)*

A popular dish in the South named after the African word for okra, gumbo often includes filé powder (ground sassafras leaves) as a thickening agent. Ground sassafras leaves were an ingredient commonly used by the Choctaw Indians; okra was introduced to the New World by the slaves. In addition to tomatoes, onion, and a variety of greens, Gumbo may also include shellfish, chicken, sausage, ham, or a combination of these ingredients.

*Take four pounds of the lean of a fresh round of beef and cut the meat into small pieces, avoiding carefully all the fat. Season the meat with a little pepper and salt, and put it on to boil with three quarts and a pint of water (not more.) Boil it slowly and skim it well. When no more scum [extraneous surface froth] rises, put in half a peck of ochras [okra], peeled and sliced and half a peck of tomatas [var.] cut in quarters. Boil it slowly till the ochras and tomatas are entirely dissolved, and the meat all to rags. Then strain it through a cullender [colander], and send it to table with slices of dry toast. This soup cannot be made in less than seven or eight hours. If you dine at two you must put on the meat to boil at six or seven in the morning. It should be as thick as jelly.*

## ⇒ 7. IRISH STEW ⇐

*(An American Lady, 1854)*

Mutton is the traditional meat in this stew, being the dominant base for the dish in Ireland. Tougher cuts of meat, such as mutton, are usually used for stews because the long cooking time tenderizes the flesh, providing a tasty way of preparing the more economical cuts.

*Put two pounds of breast of mutton into a pot, with a pint and a half of water and a pinch of salt; let it stew gently for an hour; then take off all the fat; take out the meat and cut it into small pieces; have ready four pounds of potatoes, pared and cut in halves; three or four good sized onions, peeled and sliced, and pepper and salt mixed in a cup. When you have taken the fat off the broth as closely as possible, put in a layer of potatoes; then sprinkle two or three pieces of meat with the pepper and salt, and lay them on the potatoes, then a layer of the sliced onions, then another layer of potatoes, one of mutton, then one of onions, and so on till the whole is in. Cover close and let stew very gently for another hour, shaking it frequently that it may not burn.*

## ⇒ 8. OX-TAIL SOUP ⇐

*(Harland, 1871)*

Nineteenth-century Americans quite literally ate cattle from head to tail. Most calf's head recipes disappeared from U.S. cookbooks around the turn of the century, but ox-tail soup remains a popular American dish.

*1 ox-tail*
*2 lbs. lean beef*
*4 carrots*
*3 onions*
*Thyme*

*Cut the tail into several pieces and fry brown in butter. Slice the onions and carrots, and when you remove the oxtail from the frying-pan, put in these and*

brown also. When done, tie them in a bag with a bunch of thyme and drop
into the soup-pot. Lay the pieces of ox-tail in the same; then the meat cut into
small slices. Grate over them the two whole carrots, and add four quarts of
cold water, with pepper and salt. Boil from four to six hours, in proportion to
the size of the tail. Strain fifteen minutes before serving it, and thicken with
two tablespoonful of browned flour. Boil ten minutes longer.

## ❧ 9. GREEN PEA ❧

*(Harland, 1871)*

Just as they do today, fresh green peas offered nineteenth-century
Americans a seasonal treat in the spring and early summer. Many vegetables,
especially fibrous ones such as winter greens and cabbage, were often cooked
for a length of time that would be considered excessively long by today's
standards. Some cooks boiled peas for up to 30 minutes. Others, however,
took especial care not to overcook green peas and to shell them at the last
minute in order to prolong their freshness—a tactic still followed by contemporary cooks.

*2 qts. of veal or beef broth*
*1/2 teaspoonful sugar*
*1 tablespoonful butter*
*1 qt. shelled peas*

*Bring the broth to a boil; put in the peas, and boil for twenty minutes. Add the
sugar, and a bunch of green mint. Boil a quarter of an hour more, and stir in
the butter, with pepper and salt, if the broth be not sufficiently salted already.
Strain before serving, and send to table with small squares of toasted bread
floating upon the top.*

## ❧ 10. PORTABLE SOUP ❧

*(Hale, 1852)*

Whereas dried cubes and cans of chicken, vegetable, and beef broth line
the shelves of today's grocery stores, nineteenth-century cooks prepared
their own "portable" soup. As the following recipe indicates, having portable soup on hand precluded the need to make stock or broth from scratch,
a time-consuming process. Like its more voluminous form, stock, portable
soup allowed cooks to extract the rich marrow flavor from the many bones
that would be left after the meat of an animal had been consumed. These
extractions form the base for gravies, sauces, and soups.

*Put on, in 4 gallons of water, 10 lbs. of a shin of beef, free from fat and skin,
6 lbs. of a knuckle of veal and 2 fowls, break the bones and cut the meat
into small pieces, season with 1 oz. of whole black pepper, 1/4 oz. of Jamaica*

*pepper, and the same of mace, cover the pot very closely, and let it simmer for 12 or 14 hours, and then strain it. The following day, take off the fat, and clear the jelly from any sediment adhering to it; boil it gently upon a stove without covering the sauce-pan, and stir it frequently till it thickens to a strong glue. Pour it into broad tin pans, and put it in a cool oven. When it will take the impression of a knife, score it in equal squares, and hang it in a south window, or near a stove. When dry, break it at the scores. Wrap it in paper, and put it closely up in boxes. There should always be a large supply of this soup, as with it and ketchup, no one will ever be at a loss for dressed dishes and soups.*

### ⁓ 11. SEMINOLE SOUP ⁓

*(Rutledge, 1847)*

Hickory nuts and sassafras, which are indigenous to the United States, were common ingredients in Native American cooking. As they still are today, nuts were eaten whole as snacks or ground for a flavorful addition to many dishes. Powdered sassafras root and bark are often used as a thickening agent. Sassafras root, along with sarsaparilla, is one of the key flavorings in root beer, which was invented by an American pharmacist in the mid-1800s.

*Take a squirrel, cut it up and put it on to boil. When the soup is nearly done add to it one pint of picked [shelled] hickory-nuts and a spoonful of parched and powdered sassafras leaves—or the tender top of a pine tree, which gives a very aromatic flavor to the soup.*

### ⁓ 12. TURTLE SOUP ⁓

*(Hill, 1867)*

Terrapin—technically a reptile but sorted under seafood in nineteenth-century cookbooks—and sea turtle were prized for their meat. Turtle soup, one of the first canned varieties available for commercial sale, was a labor-intensive dish and considered complicated enough by 1851 for one of the century's most popular cookbook authors, Eliza Leslie, to omit providing a recipe in her *Directions for Cookery*. Instead, she recommends: "when that very expensive, complicated, and difficult dish is prepared in a private family, it is advisable to hire a first-rate cook for the express purpose." Leslie did, however, include a recipe for mock turtle soup, another popular dish prepared from calf's head. The following recipe omits the elaborate steps required to butcher a turtle that appeared in traditional recipes for turtle soup. It does call for the addition of forcemeat balls, which are made of finely ground meat, poultry, fish, or vegetables mixed with breadcrumbs and seasonings.

*Boil the turtle very tender, remove all bones, cut the meat into small pieces; season with a tablespoonful each of marjoram, sweet basil, thyme and parsley;*

*pepper and salt to taste; one nutmeg beaten fine; a dozen cloves; the same of allspice. Tie these in thin muslin, and remove it before sending the soup to the table; stir a large tablespoonful of browned flour into a quarter of a pound of fresh butter; add this to the soup; pour over five quarts of boiling water; reduce by boiling to three quarters; boil gently. A quarter of an hour before it is done, add the green fat; and to three quarts of soup, half a pint of wine, a lemon sliced thin, the seeds removed, add force-meat balls; after simmering five minutes, take out the lemon peel. This is for a small turtle; if not fat, a slice of good ham may be added, and removed before serving.*

## MEAT

The following meat dishes are still quite popular today, with the exception of the recipes for brains and tongue, for souse, and for lamb fry, which feature variety meats—the innards and extremities of animals. The lungs, brains, heart, and tongue are not frequently used today, but other variety meats such as sweetbreads (the thymus gland), liver, and pig's feet are more common. Considered somewhat of a delicacy, sautéed sweetbreads are served in many high-end restaurants. Liver sautéed with onion or fashioned into liverwurst, a type of sausage, is eaten in many home kitchens, especially those whose cooks are influenced by Eastern European culinary traditions. Pig's feet, although not nearly so popular today, can still be found throughout the South in pickled form.

### ⊰ 13. TO BARBECUE ANY KIND OF FRESH MEAT ⊱

*(Hill, 1867)*

During the nineteenth century, enormous barbecues were often held by political candidates, who used them as venues to spread their election message. Also hosted by families who might invite hundreds of guests, barbecues could begin mid-day and last well past dark. Although hogs provided the leading barbecue meat in the South and beef led in the Southwest, both meats might appear at a given event along with lamb. In the Great Plains, buffalo was even added to the menu every now and again.

*Gash the meat. Broil slowly over a solid fire. Baste constantly with a sauce composed of butter, mustard, red and black pepper, vinegar. Mix these in a pan, and set it where the sauce will keep warm, not hot. Have a swab made by tying a piece of clean, soft cloth upon a stick about a foot long; dip this in the sauce and baste with it. Where a large carcass is barbecued, it is usual to dig a pit in the ground outdoors, and lay narrow bars of wood across. Very early in the morning fill the pit with wood; set it burning, and in this way heat it very hot. When the wood has burned to coals, lay the meat over. Should the fire need replenishing, keep a fire outside burning, from which draw coals, and scatter evenly in the pit under the meat. Should there be any sauce left, pour it over the meat. For barbecuing a joint, a large gridiron answers well; it needs constant attention; should be cooked slowly and steadily.*

### ↫ 14. HASH ↬

*(Hale, 1841)*

Also called mince meat, hash is an economical means of using up leftover meat such as pork, lamb, beef, or chicken. Although hash had long been served for breakfast or for a casual supper, by the mid-nineteenth century it had also become a popular staple of inexpensive restaurants known "hash houses" or "hasheries."

*All the pieces and bits of cold meat should be minced and warmed; if this is rightly done, the dish is generally a favorite one.*

*It is best to chop the meat very fine, (gristles and gelatinous matter from the bones may be included) then make a gravy by putting a lump of butter (what you judge necessary) into a stew pan; when it is hot, add a little flour, and stir it into the butter; then add a teacupful of broth the meat was boiled in, and a little catsup. Let this boil up, then put in the mince meat, with a little chopped parsley, pepper and salt. Let it stand and simmer a few minutes covered, but do not let it boil—it hardens the meat to boil it. Lay slices of toasted bread in the dish, and pour the meat and gravy over.*

## Beef and Veal

### ✢ DIRECTIONS FOR CLEANING CALF'S HEAD AND FEET

(Randolph, 1860)

In addition to being baked, stewed, hashed, and turned into a molded sausage known as head cheese, calf's head served as the main ingredient of mock turtle soup. Cow heel (which includes the lower portion of the leg) was boiled, stewed, or fried to make an economical meat dish. The hoof was often boiled until it turned into gelatin, which could be used to make molded desserts and side dishes.

*As soon as the animal is killed, have the head and feet taken off, wash them clean, sprinkle some pounded rosin all over the hairs, then dip them in boiling water, take them instantly out, the rosin will dry immediately, and they may be scraped clean with ease; the feet should be soaked in water three or four days, changing it daily; this will make them very white.*

## ⊰ 15. BEEF OLIVES ⊱

*(Allen, 1845)*

Beef olives were a favored dish during the nineteenth century that fell out of fashion during the twentieth century. The recipes ranged from the following economical version, which calls for leftover beef, to more extravagant ones, some of which call for dipping the rolled beef in a mixture of bread crumbs and eggs before pan frying it.

> *To dress cold beef that has not been done enough, called beef olives. Cut slices half an inch thick, and four-square; lay on them a force-meat of crumbs of bread, shallot, a little suet or fat, pepper and salt. Roll them and fasten with a small skewer. Put them into a stew-pan with some gravy made of beef bones, or gravy of the meat, a trifle of water; stew tender.*

## ⊰ 16. ROAST BEEF ⊱

*(Beecher, 1858)*

Roast beef remains a quintessential dish at the formal American table. The spare directions given here contrast with the increasing detail necessary in later years, indicating that the amount of cooking knowledge that a recipe author could take for granted dwindled dramatically over the century. As the recipe suggests, the more tender cuts of meat are usually reserved for roasts or steaks. The short loin, located behind the rib, is the most tender cut. The sirloin rests between the short loin and the tough round (from the rump to hind ankle).

> *The sirloin, and the first and second cuts of the rack, are the best roasting pieces.*
>
> *Rub it with salt; set the bony side to the fire to heat awhile, then turn it, and have a strong fire; and if thick, allow fifteen minutes to the pound; if thin, allow a little less. If fresh killed, or if it is very cold, allow a little more time. Half an hour before it is done, pour off the gravy, thicken it with brown flour, and season it with salt and pepper. It is the fashion to serve roast beef with no other gravy than the juice of the meat.*

## ⊰ 17. BEEF STEAK ⊱

*(Lea, 1873)*

The following recipe calls for basting the steak to keep it moist, which requires spooning the drippings (or, alternatively, butter or stock) back over the meat as it cooks.

> *Choose the tenderest part of beef, cut it an inch thick, broil it gently over good coals, covered with a plate; have butter, salt, pepper, and a little water in a dish; and when you turn the beef, dip it in this; be careful to have as much of*

*the juice as you can. When done, put it in a warm dish, and pour the basting over, with some more butter.*

## ⃗ 18. BRAINS AND TONGUE ⃖

*(Lea, 1873)*

Unlike today, the head was considered a delicacy in the nineteenth century and would often be cooked entire. It might be baked, boiled, prepared in ragout, curried, or hashed.

*Pour boiling water on the brains, and skin them; tie them tight in a cloth, and boil them and the tongue with the head; when done put them on a plate, chop three leaves of green sage fine, and beat up with the brains; spread them round a small dish, and after skinning the tongue, place it in the middle.*

## ⃗ 19. VEAL CUTLETS ⃖

*(Harland, 1871)*

Cutlets are thin, tender cuts of meat, usually lamb, pork, or veal. The following recipe calls for the cutlets to be fried in drippings (the fat and juice that drips from cooking meat) or lard (rendered and clarified pork fat)—the two most common mediums for frying foods in the nineteenth century. Some Americans, however, did begin to use peanut oil for frying during the Civil War, when meat shortages made lard and drippings harder to come by.

*Dip in beaten egg when you have sprinkled a little pepper and salt over them; then roll in cracker-crumbs, and fry in hot dripping or lard. If you use butter or dripping, add a little boiling water to the gravy when the meat is dished; thicken with browned flour, boil up once, sending to table in a boat.*

## Lamb and Mutton

Lamb refers to a sheep less than one year old; mutton refers to sheep more than a year old. Mutton meat is stronger and tougher than that of lamb and enjoyed far more popularity during the nineteenth century that it does today.

## ⃗ 20. LAMB FRY ⃖

*(Bryan, 1839)*

Recipes for using the innards and extremities of animals, such as the following, were quite common in nineteenth-century cookbooks.

*Cut the liver, heart and sweet-breads into smooth, thin slices, season them with salt and pepper, dredge them with flour, and fry them a light brown.*

*Having the head and feet boiled tender, minced fine, and heaped in the centre of a dish, lay the fry around it, and pour over the gravy, which should be seasoned with butter, brown flour, and chopped parsley.*

### ⊰ 21. ROAST LEG OF LAMB ⊱

*(Godey's Lady's Book, 1860)*

Aside from being cooked by a hearth fire, the following dish resembles many roast lamb recipes found today.

*Make deep incisions round the bone and in the flesh, prepare a dressing of breadcrumbs, salt, pepper, sweet marjoram, or savory, and as much butter as will make the crumbs adhere together; fill all the incisions with the dressing; season the meat with salt and pepper; roast it before a clear fire, and when nearly done, dredge flour over, and baste with the gravy; skim the fat off the gravy, and add a little flour mixed with water; let it boil once, and serve it in a gravy-boat.*

### ⊰ 22. MUTTON CHOPS ⊱

*(Hall, 1855)*

Although today's cook would likely substitute lamb or pork for the mutton chops and would cook the chops in a skillet, the following recipe is close to one that might be found in a contemporary cookbook—even down to the instruction to trim excess fat from the meat.

*Broiled: Cut from the best end of the loin; trim them nicely, removing fat or skin, leaving only enough of the former to make them palatable; let the fire be very clear before placing the chops on the gridiron; turn them frequently, taking care that the fork is not put into the lean part of the chop; season them with pepper and salt; spread a little fresh butter over each chop when nearly done, and send them to table upon very hot plates.*

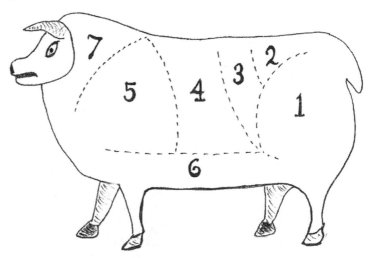

*Diagram of mutton cuts.*

### ◈ 23. SHOULDER OF MUTTON, BOILED WITH OYSTERS ◈

*(Howland, 1845)*

This recipe calls for the shoulder to be hung for "some days," a method used to tenderize tougher cuts of meat. Hanging, or aging, meat results in improved texture and flavor. Oyster sauce and stuffing were often served with meat, a practice naturally more common in those regions closest to the coastline.

*Hang it some days, then salt it well for two days, bone it, and sprinkle it with pepper and a bit of mace pounded; lay some oysters over it, roll the meat up tight, and tie it [with cooking string]. Stew it in a small quantity of water, with an onion and a few pepper-corns, till quite tender. Have ready a little good gravy [see recipe 52], and some oysters stewed in it; thicken this with flour and butter, and pour over the mutton when the tape [string] is taken off. The stew-pan should be kept close covered.*

## Pork

---

### ✦ GERMAN-AMERICAN COOKERY

Large waves of Germans immigrated in the 1830s and 1850s. They settled in large numbers in Baltimore, New York, Cincinnati, St. Louis, Chicago, Milwaukee, Missouri, and Wisconsin, where they greatly influenced middle-class cookery.

---

### ◈ 24. WESTPHALIA HAMS ◈

*(Godey's Lady's Book, 1860)*

This recipe would have been brought to the United States by German immigrants well learned in the making of flavorful hams; Westphalia, a province in Germany, is famous for its curing method.

*Prepare the hams in the usual manner by rubbing them with common salt and draining them; take one ounce of saltpetre [var. saltpeter, a crystallized salt], one-half pound of coarse sugar, and then the same quantity of salt; rub it well into the ham, and in three days pour a pint of vinegar over it. A fine foreign flavor may also be given to hams by pouring old strong beer over them and burning juniper wood while they are drying; molasses, juniper berries and highly-flavored herbs, such as basil, sage, bay-leaves, and thyme, mingled together, and the hams well rubbed with it, using only a sufficient quantity of salt to assist in the cure, will afford an agreeable variety.*

## ↭ 25. TO ROAST PIG ↬

*(Child, 1833)*

Whereas middle- and upper-class homes usually employed a cook and other servants who would handle the laborious and often bloody kitchen labor, lower-middle and lower-class families did without. As a result, they were quite accustomed to handling the tasks described here.

*Strew fine salt over it an hour before it is put down. It should not be cut entirely open; fill it up plump with thick slices of buttered bread, salt, sweet-marjoram and sage. Spit it with the head next the point of the spit; take off the joints of the leg, and boil them with the liver, with a little whole pepper, allspice, and salt for gravy sauce. The upper part of the legs must be braced down with skewers. Shake on flour. Put a little water in the dripping-pan, and stir it often. When the eyes drop out, the pig is half done. When it is nearly done, baste it with butter. Cut off the head, split it open between the eyes. Take out the brains, and chop them fine with the liver and some sweet marjoram and sage; put this into melted butter, and when it has boiled a few minutes, add it to the gravy in the dripping-pan. When your pig is cut open, lay it with the back to the edge of the dish; half a head to be placed at each end. A good sized pig needs to be roasted three hours.*

---

### ✦ SCARLET FEVER

(Hill, 1867)

In addition to culinary recipes, nineteenth-century cookbooks frequently included an array of folk remedies for common ailments and concoctions for housecleaning.

*As soon as the nature of the disease is ascertained, rub the patient night and morning with fat bacon, rubbing every part of the body but the head slowly and carefully.*

---

## ↭ 26. FRIED SALT PORK AND APPLES ↬

*(Child, 1833)*

The salt pork called for in this recipe is simply pork that has been cured with salt.

*Fried salt pork and apples is a favorite dish in the country; but it is seldom seen in the city. After the pork is fried, some of the fat should be taken out, lest the apples should be oily. Acid [sour, as opposed to sweet] apples should be chosen, because they cook more easily; they should be cut in slices, across the whole apple, about twice or three times as thick as a new dollar. Fried till tender, and brown on both sides—laid around the pork. If you have cold potatoes, slice them and brown them in the same way.*

## ◌ 27. PORK CHOPS ◌

*(Hill, 1867)*

Although today's meat comes ready butchered, nineteenth-century cooks needed to know how to handle an entire carcass from head to tail. Apples remain a popular accompaniment to pork dishes; see recipe 54 for directions on preparing apple sauce.

*Quarter the animal, remove the chine bone [back bone], cut the blade bone [the scapula or shoulder blade] from the ribs (chops are taken from the fore quarter); cut the ribs into pieces two or three inches long, one bone to a chop; if very fat, remove a part of it. Sprinkle a little finely pulverized sage over each piece; fry a light brown; serve without gravy. Fried apples, tomato sauce, or dried apple sauce are good accompaniments.*

## ◌ 28. TO MAKE SAUSAGE MEAT ◌

*(Hale, 1841)*

During the slaughter season, sausages were made from leftover meat trimmings and often preserved by curing or drying.

*Chop two pounds of lean with one of fat pork very fine—mix with this meat five teaspoonfuls of salt, seven of powdered sage, two of black pepper, and one of cloves. You can add a little rosemary, if you like.*

## ◌ 29. SOUSE ◌

*(Leslie, 1851)*

Nineteenth-century American souse is a pickle made most often with pig's feet and ears. Occasional recipes called for pickling the head along with the feet and ears.

*Having cleaned [the pig's feet and ears] properly, and removed the skin, boil them slowly till they are quite tender, and then split the feet and put them with the ears into salt and vinegar, flavoured with a little mace. Cover the jar closely, and set it away. When you use them, dry each piece well with a cloth; dip them first in beaten yolk of egg, and then in bread-crumbs, and fry them nicely in butter or lard. Or you may eat them cold, just out of the vinegar.*

*If you intend keeping them some time, you must make a fresh pickle for them every other day.*

## Game

Game such as venison was often eaten in rural areas. Small game was popular among those living in frontier regions, the rural poor, and those slaves who were allowed to carry firearms. In addition, rabbit and hare, squirrel, possum, and raccoon were caught for the table. During the nineteenth century, the widespread slaughter of deer, wild turkey, bear, and buffalo dwindled each of these species down to dangerously low numbers; public outcry eventually led to the passage of gaming laws that enabled widespread recovery.

### ❧ 30. ROASTED HARE ☙

*(Sanderson, 1864)*

Because hare can be tough, the following recipe provides instruction on hanging the carcass of an older animal, a process that tenderizes the flesh. Although the recipe here does not state it outright, the stuffed hare should be roasted.

*Hare when young is easy of digestion, and very nourishing—when old, the contrary, unless rendered so by keeping and dressing. When you receive a hare, take out the liver—if it be sweet, parboil it, and keep it for stuffing. Wipe the hare quite dry; rub the inside with pepper, and hang it in a cool place till it is fit to be dressed, that is to say, till it comes to the point of putrefaction, but not putrefied. Then paunch [remove the viscera] and skin, wash and lay it in a large pan of cold water four or five hours, changing the water two or three times; lay it in a clean cloth; dry it well, and truss. To make the stuffing, see [below]. Let it be stiff; put it in the belly, and sew it up tightly. The skin must be cut to let the blood out of the neck. Some persons baste it with skimmed milk, but we decidedly prefer dripping; it ought to be constantly basted till it is nearly done; then put a little bit of butter into your basting ladle; flour and froth nicely. Serve with good gravy and currant jelly [see recipe 121].*

*Stuffing for Hare: Three ounces of fine bread crumbs, two ounces of beef suet, chopped fine, eschalot [shallot] half a drachm [dram, or approximately 1.8 grams], one drachm of parsley, a drachm of lemon thyme, marjoram, winter savoury, a drachm of grated lemon peel, and the same of pepper and salt; mix these with the white and yolk of an egg; do not make it thin, for if it is not stiff enough, it will be good for nothing; put it in the hare and sew it up. If the liver is quite sound, parboil it, mince it very fine, and put to the stuffing.*

### ❧ 31. HUNTER'S DELIGHT ☙

*(Collins, 1857)*

The following recipe requires beating slices of deer on a kitchen dresser to tenderize them. Suet refers to the solid fat found around the kidneys and loin of beef and mutton, commonly used in nineteenth-century cooking.

*Cut slices from the ham of a deer, lay them on a dresser, beat them as you would beef-steak, season them with salt, pepper, cloves, mace, and nutmegs, then dip them in a rich egg batter. Take soft bread-crumbs, some of the venison minced fine, a little beef-suet, sweet herbs, and strew all these over the collops [slices of meat]; roll them up, put them on skewers, and roast them. Make a rich gravy with the minced meat and herbs, some butter, pepper, salt, cloves, and pour it over the roasted delights.*

### ❧ 32. FRIED SQUIRREL ☙

*(Bryan, 1839)*

Found in abundance and served most frequently in the South, squirrels were prepared like rabbit—fried, fricasseed, broiled or added to stew.

*Take a couple of fat young squirrels, case and cut them into small pieces, rinse them very clean in cold water…. [S]eason them with salt, pepper, and nutmeg, dredge them with flour, and fry them a handsome brown, in lard or butter. Stir into the gravy a spoonful of flour, one of tomato catchup, and a glass of sweet cream, and serve the squirrels with the gravy poured round.*

## Poultry and Fowl

### ❧ 33. BATTERED CHICKEN ☙

*(Rutledge, 1847)*

The following recipe is for what today would be called Southern fried chicken.

*Make a light batter with three eggs, a small tablespoonful of butter, a little wheat flour, and salt to the taste. Joint your chickens, and put them into the batter. Grease your frying-pan, throw the mixture of chicken and batter into it, fry a good brown.—This quantity of batter will suffice for one pair of chickens.*

### ❧ 34. BROILED CHICKENS ☙

*(Leslie, 1851)*

The following recipe is a nineteenth-century version of grilled chicken. The birds are split down the back and flattened before grilling, a method also known as spatchcocking.

*Split a pair of chickens down the back, and beat them flat. Wipe the inside, season them with pepper and salt, and let them lie while you prepare some beaten yolk of egg and grated bread crumbs. Have ready a hot gridiron over a bed of bright coals. Lay the chickens on it with the inside downwards, or next the fire. Broil them about three quarters of an hour, keeping them covered with a plate. Just before you take them up, lay some small pieces of butter on them.*

## ⊰ 35. CHICKEN CURRY ⊱

*(Leslie, 1851)*

By the mid-nineteenth century, curry dishes had become a common part of the British table, having been adapted from Indian recipes during England's colonial rule of India. They gained great favor in the United States, where they became a regular feature in most cookbooks until well into the twentieth century. Among the ingredients that might appear in an Indian curry sauce are cardamom, chilies, cinnamon, cloves, coriander, curry leaf, cumin, fenugreek, mustard seeds, pepper, tamarind, and turmeric.

*Take a pair of fine fowls and, having cut them in pieces, lay them in salt and water till the seasoning is ready. Take two table-spoonfuls of powdered ginger, one table-spoonful of fresh turmeric, a tea spoonful of ground black pepper; some mace, a few cloves, some cardamom seeds, and a little cayenne pepper with a small portion of salt. These last articles according to your taste. Put all into a mortar, and add to them eight large onions, chopped or cut small. Mix and beat all together, till the onions, spices, &c. form a paste.*

*Put the chickens into a pan with sufficient butter rolled in flour, and fry them till they are brown, but not quite done. While this is proceeding, set over the fire a sauce-pan three parts full of water, or sufficient to cover the chickens when they are ready. As soon as the water boils, throw in the curry-paste. When the paste has all dissolved, and is thoroughly mixed with the water, put in the pieces of chicken to boil, or rather to simmer. When the chicken is quite done, put it into a large dish, and eat it with boiled rice. The rice may either be laid round on the same dish, or served up separately.*

*This is a genuine East Indian receipt for curry.*

*Lamb, veal, or rabbit may be curried in the same manner.*

## ⊰ 36. FRICASSEE OF SMALL CHICKENS ⊱

*(Randolph, 1860)*

This was a popular way of cooking chicken or rabbit in the nineteenth century. Generally, the chicken or rabbit would be jointed, browned in butter, and stewed in liquid, usually water with perhaps a bit of wine. A variety of spices, ketchups, and herbs might be added; cream or milk is a common last-minute addition along with a squirt of lemon.

*Take off the legs and wings of four chickens, separate the breasts from the backs, cut off the necks and divide the backs across, clean the gizzards nicely, put them with the livers and other parts of the chicken, after being washed clean, into a sauce pan, add pepper, salt, and a little mace, cover them with water, and stew them till tender—then take them out, thicken half a pint of the water with two table spoonsful of flour rubbed into four ounces of butter, add half a pint of new milk, boil all together a few minutes, then add a gill [4 oz.] of white wine, stirring it in carefully that it may not curdle; put the chickens in, and continue to shake the pan until they are sufficiently hot, and serve them up.*

### ⅋ 37. WILD PIGEONS [SQUAB], STEWED ⅋

*(Harland, 1871)*

Wild passenger pigeons once flew in huge numbers; a single flock could cover up to a mile's length of sky. They were not only roasted, stewed, dried, and pickled, but also fed to slaves and hogs. Although at one point they may have numbered as many as 5 billion, their mass slaughter throughout the nineteenth century reduced their numbers so that by 1909 only two remained alive, both in cages. By 1914, they were extinct.

*Clean and wash very carefully, then lay in salt and water for an hour, Rinse the inside with soda and water, shaking it well about in the cavity; wash out with fair water and stuff with a force-meat made of bread-crumbs and chopped salt pork, seasoned with pepper. Sew up the birds, and put on to stew in enough cold water to cover them, and allow to each a fair slice of fat bacon cut into narrow strips. Season with pepper and a pinch of nutmeg. Boil slowly in a covered saucepan until tender; take from the gravy and lay in a covered dish*

Passenger pigeon.

*to keep warm. Strain the gravy, add the juice of a lemon and a tablespoonful of currant jelly [see recipe 121], thickening with browned flour. Boil up and pour over the pigeons.*

### ⇥ 38. TO ROAST A TURKEY, GOOSE, DUCK, FOWL, &C ⇤

*(Campbell, 1848)*

Whether large or small, wild or tame, birds were most often roasted to achieve maximum flavor. And, as this recipe indicates, each bird was considered best served with a particular type of sauce.

*When you roast a turkey, goose, fowl, or chicken, lay them down to a good fire. Singe them clean with white paper, baste them with butter, and dust on some flour. As to time, a large turkey will take an hour and twenty minutes—a middling one a full hour—a full grown goose, if young, an hour— a large fowl three quarters of an hour—a middling one half an hour, and a small chicken twenty minutes; but this depends entirely on the goodness of your fire.*

*When your fowls are thoroughly plump, and the smoke draws from the breast to the fire, you may be sure they are very near done. Then baste them with butter, dust on a very little flour, and as soon as they have a good froth, serve them up.*

*Geese and ducks are commonly seasoned with onions, sage, and a little pepper and salt.*

*A turkey, when roasted, is generally stuffed in the craw with forc'd meat [forcemeat], or the following stuffing: take a pound of veal, as much grated bread, half a pound of suet cut and beat very fine, a little parsley, with a small bit of thyme or savory, two cloves, half a nutmeg grated, a tea-spoonful of shred lemon-peel, a little pepper and salt, and the yolks of two eggs.*

*Sauce for a Turkey.—Good gravy in a boat; and either bread, onion, or oyster sauce in a bason [var. basin].*

*Sauce for a Goose.—A little good gravy in a boat, apple sauce in a bason, and mustard.*

*Sauce for a Duck.—A little gravy in the dish, and onions in a tea-cup.*

*Sauce for Fowls.—Parsley and butter; or gravy in the dish, and either bread sauce, oyster sauce, or egg sauce in a bason.*

SEAFOOD

---

✦ **FISH TRANSPORT**

By the 1840s, canned salmon and lobster were shipped inland via railroad, and ice-packed fresh fish was transported from Massachusetts to cities such as New York and Philadelphia. By 1851, fresh Atlantic fish was shipped as far inland as Chicago.

---

### ⊰ 39. BOILED CLAMS ⊱

*(Child, 1833)*

Clams claimed a regular place at the New England table, where they were steamed, fried, scalloped, deviled, and fashioned into chowders, fritters, and pies.

*Clams should boil about fifteen minutes in their own water; no other need be added, except a spoonful to keep the bottom shells from burning. It is easy to tell when they are done, by the shells starting wide open. After they are done, they should be taken from the shells, washed thoroughly in their own water, and put in a stewing pan. The water should then be strained through a cloth, so as to get out all the grit; the clams should be simmered in it [the water] ten or fifteen minutes; a little thickening of flour and water added; half a dozen slices of toasted bread or cracker, and pepper, vinegar and butter to your taste. Salt is not needed.*

### ⊰ 40. SLICES OF COD ⊱

*(Ellet, 1871)*

A staple of the New England diet, cod was baked, dried, salted, fashioned into cakes and balls, and placed in chowders and pies; it was also stewed as in the following recipe.

*Three slices make a small dish; put them in a baking-dish, cover them over with some good second stock, a little essence of anchovies; when done thicken the stock, and pass it through a tammy [cloth used as a strainer], pour it over your fish, season with cayenne pepper, and salt and lemon juice; if for caper [sauce] add them, if for maître d'hôtel [a sauce commonly served with fish], add cream and parsley chopped fine.*

### ⊰ 41. FISH CAKES ⊱

*(Levy, 1871)*

Like hash, fish cakes were a popular breakfast food, as they provided a tasty way of presenting leftovers from the previous night's dinner.

*Take the bones from fish of any kind; put the head and bones into a stewpan with a pint of water, a little salt, pepper, an onion and some sweet herbs to stew for gravy. Chop the fish up and mix it well with some crumbs of bread and cold potatoes, equal parts, a little parsley and seasoning. Make into a cake, with the white of an egg or a little butter or milk, egg it over and cover with bread crumbs, then fry a light brown. Pour the gravy over and stew gently for fifteen minutes, stirring it carefully twice or thrice; serve hot and garnish with slices of lemon or parsley.*

## ⫷ 42. HOT CRABS ⫸

*(Leslie, 1851)*

Found off the Atlantic and the Pacific Coasts of the United States as well as the Gulf Coast, crabs gave rise to and feature in an array of regional recipes such as Baltimore crab cake, she-crab soup (claimed by both Charleston and Savannah), Virginia's crab Norfolk, and San Francisco's crab Louis. Blue, Dungeness, and king are three of the most prized crab species in the United States.

*Having boiled the crabs, extract all the meat from the shell, cut it fine, and season it to your taste with nutmeg, salt, and cayenne pepper. Add a bit of butter, some grated bread crumbs, and sufficient vinegar to moisten it. Fill the backshells of the crab with the mixture; set it before the fire, and brown it by holding a red hot shovel or a salamander a little above it.*

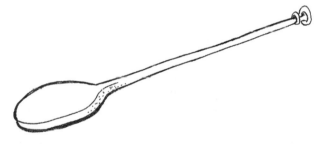

Salamander.

*Cover a large dish with small slices of dry toast with the crust cut off. Lay on each slice a shell filled with the crab. The shell of one crab will contain the meat of two.*

## ⫷ 43. TO MAKE OYSTER LOAVES ⫸

*(Randolph, 1860)*

Of all the fish and shellfish, oysters enjoyed the most popularity; they were eaten raw, incorporated into sauces, baked in pies, steamed, stewed, broiled, and roasted. Oyster loaves were just one of many nineteenth-century American inventions that starred the oyster. Other recipes include Hangtown fry, supposedly a Gold Rush invention made from breaded and fried oysters, bacon, and eggs; and oysters Rockefeller, oysters on the shell topped with a purée of green vegetables and seasoning.

*Take little round loaves [of bread], cut off the tops, scrape out all the crumbs, then put the oysters into a stew pan with the crumbs that came out of the loaves, a little water, and a good lump of butter; stew them together ten or fifteen minutes, then put in a spoonful of good cream, fill your loaves, lay the bit of crust carefully on again, set them in the oven to crisp. Three are enough for a side dish.*

## ⇥ 44. ROAST OYSTERS ⇤

*(Harland, 1871)*

The following recipe stands out for its effusive style and enthusiastic tone, illustrating just how enamored nineteenth-century Americans were with the oyster. It also demonstrates the adaptability of the mollusk; it can be served at formal dinners and casual family meals alike and is equally admired in its raw and its cooked states.

*There is no pleasanter frolic for an Autumn evening, in the regions where oysters are plentiful, than in impromptu "roast" in the kitchen. There the oysters are hastily thrown into the fire by the peck. You may consider that your fastidious taste is marvellously respected if they are washed first. A bushel basket is set to revive the empty shells, and the click of the oyster-knives forms a constant accompaniment to the music of laughing voices. Nor are roast oysters amiss upon your own quiet supper-table, when the "good man" comes in on a wet night, tired and hungry, and wants "something heartening." Wash and wipe the shell-oysters, and lay them in the oven, if it is quick; upon the top of the stove, if it is not. When they open, they are done. Pile in large dish and send to table. Remove the upper shell by a dextrous wrench of the knife, season the oyster on the lower, with pepper-sauce and butter, or pepper, salt, and vinegar in lieu of the sauce, and you have the very aroma of this pearl of bivalves pure and undefiled.*

*Or, you may open while raw, leaving the oysters upon the lower shells; lay in a large baking-pan, and roast in their own liquor, adding pepper, salt, and butter before serving.*

## ⇥ 45. TO BOIL ROCKFISH ⇤

*(Bryan, 1839)*

The southern name for Atlantic striped bass, rockfish was typically boiled; one of the most popular cookbooks of the day, however, includes a recipe for pickling rockfish in a mixture of vinegar, cloves, pepper, and mace.

*Clean the rock fish nicely, put it in a fish kettle, with enough cold water to cover it well, having dissolved in it a handful of salt. Boil it gently and skim it well. When done, drain it, sprinkle over it a handful of grated bread, with some broken bits of butter; place it before the fire, and brown it a little: then serve it up warm, garnish with slices of lemon, and accompany the rock with parsley and egg sauce [see recipe 55], a dish of mashed potatoes and a plate of sallad [obs.].*

## ❧ 46. SALMON STEAK ☙

*(Harland, 1871)*

Fresh salmon was plentiful on both the Atlantic and the Pacific Coasts. By the 1850s, large cities, such as Chicago, received shipments packed in ice. The Northeast began canning salmon and lobster as far back as the 1840s. Although no longer cooked on a gridiron or turned with a flat wire egg-beater, today's salmon steaks are commonly grilled in the same way as described here.

*Dry well with a cloth, dredge with flour, and lay them upon a well-buttered gridiron, over clear hot coals. Turn with a broad-blade knife slipped beneath, and a flat wire egg-beater above, lest the steak should break. When done to light brown, lay in a hot dish, butter each steak, seasoning with salt and pepper, seasoning with salt and pepper, cover closely and serve.*

## ❧ 47. BAKED SHAD ☙

*(Bryan, 1839)*

In addition to its meat, American shad is also prized for its roe, or eggs. A member of the herring family, the American shad weighs around three to five pounds. Because of its large size, shad is often stuffed, as it is in the following recipe.

*Stuff the shad with grated ham, bread crumbs and mashed potatoes, seasoned with butter, pepper, mace and chopped parsley; rub the outside of it with the beaten yolk of eggs; cover it with grated bread, put it into a pan of suitable size, with a little water, a gill and a half [6 oz.] of wine, and a few spoonfuls of horseradish vinegar. Roll four ounces of butter in a little flour, break it into small bits, and put them over the fish: lay on it a piece of paper, and bake it with moderate heat, raising the lid and basting it occasionally with the gravy. Serve it up warm, garnish with small force-meat balls, and pour over the gravy.*

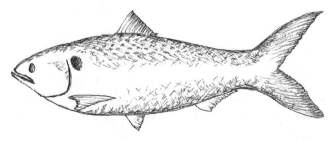

*Shad.*

## ❧ 48. FRIED TROUT ❧

*(Hall, 1855)*

Trout were plentiful in American waters until the late 1860s, by which time overfishing had depleted their numbers. By the turn of the century, however, trout were making a comeback, helped in large part by hatcheries.

*Scale, gut, clean, dry, and flour; fry them in butter until they are a rich clear brown; fry some green parsley crisp and make some plain melted butter; the butter may be poured over the fish, but it is most advisable to send it [separately to the table] in a butter tureen.*

## GRAVIES, SAUCES, CATSUPS, AND PICKLES

What is here termed gravy would be called broth or stock nowadays. Pickles and ketchups were largely served with meat, poultry, and fish. Ketchup recipes, such as for tomato, mushroom, or walnut can often resemble those for pickles. Whereas pickling places the emphasis on the ingredient pickled (we pickle cucumbers to preserve the cucumbers for future eating), ketchups emphasize the pickling liquid, which is often added as flavoring to sauces served over meat, fish, and poultry.

## ❧ 49. MUSHROOM CATSUP ❧

*(Allen, 1845)*

Ketchups were used to flavor sauces, meats, fish, and poultry. Unlike the tomato ketchup known today, mid-nineteenth-century ketchups were a savory and spicy concoction containing little, if any, sugar. As the century progressed, however, sugar began to creep into recipes.

*4 quarts of mushrooms*
*2 spoonfuls of salt*
*4 oz. of shallots*
*1 oz. of ginger*
*1 oz. of mace, in powder*
*1 cayenne pepper*
*1 oz. of cloves, all in powder*

*Wipe and clean the mushrooms, see there are none worm-eaten, sprinkle the salt in as you put the mushrooms in, and set them over a slow fire. They will produce a great deal of liquor, which you must strain, and then put in the above seasoning. Boil and skim very well. When cold, bottle and cork close. In two months boil it up again with a little fresh spice and sticks of horseradish, and it will then keep the year, which it seldom does, if not boiled the second time.*

### ঌ 50. TOMATO CATSUP ঌ

*(Hale, 1841)*

Like the mushroom ketchup in recipe 49, the following recipe contains no sugar. By the end of the century, however, tomato ketchups began to include increasingly large amounts of sugar.

*This is a very good and healthy flavor for meats, sauces, &c. Take two quarts skinned tomatos [var.], two table-spoonfuls of salt, two of black pepper, and two of ground mustard; also one spoonful of allspice, and four pods of red pepper. Mix and rub these well together, and stew them slowly in a pint of vinegar for three hours. Then strain the liquor through a sieve, and simmer down to one quart of catsup. Put this in bottles and cork it tight.*

### ঌ 51. WALNUT PICKLE [AND CATSUP] ঌ

*(Child, 1833)*

Americans imported their fondness for walnut pickle from England, where it had long been an indispensable condiment for cold meats and cheeses.

*When walnuts are so ripe that a pin will go into them easily, they are ready for pickling. They should be soaked twelve days in very strong cold salt and water, which has been boiled and skimmed. A quantity of vinegar, enough to cover them well, should be boiled with whole pepper, mustard-seed, small onions, or garlic, cloves, ginger, and horseradish; this should not be poured upon them till it is cold. They should be pickled a few months before they are eaten. To be kept close covered; for the air softens them. The liquor is an excellent catsup to be eaten on fish.*

### ঌ 52. DRAWN MEAT GRAVIES, OR BROWN GRAVIES ঌ

*(Beecher, 1858)*

Brown gravy commonly refers to that made from meat, and white refers to that made from poultry. Recipe 23, for shoulder of mutton, calls for just such a gravy as the following.

*Put into a sauce-pan fresh meat cut in small pieces, seasoned with salt and pepper and a bit of butter, and heat it half an hour, till brown, stirring so that it shall not stick.*

*Pour on boiling water, a pint for each pound—simmer three hours and skim it well. Settle and strain it, and set it aside to use. Thicken, when you need it, with brown flour, a teaspoonful to a half pint.*

## ⇥ 53. PICKLED PEACHES ⇤

*(Beecher, 1858)*

Pickled peaches were a common condiment during the nineteenth century, especially in the South, and were served as an accompaniment to meat.

*Take ripe but hard peaches, wipe off the down, stick a few cloves into them, and lay them in cold spiced vinegar. In three months they will be sufficiently pickled, and also retain much of their natural flavor.*

## ⇥ 54. APPLE SAUCE ⇤

*(Bliss, 1864)*

Apple sauce is still prepared in much the same way today. It is often served as a sweet complement to meat. The following recipe can be paired with pork chops, recipe 27.

*Pare, core, quarter and wash one dozen russet apples; stew them twenty minutes in half a tea-cupful of water over a slow fire, stir into them one table-spoonful of sugar, one table-spoonful of butter, a pinch of cinnamon, and a little nutmeg; dish and serve.*

## ⇥ 55. EGG SAUCE ⇤

*(Leslie, 1851)*

Egg sauce was a standard variation of the melted butter sauce so favored by early and mid-nineteenth-century Americans. Herbs, oysters, lobsters, or capers are also added to melted butter to form sauces. Serve with the boiled rockfish, recipe 45.

*Boil four eggs ten minutes. Dip them into cold water to prevent their looking blue. Peel off the shell. Chop the yolks of all, and the whites of two, and stir them into melted butter. Serve this sauce with boiled poultry or fish.*

## ⇥ 56. MINT SAUCE ⇤

*(Levy 1871)*

Part of our British inheritance, mint sauce is still prepared as an accompaniment to roasted lamb dishes today; it almost invariably calls for the same list of ingredients found below. Serve with the roast leg of lamb, recipe 21.

*Half a pint of vinegar, a tablespoonful of sugar, with some mint, chopped fine.*

## VEGETABLES

During the nineteenth and early twentieth centuries, vegetables enjoyed a far more minor role in the daily diet than they do today. Frequently served as side dishes, vegetables were often boiled until they were limp; some recipes call for cauliflower and cabbage to be boiled well over an hour and asparagus boiled until it could be pressed flat with a fork. It would not be until the discovery of vitamins in the early twentieth century that vegetables would be considered an essential part of a balanced meal. The discovery that boiling vegetables for a long time leaches much of their vitamin content also led to increasingly shorter cooking times and alternative cooking methods, such as steaming and stir-frying.

### ◆ 57. BEETS ◆

*(Hall, 1855)*

In addition to being pickled to serve cold as they are in the following recipe, beets were also boiled until cooked through before being stewed with a combination of shallot, parsley, butter, and vinegar.

*Break off the leaves, but do not cut beets, as that spoils both flavor and appearance; wash them and boil them until tender; then take them out into basin of cold water, and rub all the outside skin off, with the hands; then slice them thin in a dish, and just cover them with cold vinegar, and sprinkle them with pepper and salt, or quarter them, and lay them for a day or two in cold vinegar, as they are then fit for use. The tips of young beets are dressed as asparagus.*

### ◆ 58. GREENS ◆

*(Beecher, 1858)*

Greens were especially enjoyed in the spring, when they proved a refreshing tonic after months of dining on heavy winter dishes. As in the following recipe, they were frequently served on toast, drizzled with butter, and garnished with either hard boiled or poached egg.

*Beet tops, turnip tops, spinach, cabbage sprouts, dandelions, cowslips, all these boil in salted water till they are tender, then drain in a colander, pressing hard. Chop them a little, and warm them in a sauce-pan, with a little butter.*

*Lay them on buttered toast, and if you like, garnish them with hard-boiled egg, cut into slices. If not fresh [young and recently harvested], soak them half an hour in salt and water.*

### 59. TO STEW OCHRA [OKRA]

*(Hill, 1867)*

In addition to its use in gumbo, okra was often stewed with tomatoes, battered and fried, or boiled whole and dressed with butter.

*Cut it in round slices; put it in a stewpan; for a quart, add a wineglass of hot water, a tablespoonful of butter, into which as been rubbed an even teaspoonful of flour; salt and pepper to taste. Cover the stew-pan, shake it occasionally, and stew until tender; serve in a hot covered dish. A few tomatoes and a little onion stewed with the ochra is an improvement. This is excellent used as a sauce for plain boiled rice.*

### 60. ONIONS

*(Lea, 1873)*

The following recipe combines milk with the boiling water to tame the onion's bite, but some recipes from this time period call for the onions to be boiled in several changes of water in order to drown and discard any potential piquancy. Even though cooks took great care to boil out the onion's snap, some felt that, when eaten in its piquant form, the onion aided brain function and helped sooth nervous temperaments. Thus a few did eat onions in their raw or barely cooked states for medicinal purposes. However, most cookbooks assumed their readers were wary of smelling like onions, and the majority of recipes call for boiling or stewing them until they could be easily pierced with a fork.

*After they are peeled, boil them in milk and water; if small, they will cook in half an hour; when they are done, pour off the water; put in cream, butter and salt, and let them stew a few minutes. Small onions are much better for cooking, as they are not so strong.*

### 61. TO FRY PARSLEY

*(Godey's Lady's Book, 1861)*

Fried parsley is a fitting accompaniment to roast beef or lamb. As with most fried foods, it benefits from a thorough salting.

*When the parsley has been washed and thoroughly dried, throw it into lard or butter which is on the point to boil; take it up with a slice [slotted spoon or spatula] the instant it is crisp, and lay it on paper on a sieve before the fire.*

## ❧ 62. POKE TOPS ☙

*(Bryan, 1839)*

The shoots of this plant, which is native to the eastern United States, were often compared to asparagus and cooked just as the greens in recipe 58. A typically southern method of preparing greens follows. Ham hock was (and still is) often used in lieu of, or in addition to, the bacon. Because poke becomes difficult to digest and actually contains minute amounts of toxins when older, poke recipes invariably indicate that the shoots should be gathered when young and no taller than a half-foot in height.

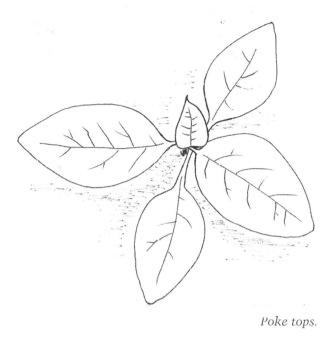

*Poke tops.*

*Poke tops, or sprouts that put forth in the spring of the year, are considered fine sallad [obs.] by many people. Gather them when very young and tender, pick them carefully, pour boiling water on, and let them stand for an hour or two, to draw out the strong taste. Having ready a pot of boiling water, in which a piece of bacon has been boiled till nearly done, put the poke into it, and let it boil with the meat till it is tender. It will take but a short time to boil it sufficiently, as it is not good when boiled very soft. Serve it with the meat, drain it well, and have salt, pepper and vinegar to season it at table.*

## ❧ 63. POTATOES, TO ROAST UNDER MEAT ☙

*(Randolph, 1860)*

As they are today, potatoes were prepared in an endless variety of ways. The more expansive cookbooks included up to twenty recipes for the tuber. In addition to the old familiars (mashed, fried, baked, and stuffed potatoes), cookbooks included recipes for potato pudding, potato cheesecake, and even potato sandwiches.

*Half boil large potatos [var.], drain the water from them, and put them into an earthen dish or small tin pan, under meat that is roasting, and baste them with some of the dripping; when they are browned on one side, turn them and brown the other; send them up around the meat, or in a small dish.*

## ❧ 64. SAUER KROUT ❧

*(Levy, 1871)*

In German sauerkraut means "sour cabbage." Since Eastern Europeans first brought sauerkraut to the United States, it has become so entwined in American culture that today it's frequently eaten on hotdogs and is an essential part of the Reuben sandwich, a decidedly American invention.

*Cut the cabbage fine, pack it tight in a clean barrel, with salt between each layer of cabbage, pound it down very tight, then lay a weight on the top, and place the cover on tight, put it in a warm cellar for three weeks, then take off the skum [var. scum] which will rise on the top, and lay a clean cloth on; the juice should always cover the krout. It will keep for years.*

## ❧ 65. SWEET POTATOES, BROILED ❧

*(Bryan, 1839)*

Sweet potatoes originated in Central and South America and were brought to the Caribbean. The Spanish introduced them to Europe, where they became one of the region's first adopted New World foods. The author of the following recipe most likely refers to them as Spanish potatoes for this reason.

*Take a fine large Spanish potato, boil it till half done, then cut it across in slices about half an inch thick, broil them on a gridiron over clear coals, the bars of which having been greased to prevent the potatoes sticking to them; turn them over once, and when both sides are a light brown: serve them up, pour over a little melted butter, and eat them at breakfast or supper. Sweet potatoes may be half boiled, sliced, floured and tried [sic] in butter.*

## ❧ 66. SUCCOTASH ❧

*(Ladies of the First Presbyterian Church, Dayton, Ohio, 1873)*

Succotash is just one of the many Indian dishes made from corn that were adopted by the colonists. The name derives from the Narragansett Indian word "msickquatash (also spelled misickquatash)." Countless variations of the dish exist; the first known recorded recipes from the eighteenth century include a range of meat such as fowl, corned beef, pork, and even bear. Many New Englanders include cranberry beans in lieu of the Lima.

*Put Lima beans on to boil, soon after breakfast; let them get well done. Have the corn boiling in a separate pot. When done, cut the corn off the cobs and have twice as much corn as beans; put the corn with the beans and let them boil. Just before serving, put in a little butter, pepper and salt.*

## ⤷ 67. TOMATOES ⤶

*(Child, 1833)*

Until the early nineteenth century, the tomato's culinary function in the United States had largely been confined to its use in ketchups and pickles. By mid-century, however, tomatoes had gained a wider acceptance by Americans. Cookbooks from this era included recipes for stewed, stuffed, baked, fried, and even sliced raw tomatoes.

*Tomatoes should be skinned by pouring boiling water over them. After they are skinned, they should be stewed half an hour, in tin, with a little salt, a small bit of butter, and a spoonful of water, to keep them from burning. This is a delicious vegetable. It is easily cultivated, and yields a most abundant crop. Some people pick them green, and pickle them.*

## ⤷ 68. TURNIPS ⤶

*(Hale, 1841)*

As they are today, turnips were often prepared as were potatoes—mashed, boiled, or sliced and baked in cream.

*Turnips should be pared; put into boiling water with a little salt; boiled till tender; then squeeze them thoroughly from the water, mash them smooth, add a piece of butter and a little pepper and salt.*

## EGGS, RICE, PASTA AND SUNDRY OTHER DISHES

### ⤷ 69. BAKED BEANS, YANKEE FASHION ⤶

*(Collins, 1857)*

Otherwise known as Boston baked beans, this dish was common throughout the North and, as the name suggests, a mainstay of Bostonians. The dish was usually baked on Saturday and eaten in the evening along with Boston brown bread [see recipe 81] and served along with fish cakes for breakfast the next day. Maple syrup or, more recently, molasses is a common ingredient not included in the following recipe.

*Take three pints of white beans, put them in cold water over night, take them out in the morning, wash and rub them well, then put them in a pot, and boil them until tender; then put them in an earthen dish.*

*Cut a neat piece of pork, place it on the top of the beans; bake them slowly until well browned. This is a fine dish for a snowy day.*

## ❧ 70. A GOOD WAY OF COOKING EGGS ❧

*(Godey's Lady's Book, 1864)*

As the following recipe indicates, eggs were often dressed in much the same way as fish; they were also frequently ground and added to sauces served with fish.

*Boil say six eggs quite hard, peel, and cut in two lengthways; put two ounces of good butter in a saucepan (enameled the best), boil till of a rich brown; have ready to hand a tablespoonful of vinegar mixed with a teaspoonful of made mustard, salt and pepper to taste, and pour this mixture into the boiling butter, mix well and pour over the eggs (which must be kept hot) so that each portion of egg receives its share of sauce; the eggs should be placed on the dish with the yelk [var. yolk] part upwards and serve up immediately, as hot as possible; the sauce must be well blended, and for this purpose use a small pastebrush; a teaspoonful of water will often facilitate the blending. The same sauce is excellent with boiled fish. 6 servings.*

## ❧ 71. HOMINY ❧

*(Leslie, 1851)*

The American Indians introduced the European settlers to hominy, dried white or yellow corn kernels that have had the hull and germ removed. The term hominy grits, or grits, refers to finely ground hominy. Grits, in turn, come in coarse, medium, or fine grind. Grits remain a common breakfast dish throughout the South.

*Wash the hominy very clean through three or four waters. Then put it into a pot (allowing two quarts of water to one quart of hominy) and boil it slowly five hours. When done, take it up, and drain the liquid from it through a cullender [var. colander]. Put the hominy into a deep dish, and stir into it a small piece of fresh butter.*

*The small grained hominy is boiled in rather less water and generally eaten with butter and sugar.*

## ❧ 72. HOPPING JOHN ❧

*(Rutledge, 1847)*

Hopping, or hoppin', John was a favorite dish of South Carolina low country plantations slaves. Unlike the rest of the South that adopted the "gang system," the low-country slaves, from South Carolina and Georgia, worked under the "task system," performing a set number of jobs each day, often leaving them time for themselves during off season. They became known as Gullahs or Geechees and developed their own language, which proved a mix of English and African. Although Hoppin' John is usually made with black-eyed peas, or cowpeas, the following recipe calls for red peas. Hoppin' John remains a popular dish throughout the South and is traditionally eaten on New Year's Day, when the black-eyed pea is touted as bringing good luck for the coming year.

*One pound of bacon, one pint of red peas, one pint of rice. First put on the peas, and when half boiled, add the bacon. When the peas are well boiled, throw in the rice, which must be first washed and gravelled [picked free of extra matter]. When the rice has been boiling half an hour, take the pot off the fire and put it on coals to steam, as in boiling rice alone. Put a quart of water on the peas at first, and if it boils away too much, add a little more hot water. Season with salt and pepper, and, if liked, a sprig of green mint. In serving up, put the rice and peas first in the dish, and the bacon on the top.*

### ⧎ 73. TO DRESS MACCARONI ⧎

*(Leslie, 1851)*

Just as with all pasta, macaroni was not a common ingredient before the late nineteenth-century wave of Italian immigration. It appeared, however, every now and again in cookbooks, most commonly those geared toward the upper-middle and upper-class reader; it was considered something of a luxury item.

*Have ready a pot of boiling water. Throw a little salt into it, and then by slow degrees put in a pound of the maccaroni, a little at a time. Keep stirring it gently, and continue to do so very often while boiling. Take care to keep it well covered with water. Have ready a kettle of boiling water to replenish the maccaroni pot if it should be in danger of getting too dry. In about twenty minutes it will be done. It must be quite soft, but it must not boil long enough to break.*

*When the maccaroni has boiled sufficiently, pour in immediately a little cold water, and let stand a few minutes, keeping it covered.*

*Grate half a pound of Parmesan cheese into a deep dish and scatter over it a few small bits of butter. Then with a skimmer that is perforated with holes, commence taking up the maccaroni, (draining it well,) and spread a layer of it over the cheese and butter. Spread over it another layer of grated cheese and butter, and then a layer of maccaroni, and so on till your dish is full; having a layer of maccaroni on the top, over which spread some butter without cheese. Cover the dish, and set it in an oven for half an hour. It will then be ready to send to table.*

*You may grate some nutmeg over each layer of maccaroni.*

*Allow half a pound of butter to a pound of maccaroni and half a pound of cheese.*

## 74. OMELET

*(Allen, 1845)*

As they are today, omelettes were often served for breakfast or as a light supper.

> *6 eggs*
> *1/2 cup of cream*
> *1/4 lb. of dripping of pork*
> *Seasoning*

> *Beat the eggs well, then add the cream; have ready some chives, or shallot, and parsley, cut very fine, with a scrape or two of nutmeg. Stir all together, mix with a very little flour and salt. Have the dripping ready, boiling hot, and pour the above into it. When one side is of a fine yellow brown, turn and do the other. Some scraped lean ham put in with the batter, is thought an improvement. A good deal of parsley should be used, and tarragon gives a fine flavor.*

## 75. TO BOIL RICE

*(Randolph, 1860)*

Served as a side dish, which often accompanied boiled meat or poultry, boiled rice was a common feature of the southern table.

> *Put two cups full of rice in a bowl of water, rub it well with the hand, and pour off the water; do this until the water ceases to be discoloured; then put the rice into two and half cups of cold water; add a tea-spoonful of salt, cover the pot close, and set it on a brisk fire; let it boil ten minutes, pour off the greater part of the water, and remove the pot to a bed of coals, where it must remain a quarter of an hour to soak and dry.*

## 76. RICE CROQUETTES

*(Ellet, 1871)*

Croquettes can be fashioned from an endless array of ingredients and into a variety of shapes, the most common of which are ovals, cylinders, and balls. Once formed, croquettes are battered and fried. They were often served as an accompaniment to a main meat dish.

> *Take half a pound of boiled rice, mix with it two table-spoonfuls of grated cheese, and a little nutmeg and mace; then take a little butter, six table-spoonfuls of cold chicken breast, minced, six bearded oysters, a little parsley and lemon peel, and mixed together with rich milk or cream. Roll out a table-spoon heaping full of the rice, and put into it as much as it will hold of the mixture, folding the edges and inclosing [var.] it; brush the balls over with*

*yolk of raw egg, roll them in cracker crumbs, and fry them light brown in
boiling lard. Serve them hot when drained.*

## ⇾ 77. HAM SANDWICH ⇽

*(Ladies of the First Presbyterian Church, Dayton, Ohio, 1873)*

In addition to ham, sandwiches were also made regularly from grated
smoked tongue. They were served at lunch or supper and were rolled on occasion rather than served flat.

*Rub one tablespoonful of mustard into one-half pound of sweet butter; spread
on thin slices of bread; cut boiled ham very thin, and place in between two
pieces of the bread.*

## BREAD AND BISCUITS

Indigenous to America, corn, in the form of cornmeal, was commonly
used for bread making. In the southern rice-growing regions, rice was also
frequently used in addition to, or in place of, flour. As it began to flourish
in the upper Mississippi Valley, flour became increasingly common over the
course of the century.

---

### ✦ OBTAINING GOOD FLOUR

(Hale, 1841)

The following directions on cleaning wheat illustrate just how time-
consuming and tedious certain kitchen tasks could be.

*The first requisite for good bread is that the flour or meal be good. Wheat
is always better for being washed; if it be at all injured by smut, it is
not fit for food unless it be thoroughly washed. In the country this is
easily done.*

*Put the grain in a clean tub, a bushel at a time; fill the tub with water,
and stir the whole up from the bottom, briskly, with your hand, or a stick.
Pour off the water and fill with clean till the water ceases to be colored
or dirty. Two or three waters usually are sufficient. Finish the washing
quickly as possible, so as not to soak the grain; then spread it thinly on
a large, strong sheet, (it is best to keep a coarse unbleached sheet solely
for this purpose, if you wash your grain,) laid on clean boards in the sun,
or where the sun and air can be freely admitted. Stir the grain with your
hand every two or three hours; it will dry in a day, if the weather be fair.*

*Fresh-ground flour makes the best and sweetest bread. If you live in
the vicinity of a mill, never have more than one or two bushels ground
into flour at a time.*

---

*Take two pounds of fine flour and rub it into one pound of warm mashed potatoes; then mix some warm milk and water with a little yeast and salt, and put it in the flour; let it rise for two hours in a warm place in winter; bake it in tins. It makes nice rolls for breakfast. By adding some sugar, eggs and currants, you can make nice buns.*

### ⊰ 84. RYE AND INDIAN BREAD ⊱

*(Hale, 1841)*

Also known as Rye 'n' Injun. Rye grew well in New England, where it was frequently mixed with corn meal and molasses to make the following bread.

*Take four quarts of sifted Indian [corn] meal; put it into a glazed earthen pan, sprinkle over it a table-spoonful of fine salt; pour over it about two quarts of boiling water, stir and work it till every part of the meal is thoroughly wet; Indian meal absorbs a greater quantity of water. When it is about milk-warm, work in two quarts of rye meal, half a pint of lively yeast, mixed with a pint of warm water; add more warm water if needed. Work the mixture well with your hands: it should be stiff, but not firm as flour dough. Have ready a large, deep, well buttered pan; put in the dough and smooth the top by putting your hand in warm water, and then patting down the loaf. Set this to rise in a warm place in the winter; in the summer it should not be put by the fire. When it begins to crack, on the top, which will usually be in about an hour or an hour and a half, put it into a well heated oven and bake it three or four hours. It is better to let it stand in the oven all night, unless the weather is warm. Indian meal requires to be well cooked. The loaf will weigh between seven and eight pounds.*

### ⊰ 85. BUCKWHEAT CAKES ⊱

*(Parkinson, 1864)*

Although treated as a cereal, buckwheat is actually an herb, which hails from Russia. Buckwheat cakes, a variety of pancakes, were a winter breakfast favorite. Like pancakes today, they were often topped with maple syrup and served with sausage or bacon.

*To a quart of buckwheat meal put a little Indian [corn] meal (say a table-spoonful) and a little salt; make them into a batter with cold water, taking care to beat it very well, as the excellence of buckwheat cakes depends very much on their being well beaten; then put in a large spoonful of good yeast, and set to rise; when sufficiently risen, bake them a clear brown on a griddle. They are usually buttered before being sent to table.*

### ⊰ 86. FOR MAKING SOUTH CAROLINA JOHNNY OR JOURNEY CAKE ⊱

*(Godey's Lady's Book, 1860)*

The American johnnycake, or jonnycake, is traditionally made with corn-meal. However rice and hominy versions are also common throughout the South.

*Half a pint of boiled rice or hominy, two eggs, one tablespoonful of butter, a little salt, flour enough to make a stiff batter; spread on an oaken board, and bake before a hot fire; when nicely baked on one side, turn, and bake the other; cut through the centre, and butter well. It pays for the trouble. This is the way our servant made it at my home in Charleston, South Carolina.*

### ⊰ 87. INDIAN MUSH ⊱

*(Bryan, 1839)*

Basically a breakfast porridge, mush is a mixture of corn meal and water or milk. As a breakfast dish, it was either cooled, sliced, and fried or spooned warm from the pot and topped with maple syrup or butter.

*Like many other of our receipts, the process of making mush is quite plain and simple, yet it is often badly prepared, and to the inexperienced some instructions are necessary. Sift some fine Indian [corn] meal, make a smooth batter of it by stirring in a sufficiency of cold water. Having ready a pot of boiling water, throw in a handful of salt, and stir in your batter till it is like very thick soup. Boil it till of the proper consistence, and stir it frequently to prevent its being lumpy, and to keep it from burning at the bottom. Mush, made in this manner, will never fail to be thoroughly done and clear of lumps, which are two common failures. Cold mush may be sliced and fried brown in butter. They are very good for breakfast.*

## PASTRY, PIES, PUDDINGS, DUMPLINGS, AND FRITTERS

The vast array of savory pies and puddings eaten during the nineteenth century reflect America's British heritage. They could be eaten as a side dish or served as the main course. Some, like Indian pudding—also known as hasty pudding—were often eaten at breakfast. As the price of sugar declined throughout the nineteenth century, puddings became increasingly sweeter and were served after the meat course. By the end of the century, savory pies and puddings had begun to disappear from the American table, although a few, such as chicken pot pie, are still served today. Dessert puddings, which proliferated throughout the nineteenth century, have also declined in popularity, with a few die-hard exceptions such as those made with bread, lemon, tapioca, or chocolate as their featured ingredient. Even the dessert pie, which is still popular throughout the United States, saw a decline beginning in the 1870s, when health food reformers warned Americans that their diet contained far too much flour and sugar. Despite such health concerns, however, pies remain a beloved part of the American diet. Some versions, such as apple pie, are ubiquitous; others, such as pecan pie, shoo-fly pie, key lime pie, or sweet potato pie have strong regional affiliations.

## Savory Pastry

### ᴈ 88. PLAIN PASTE ᴈ

*(Bryan, 1839)*

Crust was often made from suet and usually produced a dense and heavy end result. By comparison, the use of butter results in a far lighter pastry. The following recipe is suited for everyday savory and sweet dishes. The directions state that the butter should be washed before use to clean it of all salt particles. Butter was coated in salt as a preservative.

*All pastry should be made of the best materials: the flour should be superfine and quite new, and the butter fresh and sweet. For fine puff or sweet paste, every particle of salt should be washed from the butter; otherwise it will not rise well nor have a pleasant taste. For meat pies, dumplings, &c., the butter should be freely washed in cold water, to give it a sweet taste, but salt should be sprinkled in the flour, or the paste will have a flat unpleasant taste. Sift two quarts of flour, and weigh out a pound of butter; rub half of the butter into the flour, sprinkling in a little salt. Make it into a stiff paste with cold water, and roll it out into a thin sheet; divide the half pound of butter into two equal parts, break them up into small bits, and put one half over the sheet of paste, mashing it smooth with a knife; sprinkle on a little flour, roll up the paste into a scroll, and flatten it with a rolling-pin; roll it again into a sheet, put on the last portion of butter in the same manner, and springling [sic] on a little flour; fold it up, roll it into a sheet the third time, and it will be ready for use. Plain paste is generally used for pies, dumplings and breakfast cakes. By rolling in the butter in this manner, it makes the paste much lighter and more flaky than when the butter is all rubbed into the flour at first.*

### ᴈ 89. TO MAKE PUFF PASTE ᴈ

*(Randolph, 1860)*

The following recipe makes a light pastry suitable for both savory and sweet dishes.

*Sift a quart of flour, leave out a little for rolling the paste, make up the remainder with cold water into a stiff paste, knead it well, and roll it out several times; wash the salt from a pound of butter, divide it into four parts, put one of them on the paste in little bits, fold it up, and continue to roll it till the butter is well mixed; then put another portion of butter, roll it in the same manner; do this till all the butter is mingled with the paste; touch it very lightly with the hands in making—bake it in a moderate oven, that will permit it to rise, but will not make it brown. Good paste must look white, and as light as a feather.*

## Savory Pies

### ❧ 90. BEEFSTEAK PIE ☙

*(Ellet, 1871)*

Simple savory pies, such as the following, were an economical means of serving meat. The crust often took the place of bread.

*Take some good steaks, beat them with a rolling-pin, season them with pepper and salt; fill a dish with them, adding as much water as will half fill it, then cover with a good crust, and bake it well.*

### ❧ 91. CONNECTICUT THANKSGIVING CHICKEN PIE ☙

*(Webster, 1853)*

By placing the chicken between layers of butter-rich, as opposed to suet-laden pastry, this recipe transforms the common chicken pie into a more elaborate dish fit for special occasions.

*In sufficient water to prevent burning, stew old not young fowls, jointed, all but tender enough for the table. Pour all into a dish, and season with salt and pepper to taste. When about cold, place the parts in your pudding dish, lined with a thin common paste, adding about half a pound of butter to three pounds of fowl, in alternate layers. Take more of the paste; roll in nine times, studding it each time with butter, (it must be made very rich;) to be careful to roll out, each time, from you, and to roll up towards you, leaving it, at least, an inch thick. Add the upper crust; cut a lip in it; and ornament it with some of the reserved paste, having first lightly sprinkled the chickens with flour, after almost filling the dish with the liquor in which the chickens were stewed. Pin tight around the rim of the dish a cloth bandage, to prevent the escape of the juices; and bake from an hour to an hour and a half, in a quick oven. If the top burns, lay a paper over it.*

### ❧ 92. OYSTER PIE ☙

*(Ladies of the First Presbyterian Church, Dayton, Ohio, 1873)*

The following recipe relies on the liquid from the oysters themselves to moisten the pie. Wine or milk was also commonly added to the dish.

*Take a large dish, butter it, and spread a rich paste over the sides and around the edge, but not on the bottom. The oysters should be fresh and as large and fine as possible; drain off part of the liquor from the oysters; put them into a pan, and season them with pepper, salt and spice. Have ready the yolks of three eggs, chopped fine, and grated bread crumbs; pour the oysters with as much of their liquor as you please, into the dish that has the paste in it; strew over them the chopped egg and grated bread; roll out the lid of the pie and put it on, crimping the edges; bake in a quick [400–425°] oven.*

## Sweet Pastry

### ❧ 93. STANDING PASTE FOR FRUIT PIES ❧

*(Bryan, 1839)*

A standing paste is a sturdy one, which can retain the hot liquid from fruit, meat, or shellfish without tearing or leaking.

*Sift three pints of flour, rub well into it one pound of fresh butter, a spoonful of salt, and make it a good paste with sweet milk; knead it well, and beat it with a rolling-pin till quite smooth.*

### ❧ 94. APPLE PIE ❧

*(Hale, 1841)*

Apples proliferated in the United States, in large part due to the American love of cider. The enormous number of trees needed to fill the national demand eventually led to the cultivation of thousands of apple varieties well suited to eating fresh, cooking, and preserving. Many of these varieties have since been lost to commercial production.

*Apples of a pleasant sour, and fully ripe, make the best pies—pare, core and slice them, line a deep buttered dish with paste, lay in the apples, strewing in moist brown sugar and a little pounded lemon-peel or cinnamon; cover and bake about forty minutes. The oven must not be very hot.*

*When apples are green, stew them with a very little water before making your pie. Green fruit requires a double quantity of sugar.*

*Gooseberries and green currants are made in the same manner.*

### ❧ 95. PEACH PIE ❧

*(Ellet, 1871)*

Basic fruit pies such as the following were a common part of the middle- and working-class diet.

*Take mellow juicy peaches—wash and put them in a deep pie plate, lined with pie crust. Sprinkle a thick layer of sugar, on each layer of peaches, put in about a table-spoonful of water, and sprinkle a little flour on top—cover with thick crust and bake from fifty to sixty minutes.*

### ❧ 96. SWEET POTATO PIE ❧

*(Bryan, 1839)*

Grown largely in the southern Atlantic states and Georgia, sweet potatoes were a staple of southern cooking. In addition to being turned into pies, they were roasted whole, mashed, fried and made into breads and puddings.

*Peel your potatoes, wash them clean, slice and stew them in a very little water till quite soft, and nearly dry; then mash them fine, season them with butter, sugar, cream, nutmeg and cinnamon, and when cold, add four beaten eggs, and press the pulp through a sieve. Roll out plain or standing paste as for other pies, put a sheet of it over a large buttered patty-pan, or deep plate, put in smoothly a thick layer of the potato pulp, and bake it in a moderate [350–375°] oven. Grate loaf sugar over it when done, and send it to table warm or cold, with cream sauce or boiled custard.*

## Puddings

---

### ✧ GENERAL DIRECTIONS IN REGARD TO PUDDINGS AND CUSTARDS

(Beecher, 1858)

The following directions explain how puddings were cooked in a pudding-bag. Molds were also used for the fancier dessert puddings and began to replace pudding-bags toward the end of the century.

*Make pudding-bags of thick close sheeting, to shut out the water. Before putting in the pudding, put the bag in water, and wring it out, then flour the inside thoroughly. In tying it, leave room to swell; flour and Indian need a good deal, and are hard and heavy if cramped.*

*Put an old plate in the bottom of the pot, to keep the bag from burning into the pot. Turn the pudding after it has been in five minutes, to keep the heavy parts from settling. Keep the pudding covered with water, and do not let it stop boiling, as this will tend to make it water soaked. Fill up with boiling water, as cold would spoil the pudding. Dip the bag a moment in cold water, just before turning out the pudding.*

---

## ❧ 97. PUDDING SAUCE ❧

*(Rutledge, 1847)*

This pudding sauce can be served on top of sweet and savory puddings alike. It will transform the latter, such as the plain pudding [recipe 98] and the Indian pudding [recipe 101] from main or side dishes into desserts.

*Six heaping table-spoonfuls of loaf sugar, half a pound of butter, worked to a cream; then add one egg, one wineglass of white wine, one nutmeg.—When it is all well mixed, set it on the fire until it comes to boil: it is then fit for use.*

## ❧ 98. BOILED PUDDING, PLAIN ❧

*(Collins, 1857)*

As the following recipe indicates, in addition to being boiled in cloth bags, puddings were also baked in containers, much as they are today. They were eaten as a main dish, a side dish, or dessert, depending on their contents. The following basic pudding could be served alongside a meat dish, eaten as the main dish, or served with the preceding pudding sauce [recipe 97] as a dessert.

*Take three eggs, and beat them up well; add slowly, a gill [4 oz.] of milk or cream, two ounces of sugar, four ounces of flour, and a little nutmeg; taking pains to beat it into a very smooth batter. Then mince seven ounces of beef-suet very fine, and stir it in gradually, and two or three ounces of bread-crumbs. Beat it all together well, for some time, and pour it into a pudding-bag, and boil it three hours; let the water be boiling when it is put in, and do not let it cease boiling.*

*This may be baked, if you will add half a pint more of milk.*

## ❧ 99. BREAD PUDDING ❧

*(Randolph, 1860)*

As today, making bread pudding provided a way to transform stale bread into a tasty savory or sweet dish. The following recipe would have been eaten for dessert.

*Grate the crumb of a stale loaf, and pour on it a pint of boiling milk—let it stand an hour, then beat it to a pulp; add six eggs, well beaten, half a pound of butter, the same of powdered sugar, half a nutmeg, a glass of brandy, and some grated lemon peel—put a paste [place pastry dough] in the dish, [pour the batter in] and bake it.*

### ᴥ 100. GREEN CORN PUDDING

*(Beecher, 1858)*

This variation of corn pudding uses the kernels of fresh sweet corn rather than the dried, ground kernel, or cornmeal, used in Indian pudding. The following dish would have been served as a vegetable.

*Twelve ears of corn, grated. Sweet corn is best.*
*One pint and a half of milk*
*Four well-beaten eggs*
*One tea-cup and a half of sugar*

*Mix the ingredients, and bake three hours in a buttered dish. More sugar is needed if common corn is used.*

### ᴥ 101. INDIAN PUDDING, BAKED ᴥ

*(LeClercq, 1855)*

A favorite among New Englanders, Indian pudding refers to a blend of cornmeal, milk, and molasses that was usually eaten for dessert.

*Boil 3 pts milk [and] while boiling stir in enough Indian [corn] meal to make it thick as batter cake. Let it cook, when cool beat 6 eggs, add to the batter with enough molasses to sweeten it; bake in a slow [300–325°] oven 1 hour and 1/2. Dress with a sauce of sweetened cream and nutmeg.*

## Dumplings and Fritters

Dumplings come in two main forms: the drop dumpling, which is boiled in water like the egg dumpling that follows; and the filled dumpling, the original version created in Asia, which is stuffed with savory or sweet ingredients, such as the apple dumpling that follows.

### ᴥ 102. APPLE DUMPLINGS ᴥ

*(Campbell, 1848)*

These dumplings, which are boiled in pudding cloth, should be served as dessert. The cored apples were often stuffed with a mixture of cinnamon and sugar before being wrapped in pastry dough.

*Pare and core as many codlings [small green apples] as you intend to make dumplings. Make a little cold butter paste. Roll it to the thickness of one's finger, and wrap it round every apple singly; and if they be bound singly in pieces of cloth, so much the better. Put them into boiling water, and they will be done in half an hour. Serve them up with melted butter and white wine; and garnish with grated sugar about the dish.*

## ❧ 103. EGG DUMPLINGS ☙

*(Godey's Lady's Book, 1869)*

Dumplings such as these were commonly served alongside meat much as we serve potatoes today. They remain a favored item on the German-American table.

*Make a batter of a pint of milk, two well-beaten eggs, a teaspoonful of salt, and flour enough to make a batter as thick as for pound-cake. Have a clean saucepan of boiling water; let the water boil fast; drop in the batter with a tablespoon. Four or five minutes will boil them. Take them with a skimmer on a dish; put a bit of butter and pepper over them, and serve with boiled or cold meat. To serve sweet, put butter and grated nutmeg, with syrup or sugar over it.*

## ❧ 104. GREEN CORN FRITTERS ☙

*(Ellet, 1871)*

Also known as corn oysters, these pan-fried fritters were eaten as a vegetable dish.

*Six ears of boiled corn, grated, two eggs, a little milk and just enough flour to mix it. Drop a spoonful of the batter into a frying-pan, and fry in butter.*

## ❧ 105. FRUIT FRITTERS ☙

*(Beecher, 1858)*

Usually eaten as breakfast treats today, these deep-fried fruit fritters were a popular dessert.

*A pint of milk*
*A pint and a half of flour*
*Two teaspoonfuls of salt*

*Six eggs, and a pint of cream if you have it; if not, a pint of milk, with a little butter melted in it. Mix with this, either blackberries, raspberries, currants, gooseberries, or sliced apples or peaches, and fry it in small cakes in sweet lard. Eat with a sauce of butter beat with sugar, and flavored with wine or nutmeg, or grated lemon peel.*

## CAKES, COOKIES, CUSTARDS, AND CREAMS ☙

During the nineteenth century baking cakes was a national pastime among women. Elaborate layered cakes filled with creams, custards, and jellies were frequently made in the home kitchen. Such rich desserts were often served on special occasions or when guests were expected for dinner. Cake bakers were able to make the end product lighter with the addition of chemical leaveners, such as saleratus (called baking soda by the 1850s). When combined with an acid, such as buttermilk, yogurt, or cream of

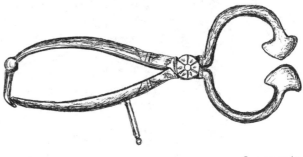

*Sugar snip.*

tartar, baking soda produces carbon dioxide gas bubbles. The sugar used in these desserts came in hard-packed loaves that varied in color from off-white to light brown, dependent, in large part, on the amount of molasses that remained in the sugar. To use the sugar, the cook broke a piece from the loaf using a sugar snip and grated or ground it in a mortar and pestle.

## Cakes and Cookies

### ❧ 106. ICING FOR A CAKE ☙

*(Parkinson, 1864)*

The following white icing recipe can be used to top the cupcakes, lady cake, or sponge cakes found in this section. The recipe calls for a lawn sieve, which is a fine sieve made of lawn fabric or silk.

*Take one pound of double-refined sugar, pound it fine, and sift it through a lawn sieve; then beat the whites of three eggs in a very clean pan, with a whisk, till they are a strong froth, and hang round the pan, leaving the bottom clear; then, with a wooden spoon, beat in your sugar, a little at a time, with about a tea-spoonful of lemon-juice—beat it till it becomes a nice thick smooth batter, and will hang round the pan to any thickness you may choose to spread it. Then, when your cake is nearly cold, spread your icing nicely over the top, and round the sides, with a pallet-knife; let it stand in a warm place, where it will be safe from hurt, and it will soon dry.*

### ❧ 107. BLACK CAKE ☙

*(Ladies of the First Presbyterian Church, Dayton, Ohio, 1873)*

The black cake, also known as fruit cake, is an Americanized version of the British plum cake. The addition of molasses darkens the cake.

*One pound and one quarter of butter; one pound of brown sugar; one of flour; three of raisins, seeded and chopped; two of currants; one of citron, cut thin and small; one of figs, chopped; thirteen eggs; one wine glass of Madeira wine, and two of brandy; one teacupful of molasses; one large nutmeg, grated; two teaspoonsful of cinnamon; one of mace, and one of cloves. Beat the butter and sugar until very light; then stir in one fourth of the flour; whisk the eggs, very stiff, and add them gradually; then the remainder of the flour, one half at a time; after beating well, add the wine, brandy, and spices, then mix all the fruit together, and add one third at a time. Beat well; butter and line the pan with white paper; put in the mixture, and smooth with a knife. Bake in a moderate [350–375°] oven, about four hours.*

### ❧ 108. BOSTON CREAM CAKES ❧

*(Ellet, 1871)*

The following recipe calls for a bain-marie, the French term for a "water bath." The container holding the contents to be cooked is placed in a pan into which water is poured. The pan is then gently heated over a low flame or in an oven set at low temperature. This allows for delicate creams, custards, and so forth to cook without curdling. The cakes are baked in "patty-pans, not scolloped" [var. scalloped], which means that they should be placed in small tin pans with flat, rather than ridged, sides and bottoms.

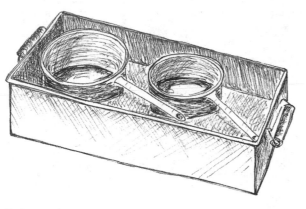
*Bain-marie.*

*Take half a pint of cream from a quart of milk [before homogenization, milk would naturally separate so that the cream rose to the top], and boil it with vanilla and cinnamon; strain and mix it with the rest of the milk; when cold, add the yolks of twelve eggs and quarter of a pound of loaf-sugar, and bake the custard in a bain-marie; have ready a batter made of half a pound of flour and the same of butter, in a pint of milk, with eight eggs, and bake it in buttered deep patty-pans, not scolloped [var. scalloped, or shaped like a scallop shell]; when browned, open a slit in the side of each while hot, and put in with a spoon as much of the custard as it will hold; close the slit smoothly, and set the cakes away.*

### ❧ 109. CUP CAKES ❧

*(Bryan, 1839)*

An American invention, these little cakes are quick and economical to make. The ingredients are measured in cups, hence the name, rather than weighed. They also take less time to bake than a traditional cake because of their small size. Cup cakes were often served at tea.

*Mix together one cup of butter, two of sugar, three of flour, four beaten eggs, a spoonful of cinnamon and a few spoonfuls of rose or lemon brandy. Commingle it very well and bake it in small buttered pans with moderate heat.*

### ❧ 110. GINGER SNAPS ❧

*(Ladies of the First Presbyterian Church, Dayton, Ohio, 1873)*

These ginger cookies are a crisp variation of the softer gingerbread, a confection that dates back to the Middle Ages. Instead of the honey, or more recently golden syrup, used in traditional gingerbread, the American ginger snaps and breads call for molasses. Byproducts of refined sugar, golden syrup and molasses are the liquid left over after sugar cane has been boiled and the resulting sugar crystals removed. Golden syrup is lighter and sweeter than molasses.

*One pint of molasses; one and one half coffee cups of butter; two and one half cups of sugar; one half cup of water; two eggs; one tablespoonful of ginger; one heaping teaspoonful of soda. Mix all together with flour to make a soft dough; roll very thin, and bake in a quick [400–425°] oven.*

### ❧ 111. LADY CAKE ❧

*(Harland, 1871)*

The lady, also known as silver, cake is an American adaptation of the traditional pound cake. Whereas the pound cake includes both egg whites and yolks, the lady cake uses only the whites, which make a light-colored and airy end result. By the 1850s, these cakes had become quite fashionable and lady, or silver, cake recipes appeared in most cookbooks.

*1 lb. sugar*
*3/4 lb. sifted flour*
*6 oz. butter*
*The whipped whites of ten eggs.*

*Flavor with bitter almond, and bake in square, not very deep tins. Flavor the frosting with vanilla. The combination is very pleasant.*

### ❧ 112. STRAWBERRY SHORTCAKE ❧

*(Levy 1871)*

Strawberries, along with peaches and apples, were among the most popular American fruits. In the 1850s, the popularity of strawberries spiked into what some called "strawberry fever." A variety of fruits were commonly paired with the American shortcake, a rich, sweet biscuit. By mid-century, however, the strawberry had become the nation's most popular choice, a position it holds unrivalled today.

*Take half a cup of butter, one quart of flour, one quart of milk, one teaspoonful of soda, and make into a dough; roll it out thin and bake it. When done split it, and spread with butter and fresh strawberries.*

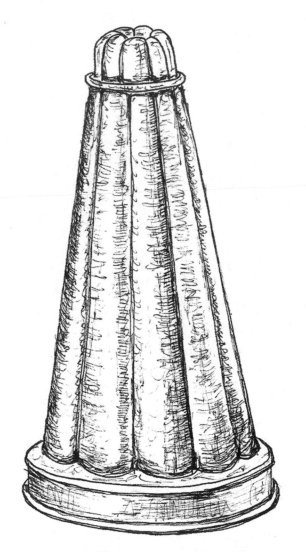

*Ice cream mold.*

## Custards and Creams

All custards contain a mixture of beaten egg with milk or cream. Sweet custards are still common today, but savory custards are less prevalent. One exception would be the quiche, which is a custard baked in a crust. Creams, as the name implies, are cream-based concoctions. Although ice cream dates back to the sixteenth century in Italy, it did not become a treat available to the average American until the nineteenth century. Today ice cream is one of the most popular foods consumed in the United States.

### ᪥ 113. CHARLOTTE RUSSE (RUSSIAN CHARLOTTE) ᪥

*(Rutledge, 1847)*

The following recipe describes how to make the traditional charlotte russe, which consists of a mold lined with lady fingers and filled with Bavarian cream. The classic version found here calls for isinglass, a gelatin made from the air bladders of fish, rarely used today. A simpler version began to appear in American cookbooks later in the century.

*One pint of milk made into a custard with the yolks of six eggs, and six ounces of white sugar, flavored with vanilla bean, one ounce of isinglass dissolved in* milk and mixed with custard, one pint of cream, whipped to a froth, and mixed gradually with the custard; stirring the whole constantly with a large spoon. The mould to be lined with light sponge cake, cut in strips, and placed on the bottom around the slices; then filled with the mixture, and the top covered in the same manner, with the cake. The mould to be surrounded for some hours with ice, until the Charlotte is completely frozen; then turned out as you would ice cream.

---

### ✢ TO MILK

(Hill, 1867)

As the following directions illustrate, dairy products quite often came directly from the family cow.

*No animal better repays kind and generous treatment than the cow. In winter she should be well housed, and a sufficient quantity of dry straw provided for a litter, and this changed occasionally. Regular and proper feeding. She should be curried and rubbed with the same care bestowed upon the horse. How rarely anything of the kind is done! The miserable, half-frozen condition of this valuable animal during the cold weather, without shelter of any kind, turned loose to pick up a precarious and scanty living, or only supplied with a few dry shucks thrown upon the ground, perchance a little dirty slop water, is a reproach to the master. The quality and quantity of milk and butter which would be yielded when well treated, is of itself (it would seem) an irresistible argument in favor of providing liberally for her comfort, to say nothing of her mute appeals to man's humanity.*

---

## ⊰ 114. FLOATING ISLAND ⊱

*(Hill, 1867)*

Whereas the previous recipe calls for isinglass, the following instructions list "hog's foot or calf's foot jelly," another form of gelatin. Before the advent of commercial gelatin in the late nineteenth century, cooks either used the relatively expensive isinglass or they boiled hog's or calf's feet and knuckles to obtain the jelling agent used to mold salads and desserts and to thicken soups.

*Place slices of sponge [cake] or Naples biscuit [ladyfingers] at the bottom of a large glass stand. Pour the dish half full of good boiled custard. Beat to the whites of the eggs six table spoonfuls of hog's foot or calf's foot jelly to a stiff froth. Place this irregularly on the top of the custard.*

*If it is not convenient to use either of the jellies mentioned, any kind of fruit jelly will answer, using four tablespoonfuls.*

## ❧ 115. LEMON CUSTARD ❧

*(An American Lady, 1854)*

The following instructions call for a "salamander," which consists of a metal disc joined to a long wooden handle. The metal disc is heated in the fire and then passed closely over the top of the custard to brown it.

*Take the yolks of ten eggs beaten, strain them, and whip them with a pint of cream; boil the juice of two lemons sweetened with the rind of one, when cold strain it to the cream and eggs; when it almost boils, put it into a dish, grate over the rind of a lemon, and brown it with a salamander.*

## ❧ 116. RICE CUSTARD ❧

*(Sanderson, 1864)*

As with all rice dishes, rice custard was a special favorite in the southern rice-growing regions. The Carolina rice called for below remains one of the most popular types of rice eaten in the United States. It is a generic term used for long-grained rice, which was first planted in South Carolina more than 300 years ago.

*Take a cup of whole Carolina rice, and seven cups of milk; boil it, by placing the pan in water, which must never be allowed to go off the boil until it thickens; then sweeten it, and add an ounce of sweet almonds pounded.*

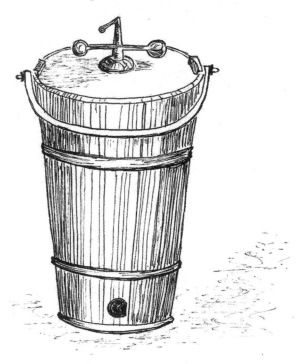

## ❧ 117. PEACH ICE CREAM ❧

*(Bryan, 1839)*

Although George Washington and Thomas Jefferson enjoyed ice cream in the eighteenth century, it would not become a treat available to the average American until the next century. By the 1830s, ice cream could be purchased in public gardens and "saloons" as an expensive sweet. It could also be made (and had been among the wealthy for centuries) by placing cream into a covered pail and setting the pail into a container of a few inches wider circumference. A mixture of ice and salt was placed in the gap

*Ice cream freezer.*

between the two containers. The cream was stirred on occasion until the desired consistency was obtained. In 1846, an ice cream freezer was invented for home use, which enabled Americans to churn ice cream far more easily. The cream could be churned by simply turning a handle on the outside of the machine; previously the pot containing the cream had to be removed from the ice and opened before it could be stirred, a tedious and time-consuming process.

*Select peaches that are very ripe and soft, peel them, extract the stones, and mash them to a marmalade. Having one quart of peach pulp, mix with it one pound of powdered sugar, a grated nutmeg and a tea-spoonful of powdered cinnamon; stir it into a quart of rich sweet cream and freeze it as directed. If cream is not to be had, substitute a quart of rich sweet milk, stir into it the beaten yolks of five or six eggs, simmer it till the eggs are sufficiently cooked, set it by till cold, and then stir it into the peaches, &c. [and remaining ingredients] as before directed.*

### ❧ 118. VANILLA ICE CREAM ❧

*(Ellet, 1871)*

The following recipe calls for a vanilla bean—the fruit pod of an orchid variety that is indigenous to tropical America. Picked when green, the fruit is boiled for a period of seconds before being dry cured for many months in the sun, during which time it turns into the dark, fragrant bean used to flavor creams, custards, cakes, icings, and countless other confections. The following mixture would naturally need to be churned and frozen.

*One quart cream, eight ounces sugar, crushed, half a vanilla bean. Boil half the cream with the sugar and bean, then add the rest of the cream, and cool and strain it.*

## PRESERVES

### ❧ 119. YANKEE APPLE BUTTER ❧

*(Ellet, 1871)*

A thick preserve, apple butter was an ever-present feature of the Pennsylvania Dutch table, appearing at meals throughout the day. Apple butter was prepared and eaten in huge quantities and was often accompanied by a complementary array of preserves and pickles, which added the "seven sweet and seven sour" notes that the Pennsylvania Dutch felt balanced out a meal.

*Boil cider down one half; put in as many apples as the liquor will contain, stew them soft; then take them out and put in fresh apples. When they are cold boil them again in the cider till they are pulpy and thick. Add different kinds of spice, a little before it is done. Keep in covered jars.*

### ﷽ 120. CANDIED ORANGE OR LEMON-PEEL ﷽

*(Godey's Lady's Book, 1862)*

These candied peels, now relegated to specialty food shops, are used in cakes and confections or simply eaten on their own.

*Take the fruit, cut it lengthwise, remove all the pulp and interior skin, then put the peel in strong salt and water for six days; then boil them in spring water until they are soft, and place them in a sieve to drain; make a thin syrup with a pound of sugar candy to a quart of water; boil them in it for half an hour, or till they look clear; make a thick syrup with sugar and as much water as will melt it; put in the peel, and boil them over a slow fire until the syrup candies in the pan; then take them out, powder pounded sugar over them, and dry them before the fire in a cool oven.*

### ﷽ 121. CURRANT JELLY ﷽

*(Randolph, 1860)*

A smooth preserve, jelly is basically a jam that has been strained to remove all solid pieces of fruit. Currants have been a popular jelly fruit for Americans since shortly after the first colonialists landed.

*Pick full ripe currants from the stem, and put them in a stone pot; then set it in an iron pot of water—take care that no water gets in: when the currants have yielded their juice, pour them into a jelly bag—let it run as long as it will without pressing, which must be reserved for the best jelly; you may then squeeze the bag to make inferior kind. To each pint of this juice, put one pound of loaf sugar powdered—boil it fifteen or twenty minutes—skim it clean, and put it in glasses; expose them daily to the sun to prevent fermentation.*

### ﷽ 122. PRESERVED APPLES ﷽

*(Bryan, 1839)*

Preserves are typically made from fruit cooked with its equal weight in sugar. The following recipe calls for the addition of egg whites to the boiling sugar syrup, a step that clarifies the mixture of any impurities, which will cling to the egg white and rise to the surface from where they can be skimmed. During this period, most preserves were sealed with paper dipped in brandy, as the alcohol helped keep the mouth of the jar sterile.

*Take large ripe apples that are firm and sufficiently acid to cook tender; pare them, extract the cores smoothly, and fill the cavities with fresh lemon rind, cut in very thin slips. Boil them till half done in a small quantity of water, and weigh them. Weigh an equal quantity of loaf sugar, dissolve it in the syrup in which the apples were boiled, mix in the white of one egg to every five pounds of sugar, boil it fast for a few minutes till the scum rises, which carefully remove, and then put in your apples. Add enough lemon juice to flavor them well, and boil them slowly and steadily till they are quite transparent, but be careful not to break them. Raise them with a perforated ladle, that the syrup may drain from them into the kettle; spread them out on dishes, set them in the open air till they get perfectly cold, and then put them up in jars. Boil the syrup thick, color it red with sanders [dye made from sandalwood] or cochineal [dye made from insects], pour it over the apples while hot, and next day cover them with paper dipped in brandy.*

### ☙ 123. TO PRESERVE PEACHES ❧

*(Rutledge, 1847)*

One type of preserve was made to keep fruit for winter and another for using in pies and tarts. The following recipe will keep the fruit for winter. The sugar and brandy aid in preserving the peaches.

*Gather your peaches full grown, but not ripe enough for eating; allow three-fourths of a pound of sugar to every pound of fruit; pare and put them into a bowl, sprinkling sugar between each layer; let them lie twelve hours, in which time the juice will be drawn; then put them into the preserving-kettle, and boil until transparent. Before putting the peaches into the kettle, pour in a glass of brandy.*

### ☙ 124. TO PRESERVE STRAWBERRIES ❧

*(Leslie, 1851)*

In addition to being made into the preserves, jams, and jellies so familiar today, strawberries were also fashioned into cordials and wine. The following recipe recommends gathering the strawberries during dry weather, a step that helps prevent the growth of mold on the picked berries.

*Strawberries for preserving should be large and ripe. They will keep best if gathered in dry weather, when there has been no rain for at least two days. Having hulled, or picked off the green [stem], select the largest and firmest, and spread them out separately on flat dishes; having first weighed them, and allowed to each pound of strawberries a pound of powdered loaf-sugar. Sift half the sugar over them. Then take the inferior strawberries that were left, and those that are over-ripe; mix with them an equal quantity of powdered sugar, and mash them. Put them into a basin covered with a plate, and set them over the fire in a pan of boiling water, till they become a thick juice; then strain it through a bag and mix with it the other half of the sugar that you have allotted to the strawberries, which are to be done whole. Put it into a porcelain kettle, and boil and skim it till the scum ceases to rise; then put in the whole strawberries with the sugar in which they have been lying, and all the juice that may have exuded from them. Set them over the fire in the syrup, just long enough to heat them a little; and in a few minutes take them out, one by one, with a tea-spoon, and spread them on dishes to cool; not allowing them to touch each other. Then take off what scum may arise from the additional sugar. Repeat this several times, taking out the strawberries and cooling them till they become quite clear. They must not be allowed to boil; and if they seem likely to break, they should be instantly and finally taken from the fire. When quite cold, put them in with the syrup into tumblers, or into white queen's-ware [a type of stone or ceramic ware] pots. If intended to keep a long time it will be well to put at the top a layer of apple jelly.*

# 2
## 🌿 1876–1910

### MAJOR FOODSTUFFS

- Meat: beef and veal; pork; mutton and lamb
- Game: hare, possum, rabbit, squirrel, venison
- Poultry and Fowl: chicken, duck, goose, grouse, guinea fowl, pigeon, quail, turkey
- Fish: bass, catfish, cod, eel, flounder, haddock, herring, mackerel, perch, pompano, salmon, shad, snapper, trout, tuna, whitefish
- Shellfish: clam, crab, lobster, oyster, shrimp
- Vegetables: asparagus, beans, beets, cabbage, carrots, celery, corn, cucumbers, okra, parsnips, peas, potatoes, radishes, rhubarb, squash, tomatoes, turnips
- Fruits: apples, cherries, grapes, peaches, pears, rhubarb, strawberries
- Grains: corn; rice; wheat flour spread in popularity as steel mills began to replace stone mills and large companies drove smaller mills out of business.
- Dairy: cow's milk, cream, and cheese (the increasing availability of iceboxes and regular ice delivery enabled Americans to incorporate more dairy safely into their diet).

## COOKING METHODS

### Heat Sources

- Cookstoves fueled by oil, wood, coal, and, increasingly, gas

### Preservation Methods

- Ice boxes greatly increased the longevity of perishable goods such as dairy, meat, and seafood

### Preparation

- The egg beater, patented in 1870, eased the preparation time for egg-based dishes such as soufflés and cakes.
- The hand-cranked meat grinder spurred the popularity of minced meat dishes.
- The introduction of powdered gelatin spurred the rise of jelled salads and desserts.

## PREVALENT CULTURAL INFLUENCES

- British
- French
- Spanish
- Dutch
- African American
- German
- Scandinavian
- Mexican

## KITCHEN AMENITIES

Bug screens began to appear over kitchen windows in the 1890s, vastly reducing the number of pests that made their way into the kitchen and, by extension, the dishes it turned out. Late-nineteenth and early-twentieth-century cooks were increasingly aided by one or two water pumps that delivered the water cooks previously carted by hand.

## SPECIAL GADGETS

The hand-cranked meat chopper spread the popularity of dishes such as croquettes, meat loafs, hashes, and Hamburg or Salisbury steak (versions of the hamburger patty). Cooks also began using potato peelers and slicers, measuring spoons and cups, spatulas, spice mills, juice extractors, and more sophisticated kitchen knives.

## FOOD PRESERVATION

By the 1880s, most middle- and upper-class kitchens were equipped with ice boxes or chests, which kept perishables cool, but not frozen. The temperature within the ice boxes varied widely depending on how much time had elapsed since the ice had been delivered (some homes had daily delivery) and how often the box door had been opened. As the United States became more urban, butcher shops and grocery stores became increasingly responsible for the preparation and distribution of meat provided by slaughterhouses. Milk was delivered by hand to city dwellers, although those living in the country still relied on their own or a neighbor's cow for the milk they consumed.

*1890s ice box.*

## COOKING METHODS

Cooks relied primarily on oven or range cookery. The cookstove, as it still does today, often contained a range and an oven. Unlike cook stoves today, however, those from the nineteenth century were attached to a chimney flue via a stove pipe. Once fired, the cookstove required careful regulation through a set of dampers—the oven damper, the chimney damper, the front damper—which regulated air circulation and heat.

*Victorian wood-burning stove.*

The early stoves were fueled by oil, wood, or coal; gas stoves entered the market in the 1850s. These first gas stoves were more expensive to buy and to fuel, as gas manufacturing was still in its relative infancy. Not only more expensive, gas stoves could also prove dangerous, occasionally acquiring leaks or exploding. Despite these dangers, gas stoves burned far more cleanly and required significantly less labor to use and maintain than either wood or coal stoves. As a result, improved gas stoves continued to enter the market; by 1920, they were common throughout the United States.

## DINING

The number of dining implements skyrocketed after the Civil War, and the middle classes bought them en masse, seeing them as markers of civility and distinction. Just a few such items include celery vases, orange spoons, and sardine boxes. Over the course of the century, a gradual switch from French (sometimes called English) to Russian service occurred among the upper and middle classes. With French service, an array of individual dishes were placed on the table before the meal began. The first course of dishes usually included soup, fish, and side meat or egg dishes. Next came a course composed of a mix of the following: a roast, side vegetables, salads, soufflés, sweet or savory pies, sweet custards; the meal ended with a third round of dishes that formed the dessert course. In contrast, Russian service consisted of a series of courses delivered to the table by a wait staff. The upper and upper middle classes might serve 8 to 12 courses, and the middle class might serve 4 or 5, roughly in the following order: first course—soup, fish, and potatoes; second—a roast garnished with vegetables; optional third—game; third or fourth—salads and vegetables; final course—dessert.

## MEALS

Many African Americans continued to cook for wealthy and middle-cla[...] families after the Civil War, but growing numbers also worked as promine[...] chefs and caterers throughout the country. In addition to African America[...] cooks, families in the North also hired French cooks; families in the rapidly expanding West relied heavily on Chinese cooks, who were often trained in French techniques. If the meals of the wealthy were heavily influenced by French cuisine, the meals of the middle and lower classes were heavily influenced by German cuisine, particularly in the Midwest.

Breakfast became lighter as the amount of physical labor performed by the average American shrank. The British-inspired breakfast of steaks and pies gave way to the bacon, eggs, and toast still served in diners throughout the United States. Pies, however, were still served on occasion for lunch and dinner.

During this time, immigrants flooded into the United States, influencing the American table in unmistakable ways. In particular, many Europeans and Asians immigrated to the northern United States, which became increasingly urban, industrial, and international after the Civil War. Westward expansion also gave rise to new cooking methods and ingredients as groups from different classes and different parts of the world worked together to build new cities. For example, the Centennial Exhibition held in Philadelphia in 1876 included French, German, and Tunisian restaurants, along with regionally influenced American eateries.

## POPULAR RECIPES

By the late nineteenth century, savory pies had all but disappeared from cookbooks with the exception of the occasional oyster and chicken versions. In turn, savory puddings were largely limited to recipes for green corn or Yorkshire puddings. Those few savory pie and pudding recipes included here and there were no longer housed in the pie and pudding section, which became devoted solely to sweets. These changes are reflected in this chapter; savory puddings, pies, dumplings, and fritters are thus located in the meat and vegetable sections.

Although plum pudding was still commonly served for special occasions, heavy puddings began to decline. Aided by the powdered gelatin that went on the market in the 1890s, desserts became lighter. Commercial gelatin meant that cooks no longer had to boil calves feet for hours to obtain the thickening agent used to set jellied desserts and salads. As a result, layer cakes grew in popularity. The flavors of ice cream also flourished as did the ice-cream soda, supposedly invented in 1874. The ice-cream sundae also came into its own.

By the turn of the century, Italians had spread the use of pasta, which had previously been eaten predominantly by the wealthy. During this time, the

tamales, tacos, and enchiladas of Mexican American cooking gained a hold in kitchens beyond the Southwest.

Sandwiches became more common and were often served at tea and at the growing number of lunch establishments. Salads, ranging from chicken to shrimp and avocado to green leaf, also began to appear more frequently at the dining table. Meat, vegetable, and starch croquettes spiked in popularity, with some cookbooks devoting an entire section to them. Chafing dishes, serving dishes that are heated from below, became ubiquitous at middle- and upper-class tables throughout the nation; many chafing dish recipes were rich meat- and cream-based concoctions. Cookbooks also began to include recipes calling for canned foods such as corn, tomatoes, peas, beans, and fish.

## SOUPS, CHOWDERS, AND STEWS

During the tail end of the nineteenth century, soups gained in popularity, largely because many could be prepared with little expense. Several of the following still number among the nation's most beloved soups, including black bean, tomato, and potato.

*Soup tureen.*

### 125. BLACK BEAN SOUP

*(Rorer, 1898)*

The following version of black bean soup is still served in many homes today. Excluding the hard boiled eggs, this soup can be prepared cheaply. Many versions also dress up the soup for company with a splash of sherry, an addition still common today.

> 1 pint of black turtle beans
> 1 quart of good stock
> 1 lemon
> 1 1/2 quarts of boiling water

*2 hard boiled eggs*
*1 level teaspoonful of salt*
*1 saltspoonful of pepper*

*Wash the beans, drain, cover with cold water and soak over night. In the morning, drain again, and cover with the boiling water. Cover the kettle, and boil slowly for about two hours until the beans are very tender; add the salt, pepper and stock. Press the whole through a colander, then through a sieve. Rinse the kettle; return the soup to it, and bring to boiling point. Cut the eggs and lemon into slices and put them into the tureen; pour over the boiling thick soup, and serve. If you use wine, put four tablespoonfuls into the tureen with the egg and lemon.*

## ⊰ 126. KENTUCKY BURGOUT [BURGOO] ⊱

*(Fox, 1904)*

Most often spelled burgoo, the following stew was common throughout Tennessee and Kentucky, where it was frequently served at large picnics and political rallies. Comparable to Brunswick stew (recipe 2), burgoo can include a range of meats and vegetables. Smaller birds such as quail or pigeon might be used in the following version.

*6 squirrels*
*6 birds*
*1 1/2 gallons of water*
*1 teacup of pearl barley*
*1 quart of tomatoes*
*1 quart of corn*
*1 quart of oysters*
*1 pint of sweet cream*
*1/4 pound of butter*
*2 tablespoons of flour*
*Season to taste*

*Boil the squirrels and birds in the water till tender and remove all the bones. Add barley and vegetables and cook slowly for 1 hour. Ten minutes before serving add the oysters and cream with butter and flour rubbed together. Season and serve hot.*

## ⊰ 127. CHERRY SOUP ⊱

*(Aunt Babette, 1889)*

Popularized by Scandinavian immigrants, cold fruit soup was served throughout the Midwest during the summer months. Many recipes, such as the following one, called for the palm starch sago (similar to tapioca) as a thickener. Like cherry, strawberry and rhubarb were also frequently used as fruit soup bases in the United States.

*This delicious soup is to be eaten cold; it is a summer soup. Use large, dark red or black cherries, a quart is sufficient. Take a bottle of claret, or any other red wine, and twice as much water as you have wine; half a cup of pearl sago [a thickener made from palm starch], a few slices of lemon and some cinnamon bark or stick cinnamon, cook about one-half hour, cherries and all. If you find that the soup is too thick add more wine and water, sweeten to suit the taste; a cupful of sugar is the most I ever use.*

*Strawberry, blueberry and raspberry soups may be prepared according to above receipt.*

### ⊰ 128. CHILI CON CARNE ⊱

*(California Women, 1905)*

Although competing stories of its exact origins exist, chili con carne undoubtedly sprang from the Southwest. Named after its required ingredients, chili peppers and beef, chili is an economical dish, which, like burgoo, can be cooked in huge quantities. Representatives of San Antonio, the city most often associated with chili, served Texas chili at the 1893 Chicago World's Fair, helping to spread the dish beyond the Southwest. Although the following recipe calls for bayou beans, or red beans, some chili aficionados argue that beans do not belong in an "authentic" version. By the 1890s, chili con carne had become so widespread that prepared chili powder, often including dried red pepper, cumin, and oregano, appeared on the market. By the early 1900s, commercially canned versions began to appear.

*Take a good-sized piece of soup meat (not a soup bone), boil till thoroughly tender; take out of water; mince very fine; have ready two good-sized onions, also minced fine. Put into a skillet a tablespoonful of butter, and after having coated the meat with flour, turn same [meat and flour mixture] with the onions into the skillet and brown. Add to it the water in which the meat was boiled and one teacup of bayou beans [red beans] that have been boiled done; boil slowly for about three hours. Just before taking from the fire, add salt to taste and a heaping tablespoon of chili powder or sufficient to make it hot; must be rich and hot with pepper to be good. On a cool, damp evening, this is a most palatable dish.*

### ⊰ 129. CLAM CHOWDER ⊱

*(Farmer, 1896)*

The first recipe for fish chowder in the United States appeared in the eighteenth century; by the early nineteenth century chowders were eaten up and down the Atlantic Coast. Westward expansion soon gave rise to Pacific Coast versions, which made use of local fish and shellfish. Ingredients vary from region to region. One of the many clam chowder versions that proliferated in New England includes milk, potatoes, and onions, as does the following version. By the 1830s, tomatoes had become a frequent ingredient in Rhode Island; this trend, which spread into southern states, was decried by chowder hounds in Massachusetts and Maine. Many of their descendents carry this sentiment today, believing that tomatoes have no place in clam chowder.

*1 quart clams*
*4 cups potatoes cut in 3/4 inch dice*
*1 1/2 inch cube fat salt pork*
*1 sliced onion*
*1 tablespoon salt*
*1/8 teaspoon pepper*
*4 tablespoons butter*
*4 cups scalded milk*
*8 common crackers*

*Clean and pick over clams, using one cup cold water; drain, reserve liquor, heat to boiling point, and strain. Chop finely hard part of clams; cut pork in small pieces and try out [melt, or render]; add onion, fry five minutes, and strain into a stewpan. Parboil potatoes five minutes in boiling water to cover; drain and put a layer in bottom of stewpan, add chopped clams, sprinkle with salt and pepper, and dredge generously with flour; add remaining potatoes, again sprinkle with salt and pepper, dredge with flour, and add two and one-half cups boiling water. Cook ten minutes, add milk, soft part of clams, and butter; boil three minutes, and add crackers split and soaked in enough cold milk to moisten. Reheat clam water to boiling point and thicken with one tablespoon butter and flour cooked together. Add to chowder just before serving.*

*The clam water has a tendency to cause the milk to separate, hence is added at the last.*

## ⇥ 130. GREEN CORN SOUP ⇤

*(Women of the First Congregational Church, Marysville, Ohio, 1876)*

Of Pennsylvania Dutch origin, chicken and corn soup remains a favorite of the midwestern table. Noodles (recipe 197) are a frequent addition.

*Simmer a fat chicken slowly for several hours; an hour before dinner add corn cut from a dozen ears, and just before taking from the fire, add one pint sweet milk and one egg beaten light with a teaspoon flour. This can be made in winter with dried corn, but the corn must be soaked over night, and requires longer cooking.*

⊰ 131. GUMBO FILÉ ⊱

*(The Ladies Association of the First Presbyterian Church, Houston, Texas, 1883)*

The okra gumbo found in Chapter 1 (recipe 6) is the first known printed recipe. By the time the following recipe was published, however, the dish enjoyed a standard place in southern cookbooks; the *First Texas Cookbook* (from where the following recipe hails) devotes one-third of its soup entries to variations of the dish. This recipe does not include any okra, because it relies on filé powder as a thickening agent. Filé, made from the dried, ground leaves of the sassafras tree, was used as a seasoning by the Choctaw Indians of Louisiana. It is a frequent ingredient in Louisiana gumbos. The powder is added once the gumbo has been taken off the fire, as filé tends to become tough and stringy when cooked.

*Take a large fat hen and cut in pieces as for frying; two large onion, cut very fine, and fifty oysters. After the chicken is cut up, soak in salt and water quarter of an hour, then rinse in clear water. In a deep pot, put one large tablespoonful of lard: as soon as it is hot add two tablespoonfuls of sifted flour, stirring all the time; as soon as it is a light brown put in the onions, and when they are brown, put in the chicken, with a little salt, and red and black pepper; stir well and frequently, and let simmer slowly for half an hour, then add half a can of tomatoes, and half an hour after, a quart of boiling water as will make a good tureen of soup, and let it boil slowly until ready to serve. About ten minutes before serving, add a tablespoonful of filé very slowly to prevent its getting into lumps. This is without oysters. When you use them boil the oysters and liquor together, then take out the oysters, put them in a dish and add them to the gumbo about a quarter of an hour before it is done; put the boiling liquor into the gumbo at any time, first skimming well, and put less water in the gumbo. Have a dish of boiled rice at table, and, when serving the gumbo, put a spoonful in each plate, and pour the gumbo over it.*

⊰ 132. NOODLE SOUP ⊱

*(Shuman, 1893)*

Noodle soup recipes such as the one here were brought to the United States by German immigrants.

*To make a good stock for noodle soup, take a small shank of beef, one of mutton, and another of veal; have the bones cracked and boil them together for twenty-four hours. Put with them two good sized potatoes, a carrot, a turnip, an onion, and some celery. Salt and pepper to taste. If liked, a bit of bay leaf may be added. When thoroughly well done, strain through a colander and set aside until required for use. For the noodles, use one egg for an ordinary family, and more in proportion to quantity required. Break the eggs into the flour, add a little salt, and mix into a rather stiff dough. Roll very thin and cut into fine bits. Let them dry for two hours, then drop them into the boiling stock about ten minutes before serving.*

### ⇥ 133. IRISH POTATO SOUP ⇤

*(Gillette, 1887)*

The white, or Irish potato, played an indispensable role in the American diet. Among the middle and upper classes it was often married with rich cream, eggs, butter, and cheese and fashioned into elaborate dishes ranging from soufflés to cheesecakes. Among the lower classes it helped "fill out" an array of savory dishes, especially soups and stews that might include a scant piece of meat or fat for flavoring. A variation of the following potato soup recipe still makes its way onto many American dinner tables.

*Peel and boil eight medium-sized potatoes with a large onion, sliced, some herbs, salt and pepper; press all though a colander; then thin it with rich milk and add a lump of butter, more seasoning, if necessary; let it heat well and serve hot.*

### ⇥ 134. TOMATO SOUP ⇤

*(Women of the First Congregational Church, Marysville, Ohio, 1876)*

Although appearing in ketchups and pickles in the early nineteenth century, tomatoes were slower to gain a starring role in vegetable dishes. By mid-century, however, they had become a familiar part of the American kitchen; within another 20 years, tomatoes had become one of the nation's most popular canned goods. When used in soups and sauces, tomatoes are usually peeled, as they should be for the following recipe. To peel a tomato, score the bottom gently with a knife, plunge the tomato into boiling water for 30 to 40 seconds. Remove and plunge into cold water. The skin should slip off easily when peeled back from the scored section.

*One gallon of stock made from nice fresh beef, skim and strain, take three quarts tomatoes, remove skin and cut out hard center, put through a fine sieve and add to the stock; make a paste of butter and flour and when the stock begins to boil, stir in half a teacup, taking care not to have it lumpy; boil twenty minutes, seasoning with salt and pepper to taste. When out of season, canned tomatoes will answer, two quarts being sufficient.*

MEAT

---

> ✦ **MEAT PACKING AND TRANSPORT**
>
> In 1879, the Chicago meatpacker Gustavus F. Swift began regular transport of midwestern meat to eastern cities. Previously cattle had been sent East on hoof. Swift fattened, slaughtered and dressed the beef in Chicago and sent it to market in refrigerated railroad cars, making fresher and less expensive meat available to more Americans.

---

### ⇌ 135. COOKING COLD MEATS ⇋

*(The Ladies Association of the First Presbyterian Church, Houston, Texas, 1883)*

The following economical recipe for using leftover meats includes two American favorites—mashed potatoes and ketchup. The ketchup called for here would have resembled that found in recipe 50 far more than it would that which lines supermarket shelves today.

*Chop the meat fine, season with salt and pepper, a little onion and tomato catsup [see recipe 50]. Fill a pan two-thirds full, cover it with potatoes which have been well salted and mashed with milk. Lay bits of butter over the top, and set it in the oven for fifteen or twenty minutes.*

## Beef and Veal

### ⇌ 136. BEEF À LA MODE ⇋

*(Tyree, 1879)*

A recipe included in most late nineteenth-century cookbooks, beef à la mode varies from a relatively simple dish of steamed beef stuffed with salt pork, allspice, and cloves to a more elaborate version such as the following. In whatever form it takes, the dish requires stuffing the beef with a mixture of spiced fat to add extra flavor.

*Take a round or a rump piece of beef, take out the bone, the gristle and all the tough pieces about the edges. Fill the cavities from which the bone was taken, with suet, and fat salt pork.*

*Press this so as to make it perfectly round, pass around a coarse, strong piece of cloth, so as to hold it firmly in shape. If the round is six inches thick, the cloth must be six inches wide, leaving the top and bottom open. With a larding needle, fill this thickly with strips of fat pork, running through from top to bottom and about one inch apart each way. Set this in a baking-pan, pour over:*

*1 teacup boiling water*
*1 teacup boiling vinegar; mixed*

*Add to this one heaping tablespoonful brown sugar and a bunch of herbs.*

*Sprinkle over the beef liberally with salt and black pepper; chop one small onion fine, and lay over the top of the beef. Simmer this for two or three hours, basting frequently and keeping an inverted tin plate over the beef except when basting. If the gravy stews down too much, add stock or broth of any kind. Turn it over, and let the top be at bottom. When it is done and tender, skim the fat from the gravy. Pour over:*

*2 tablespoonfuls celery vinegar*
*2 tablespoonfuls pepper*
*2 tablespoonfuls made mustard*
*1 wineglassful acid fruit jelly*

*Simmer and bake for two hours longer, frequently basting, that it may be soft and seasoned through and through. Take the beef from the pan and remove the cloth; place in a large flat dish, pour over the gravy, and over this one teacup of mushroom sauce [see recipe 170]. Sift finely powdered cracker over the top and garnish with grated or scraped horseradish and parsley.*

## ᕯ 137. BEEFSTEAK SMOTHERED IN ONIONS ᕬ

*(Women of the First Congregational Church, Marysville, Ohio, 1876)*

A particular favorite in the Midwest, beefsteak was often eaten at breakfast or at dinner. Like onions, tomatoes and mushrooms were regular ingredients in beefsteak recipes.

*Fry brown four slices of breakfast bacon, take out bacon and put in six onions sliced thin, fry about ten minutes stirring constantly, take out all except a thin layer and upon it lay a slice of steak, and then a layer of onions, then steak, covering thick with onions. Dredge each layer with pepper, salt, and flour; pour over this one cup boiling water, cover tight and simmer half an hour. When you dish, place the steak in the centre of the dish, and heap the onions around it.*

## ᕯ 138. CORNED BEEF HASH ᕬ

*(Farmer, 1896)*

Corning, or brining, is a common way of preserving beef. The term *corn* can refer to a small particle; here it refers to the salt particles essential to the corning preservation method.

*Remove skin and gristle from cooked corned beef, then chop the meat. When meat is very fat, discard most of the fat. To chopped meat add an equal quantity of cold boiled chopped potatoes. Season with salt and pepper, put into a hot buttered frying-pan, moisten with milk or cream, stir until well mixed, spread evenly, then place on a part of the range where it may slowly brown underneath. Turn, and fold on a hot platter. Garnish with sprig of parsley in the middle.*

---

### ✈ TO RESTORE TAINTED MEAT

(Ellet, 1871)

Nineteenth-century cookbooks devoted sections to describing how to detect good meat from bad. They also dealt with how to "restore" or "freshen" stale meat

*Pour a few drops of hydrochloric acid in water till of a slight sour taste, and immerse the tainted meat in it for an hour or so, and it will become quite sweet again.*

---

### ⇛ 139. TO ROAST BEEF IN A STOVE ⇚

*(Hearn, 1885)*

Cookstoves were a welcome improvement in home kitchens, but many cooks conceded that meats roasted in the hearth were superior in flavor and texture; direct high heat browns the outside of a roast which not only provides sapid aromas and flavor, but also seals in much of the moisture. The author of the following recipe provides a few tips for keeping an oven-roasted piece of meat well moistened.

*A fine roasting piece of beef may, if properly managed, be baked in a stove so as to resemble beef roasted before a large, open fire. Prepare the meat as if for roasting, season it well with salt, pepper, and a little onion if liked. Set the meat on muffin rings, or a trivet [a raised heat-proof ceramic or metal stand] in a dripping pan, and pour into the pan a pint or so of hot water to baste the meat with. Keep the oven hot and well closed on the meat; when it begins to bake, baste it freely, using a long-handled spoon; it should be basted every fifteen minutes; add hot water to the pan as it wastes, that the gravy may not burn; allow fifteen minutes to each pound of meat unless you wish it very rare. Half an hour before taking it up, dredge flour thickly over it, baste freely, and let it brown. Take the meat from the pan, dredge in some flour and seasoning if needed; throw into the gravy a cup of water, let it boil up once, and strain into a sauce boat or gravy tureen.*

### ❧ 140. HAMBURGER STEAK ❧

*(Aunt Babette, 1889)*

Hamburg, or hamburger, steak was popularized by German immigrants. By the late 1880s, it was served at more casual restaurants, as well as by many home cooks, some of whom made use of their new meat grinders to perform the mincing work they had previously done by hand.

*[Hamburger] is made of round steak chopped extremely fine and seasoned with salt and pepper. You may grate in part of an onion or fry with onions.*

### ❧ 141. VEAL SWEETBREAD ❧

*(Women of the First Congregational Church, Marysville, Ohio, 1876)*

Sweetbread (thymus gland) recipes flourished during this time. They were turned into omelettes and salads, baked, broiled, creamed, and fried, as in the following recipe.

*Slice, put in cold water, drain, and place in skillet prepared with hot drippings, when brown on under side then turn; make a stiff batter of two eggs, half pint milk, flour to thicken, and salt to taste, and into it dip each slice, return to the skillet and fry brown over a moderate fire.*

## Lamb and Mutton

### ❧ 142. ROAST LAMB ❧

*(Shuman, 1893)*

One way of preventing roasted meat from drying out is to keep it well moistened with fat. Toward this end, the following recipe calls for wrapping bacon around the lamb before oven roasting.

*Brush three ounces of melted butter over the inner part of a well trimmed quarter of lamb, and strew thick with finely grated bread crumbs, seasoned with salt, pepper and parsley; roll and skewer four or five slices of bacon to the outer side; put in rather quick [approximately 375°] oven. When thoroughly done (not over cooked) remove the bacon and baste the meat with well beaten yolk of egg and gravy; cover thick with bread crumbs and brown nicely. Garnish the platter on which it is served with sprays of mint. Mint sauce should be an accompaniment. This makes not only an attractive looking, but delicious roast of lamb.*

### ᵈᵌ 143. BREAST OF MUTTON STEWED WITH CARROTS ᵈᵌ

*(Aunt Babette, 1889)*

The more tender meats are reserved for roasting; tougher ones are often tenderized by cooking at a low temperature in liquid for a long time. The following recipe calls for a porcelain-lined kettle and a spider. The porcelain lining, which became widespread toward the end of the nineteenth century, protects the metal from acidic foods. The spider is a skillet with legs to straddle a direct heat source, such as coals or embers.

*Salt the mutton on both sides, adding a little ground ginger; put on to boil in cold water in a porcelain-lined kettle and cover up tightly and stew slowly. In the meantime pare and cut up the carrots and add these and cover up again. Pare and cut up about half a dozen potatoes into dice shape and add them three-quarters of an hour before dinner. Cover up again, and when done, make a sauce as follows: Skim off about two tablespoonfuls of fat from the mutton stew, put this in a spider and heat. Brown a tablespoonful of flour in the fat, add a heaping tablespoonful of brown sugar, some cinnamon and pour the gravy of the stew into the spider, letting it boil up once, and then pour all over the carrots and stew until ready to serve.*

## Pork

### ᵈᵌ 144. HAM COOKED IN WINE ᵈᵌ

*(Fox, 1904)*

The following recipe, which calls for an old (hence tough) ham, incorporates several tenderizing methods. In particular, soaking, slow simmering, and the addition of vinegar and sherry (as with any acid) to the cooking liquid help to break down tough fibers. The use of the commercial brand Coleman's mustard speaks to the burgeoning market for preground spices and condiments; the sale of powdered mustard in the United States dates back to the eighteenth century.

*Scrub well and soak an old ham in plenty of water for 48 hours. Weigh ham and allow 1/2 hour for each pound, place in large ham boiler and fill with cold water; let simmer (not boil) gently the allotted time. When half the time is up, pour off the water; fill again with fresh boiling water, into which put 1/2 cup of vinegar, a bay leaf and a few cloves, and finish cooking. Let the ham remain in the water until cool. Then remove the skin. Mix 2 tablespoonfuls of "Coleman's Mustard" with vinegar, spread over the ham, brush with the yolk of an egg. Sprinkle with bread-crumbs and sugar, pin [sic] on the fat side with cloves and a few raisins.*

*With a sharp knife make incisions all through the ham, holding back the openings and pouring in 1/2 pint of sherry. Place in the oven for 1/2 hour, basting every 5 minutes. Do not cut until perfectly cold.*

### ᵥ§ 145. SCALLOPED HAM ᵹ

*(The Ladies Association of the First Presbyterian Church, Houston, Texas, 1883)*

The following recipe provides a use for leftover bits of ham. It might, for example, be made from the leftovers from recipe 144 and served for lunch or a light dinner.

*Take pieces of Ham, not fit for slicing, chopped fine; take an equal quantity of crackers, roll and moisten with milk. Into a patty-pan put layer of ham and then of cracker. In centre of each pan make a depression with spoon, into which break one egg (being careful not to break the yelk [var. yolk]; season with salt, pepper and butter. Put in the oven, by time egg is cooked the whole will be ready to serve. Send to table in pans.*

### ᵥ§ 146. BAKED FRESH PORK ᵹ

*(Corson, 1885)*

A comparison between the roast pig recipe 25 in Chapter 1 and the following recipe illustrates several of the ways that home cookery changed between the early and the late nineteenth century. The most notable difference is that the meat for this later recipe is procured from a market and may have had the skin already removed. The recipe does, however, require that the cook know how to disjoint the pig and be familiar with handling the skin should it have been left on by the butcher. As they still are today, baked apples were considered a tasty accompaniment to pork.

*If the skin is left on the pork, as it is in some markets, scrape it with a dull knife, wash it thoroughly with a wet cloth, and score it in little squares; if the skin has been removed, trim off some of the superfluous fat. Using a sharp, thin knife, cut out the chine or backbone, disjointing it from the ends of the ribs, so that the meat may be carved with ease; put in the dripping-pan a few slices each of carrot, turnip, and onion, a dozen whole cloves, a level teaspoonful of peppercorns, and a few leaves of parsley or celery; lay the pork on these vegetables, put the pan in a moderate oven, and brown the meat; when the meat is brown, season it with salt, pepper, and powdered sage, and finish cooking it, allowing fifteen minutes to each pound of meat. An hour before the pork is done, prepare the garnish for it as follows: Peel a dozen small white onions without breaking the layers apart, put them into a pan with a teaspoonful of sugar, a tablespoonful of butter, and a little salt and pepper; set the pan in the oven, and occasionally shake it to move the onions about and insure their uniform browning; after the onions are prepared, wash four tart apples, quarter, them, remove the cores, place them in a pan just large enough to hold them, with a tablespoonful of butter distributed over them and bake them until they are tender, but not at all broken; keep the onions and apples hot to serve with the pork. When the pork is done, put it on a hot dish; arrange the apples and onions in little groups around it, and serve it with a dish of plain boiled potatoes and brown gravy. To make the gravy, after the pork is taken from the baking-pan, pour out nearly all the drippings, leaving in the scraps of vegetables; set the pan over the fire, stir in a heaping tablespoonful of flour until it is brown, and then a pint of boiling water, adding the water gradually; season the gravy thus made, palatably with salt and pepper, let it boil for a moment, and then strain it, and serve it with the baked pork.*

## ⊰ 147. MEXICAN-STYLE SAUSAGE ⊱

*(Pinedo, 1898)*

The following recipe, which was published in San Francisco in 1898, comes from the first cookbook written by an Hispanic in the United States. Mexican-style sausages, or chorizos, are characterized by the addition of chili peppers. The pasilla chili called for in the following recipe is the dried form of the chilaca, a pepper packing under half the heat of a jalapeño.

*Finely mince some pork. If the meat is lean, supplement it with fat chopped as finely as possible. The day before making the chorizos, thoroughly wash a good quantity of red pasilla chiles in cold water, and let them soak. The following day empty the chiles into a sieve and drain them of all the water.*

*Grind the chiles in the metate [mortar] and soak them with vinegar. As you grind the chiles, also grind in some peeled garlic cloves.*

*When the sauce is ready, flavor it with salt and oregano, pour into the meat and fat, and mix well with several turns.*

*When the sausage meat is prepared, fill the casing, which already has been bleached [to sanitize] for this purpose. Tie both ends of each chorizo with string, making them the size that you wish. Then hang them on a string so they can air-dry in a cool place.*

## ⊰ 148. SCRAPPEL [SCRAPPLE] ⊱

*(Gillette, 1887)*

The following sausage recipe is an Americanized version of the black, or blood, pudding. Scrapple, thought to have originated at the hands of

German-American butchers, omits the blood and substitutes cornmeal, or often buckwheat, for common European grains. As the following recipe indicates, scrapple is often eaten at breakfast.

*Scrappel is a most palatable dish. Take the head, heart and any lean scraps of pork, and boil until the flesh slips easily from the bones. Remove the fat, gristle and bones, then chop fine. Set the liquor in which the meat was boiled aside until cold, take the cake of fat from the surface and return to the fire. When it boils, put in the chopped meat and season well with pepper and salt. Let it boil again, then thicken with corn-meal as you would in making ordinary corn-meal mush, but letting it slip through the fingers slowly to prevent lumps. Cook an hour, stirring constantly at first, afterwards putting back on the range in a position to boil gently. When done, pour into a long, square pan, not too deep, and mold. In cold weather this can be kept several weeks. Cut into slices when cold, and fried brown, as you do mush, is a cheap and delicious breakfast dish.*

## Game

### ❦ 149. TO BARBECUE SQUIRREL ❧

*(Tyree, 1879)*

Although venison and rabbit recipes continue to appear in modest numbers in twentieth-century cookbooks, squirrel recipes have virtually dwindled to extinction, except in the South where squirrels continue to make their way into burgoo (recipe 126) and Brunswick stew (recipe 2) and into the occasional oven or frying pan.

*Put some slices of fat bacon in an oven. Lay the squirrels on them and lay two slices of bacon on the top. Put them in the oven and let them cook until done. Lay them on a dish and set near the fire. Take out the bacon, sprinkle one spoonful of flour into the gravy and let it brown. Then pour in one teacup of water, one tablespoonful of butter, and some tomato or walnut catsup [see recipes 50 or 51]. Let it cook, and then pour it over the squirrel.*

### ❦ 150. VENISON AND RABBIT PIE ❧

*(Aunt Babette, 1889)*

Venison was such a sought-after meat in the colonies that it had virtually disappeared in New England by the late nineteenth century. The following recipe, however, hails from the Midwest, a region where deer continued to flourish as it did in frontier and southern cooking. By the beginning of the twentieth century, however, the number of venison recipes found in cookbooks had dwindled considerably.

*Make a paste of one pound of flour. Rub twelve ounces of butter into this and add the yelks [var. yolks] of two eggs, a teaspoonful of salt and ice-water enough to mix lightly. Roll and line a deep pie-plate with this and fill with the meat of venison or rabbit, which has been previously stewed in the following manner: Cut the raw meat from the bones into small pieces and put them into a stew-pan with one onion. Add salt, pepper, nutmeg, and just enough cold water to cover, and boil until tender. Before filling this in the pie-crust, roll some flakes of butter in flour and put over the pie. Cover with a thick layer of pastry, make a hole in the center of the top crust and bake slowly. In the meantime heat some port wine, into which you have thrown a few cloves and blades of mace. When the pie is nearly baked, pour this mixture into the pie through the hole in the top crust by means of a funnel. Brush the top of the pie with beaten egg and return to the oven and bake a light brown.*

## Poultry and Fowl

---

### ✦ TO DRESS A CHICKEN

(Kander, 1903)

*Singe chicken by holding it over blazing paper. Remove pin feathers with the point of a knife. The internal organs should be removed as soon as killed. Make an opening at the vent, or under one of the legs, and remove them, taking care that the gall bladder, near the liver, is not broken. Remove the windpipe and pull the crop [pouched enlargement of a bird's gullet] out from the tail end of the neck, remove the oil-bag from the tail. Take out lungs and kidneys. Press the heart to extract any blood. Take off the inner coat of gizzard; this, with the heart and liver, are called giblets. Wash chicken with cold water.*

---

### ⤙ 151. CHICKEN CROQUETTES ⤚

*(Burr, c. 1886)*

Croquettes became quite fashionable at the turn of the century. They were made from such diverse base ingredients as hare, lamb, crab, cheese, lentils, nuts, oysters, squash, and even spaghetti. Just as the chicken in the following recipe, the main ingredient is finely chopped, moistened with a white sauce, fashioned into a cylinder, dipped in egg and breadcrumbs, and fried.

*The meat of one chicken (no skin) chopped fine, one-third the quantity of fine bread crumbs, one-third cup butter, one tablespoonful of salt, one-half teaspoonful of pepper—or, better still, "season to taste,"—three medium-sized boiled potatoes chopped very fine. Mix meat, crumbs and potatoes, then season and add the melted butter, and mix it well in; then add milk enough to make it quite moist, but still so that the croquettes will stay in form; roll in beaten egg and then in cracker-crumbs and fry in hot lard, and if you wish complete success use always a wire frying-basket.*

### ⊰ 152. COUNTRY FRIED CHICKENS ⊱

*(Hearn, 1885)*

The country gravy that accompanies these fried chickens and for which the dish takes part of its name is also served with country-fried steak. Both dishes are still eaten frequently in the Midwest, South, and Southwest.

*Take a young fat chicken, cut it up. Pepper and salt it, dredge it over with flour, and set it by while you mix a cup of lard, and some slices of fat bacon in a frying pan. Let the lard get very hot, then drop in a few pieces of the chicken, always allowing room in the pan for each piece to be turned without crowding. As fast as you fry the pieces, put them on a dish over hot water to keep the heat in them while you make the gravy. Pour off some of the grease the chicken was fried in, and then dredge into the frying pan some flour; let this brown nicely and then pour into it a cup of sweet milk, little at a time; let if froth up, and then place your chicken back into the gravy for three minutes. If you like the chicken brown and dry, pour the gravy under it on the dish for serving.*

### ⊰ 153. CANVAS-BACK DUCK ⊱

*(Gillette, 1887)*

The canvasback duck was one of the most prized, and hence costly, waterfowls of the nineteenth century. It was populace enough at mid-century to be shipped from the Chesapeake Bay to the major cities throughout the United Sates. By the turn of the century, however, the canvasback, along with many other water fowl, had been hunted in such numbers that they were approaching extinction.

*The epicurean taste declares that this special kind of bird requires no spices or flavors to make it perfect, as the meat partakes of the flavor of the food that the bird feeds upon, being mostly wild celery; and the delicious flavor is best preserved when roasted quickly with a hot fire. After dressing the duck in the usual way, by plucking, singing, drawing, wipe it with a wet towel, truss the head under the wing; place it in a dripping-pan, put it in the oven, basting often, and roast it half an hour. It is generally preferred a little underdone. Place it when done on a hot dish, season well with salt and pepper, pour over it the gravy it has yielded in baking and serve it immediately while hot.*

## ❧ 154. BROILED SQUABS [PIGEONS] ❧

*(Aunt Babette, 1889)*

Quail and grouse, like squab, were commonly broiled and serve on toast in the following fashion.

*Squabs are a great delicacy, especially in the convalescent's menu, being peculiarly savory and nourishing. Clean the squabs; lay them in salt water for about ten minutes and then rub dry with a clean towel. Split them down the back, [place on a gridiron] and broil over a clear coal fire. Season with salt and pepper; lay them on a heated platter and butter or grease them liberally with goose fat and cover with a deep platter. Now toast a piece of bread for each pigeon, removing the crust. Dip the toast in boiling water for an instant. In serving lay a squab upon a piece of toast. Crabapple jelly [recipe 224] is a nice accompaniment.*

## ❧ 155. A GOOD ROAST TURKEY ❧

*(Shuman, 1893)*

Wild and domestic turkeys, which had been imported from England, along with the new varieties they interbred have been an important component of the American diet since Colonial times. By the mid twentieth century, however, many of the early American breeds had begun to dwindle as the turkey industry became consolidated. In the last couple of decades, however, heritage turkey farms have begun to breed some of the most popular eighteenth- and nineteenth-century breeds, including the Bronze, Narragansett, and Bourbon Red.

*An ordinary turkey weighing eight to ten pounds requires at least two hours for proper and thorough cooking. Prepare your fowl and rub dry with a clean towel; then mix a little pepper and salt and rub both inside and outside of the turkey before putting in the dressing. Grate stale bread, about three cups; then add a small teaspoon of pepper and the same amount of powdered sage or sweet marjoram, salt and a little salt fat pork chopped very fine or a piece of butter the size of an egg; use warm water to mix the whole to the consistency of thick batter; beat an egg and stir into it the last thing; stuff the breast with half of the dressing, then sew up with coarse white thread and put the remaining dressing into the body and sew up. Take skewers of wood or iron and pin the wings closely to the sides, then turn the neck back and pin that firmly. One can use twine and tie them if they haven't the skewers. Force the legs down and tie tightly to the body before placing the turkey in the dripping pan with nearly a pint of water. Have a brisk fire and baste the turkey at least every fifteen minutes with these drippings. This frequent basting is of great importance as it keeps in the juices and allows thorough cooking. Turn the turkey two or three times during the cooking. During the last half hour dredge with flour and butter freely. The crisp pasty look so desirable and appetizing comes from this. Cook gizzard and liver in a sauce pan on the stove until thoroughly tender, then chop very fine and put them in the gravy to boil thoroughly in the dripping pan in the gravy which is delicious, and to be served from a tureen.*

## SEAFOOD

### ᴥ 156. CODFISH BALLS ᴥ

*(Rorer, 1898)*

Salted fish such as herring and cod provided an economical source of protein available year-round. Thus they were often prepared in homes of modest means, where they might be eaten as a main dish; middle-class Americans also ate codfish balls, usually as an entrée, or side dish, rather than as a main source of protein.

*1/2 pound of codfish*
*1 tablespoonful of butter*
*1 saltspoonful of pepper*
*4 good-sized potatoes*
*Yolks of two eggs*
*1/2 teaspoonful of salt*

*Boil and mash the potatoes. Pick the codfish apart; scald it; drain; cover with cold water; bring to scalding point again. Do this three times; then press it dry and add to the potatoes, and all the other ingredients. Mix thoroughly; form into balls a little larger than English walnuts; dip in beaten egg, roll in bread crumbs and fry in hot fat. Serve plain or with tomato sauce [recipe 171].*

### ᴥ 157. BAKED CRAB ᴥ

*(The Ladies Association of the First Presbyterian Church, Houston, Texas, 1883)*

The "made mustard" called for in the following recipe refers to the condiment rather than the powdered form. Also known as prepared mustard, "made mustard" consists of powdered mustard seeds mixed with a liquid. The recipe also calls for Worcestershire sauce, which by mid-century could be purchased from a store. Many women, however, still made it from scratch; it commonly includes garlic, soy sauce, tamarind, onions, molasses, lime, anchovies, and vinegar.

*Make a dressing as follows: One tablespoonful of made mustard, one teaspoonful of Worcestershire sauce, three tablespoons of sweet oil, cayenne pepper, black pepper and salt to taste and vinegar enough to mix well. Take the meat from one dozen large crabs or one can of crabs, put in a dish and pour over the dressing, mixing it well in, then add six soda crackers rolled fine, one raw egg, and mix all well together, then put into a dish or the shells, sprinkle over them cracker crumbs, put little pieces of butter on top and bake.*

### ⇛ 158. FRIED EELS ⇚

*(Farmer, 1896)*

Although not a large part of the American diet today, eel played a more frequent role in the nineteenth century. In addition to frying, stewing was a standard method of preparation.

*Clean eels, and cut in two-inch pieces. Sprinkle with salt and pepper, dip in corn meal, and sauté in pork fat.*

---

### ✦ TO KEEP BUTTER FRESH

(Women of the First Congregational Church, Marysville, Ohio, 1876)

Before the advent of the refrigerator, cookbooks abounded with advice on how to keep dairy and eggs fresh.

*Work [butter] until solid, make into rolls, take two gallons water; one pint white sugar, one level tablespoon saltpetre; make the brine strong enough with salt to bear an egg, boil and skim. Let cool, pour over butter and keep under brine with a weight. Butter will keep for a year as sweet as when churned.*

---

### ⇛ 159. PLANKED FISH ⇚

*(Kander, 1903)*

In plank cookery, a technique learned from the Native Americans, the fish (or less frequently fowl or meat) is placed on a well-oiled board made of particularly fragrant wood so that the flesh absorbs the wood's aroma. Although the following recipe is adapted for the oven, plank cookery is well suited for the hearth fire.

*Fish is planked when baked on a board (hickory, oak, or ash) in the oven. Place the board in oven until very hot. Place the fish on board, season with salt and pepper and a little butter, or split it and place it skin down on the board; brush with butter and dust with salt and pepper. Baste often with melted butter and bake until a golden brown. Serve with parsley, lemon or pickles sliced. Whitefish is best served in this style.*

### ৪ 160. OYSTER COCKTAIL ৪

*(Curtis, 1903)*

A version of this recipe made with shrimp can be found on many contemporary all-American restaurant menus. Although grocery stores do not always carry fresh horseradish root, they do usually stock a prepared horseradish sauce (see recipe 169 for a homemade version) in the condiment section. Oyster cocktail might be served first at a multicourse dinner.

*Seven teaspoons of horse-radish, seven teaspoons of vinegar, ten teaspoons of lemon juice, one teaspoon of tabasco sauce, salt to taste, one quart of oysters for twelve people. Serve in glasses.*

### ৪ 161. ESCALLOPED [SCALLOPED] OYSTERS ৪

*(Shuman, 1893)*

A scalloped dish generally calls for layers of the featured ingredient (often potatoes) to be coated with cream sauce and topped with bread crumbs before baking. The following version omits the cream and relies instead on egg, butter, and oyster liquor for the sauce. A scalloped dish is to be distinguished from an escalope, usually a thin piece of meat or fish that has been breaded and fried. The addition of the "E" by this recipe's author conflates the spelling of the two distinct dishes. The following dish might be served as a light main dish for lunch.

*Spread cracker crumbs on bottom of baking dish; then place bits of butter and a layer of oysters, which must be sprinkled with salt and pepper. Make alternate layers of oysters, cracker crumbs, salt, pepper, and butter until dish is full. Have crumbs on top. Now make a small incision in center and pour in one well beaten egg, with a small quantity of oyster liquor. Put in hot oven and brown nicely.*

### ৪ 162. BROILED POMPANO ৪

*(Corson, 1885)*

Pompano is a prized fish most often found along the Gulf Coast and the Atlantic. The author of this recipe pairs the pompano with cucumber sauce (see recipe 167).

*Have the fish scaled, drawn, and thoroughly washed in cold water; score it on the bone on both sides, making three or four cuts across the fish; season it lightly with salt and pepper, place it between the bars of a buttered double wire*

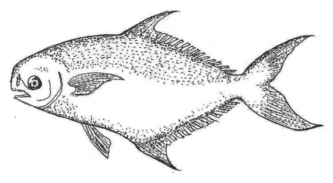

*gridiron, and quickly broil it over a hot fire for about five minutes on each side, or until the flesh begins to cleave from the bones. Serve it on a hot platter, with a tablespoonful of butter spread over it, and a little salt and pepper dusted on it. Pompano is excellent when fried or boiled.*

*Pompano.*

## GRAVIES, SAUCES, CATSUPS, AND PICKLES

### ⅊ 163. CAULIFLOWER PICKLE ⅊

*(Women of the First Congregational Church, Marysville, Ohio, 1876)*

Vegetable pickles such as the following were often served in late winter, when fresh vegetables were in short supply.

*Choose such as are fine and full size, cut away all the leaves, and pull away the flowers by bunches; steep in brine two days, drain, put into bottles with whole black pepper, allspice and stick cinnamon; boil vinegar and with it mix mustard smoothly, a little at a time, and just thick enough to run into jars; pour over the cold cauliflower and seal while hot.*

### ⅊ 164. CHOW-CHOW ⅊

*(Tyree, 1879)*

Since the mid-1800s, Americans have used the term chow-chow to describe a mixed vegetable and mustard pickle. The relish may have been introduced to the United States by Chinese railroad workers. The following version includes very little sugar, but some chow-chow recipes called for up to two pounds of sugar

*Gravies, sauces, and pickles.*

for a one-gallon recipe. Others included as little as an ounce of mustard seeds.

*The recipe is for one gallon pickle; for more, the quantities must be increased, of course. The ingredients consist of:*

*1/2 peck green tomatoes*
*1 large head of cabbage*
*6 large onions*
*1 dozen cucumbers*
*1/2 pint grated horseradish*
*1/2 pound white mustard-seed*
*1/2 ounce celery-seed*
*A few small onions*
*1/4 teacup ground pepper*
*Turmeric, ground cinnamon*
*A little brown sugar*

*Cut the cabbage, onion and cucumbers into small pieces, and pack them down in salt one night; then put in vinegar, poured over hot. Do this three mornings. The third morning, mix one box [1/2 pound] ground mustard with one-quarter pint salad oil. To be mixed in while warm.*

### ⊰ 165. DILL PICKLES ⊱

*(Aunt Babette, 1889)*

Whereas a vast array of vegetables and fruits were commonly pickled in the nineteenth century, cucumbers have become by far the most well-known contemporary pickle variety. Today's Kosher dill pickles, those prepared according to Jewish dietary law, are often pickled using many of the same ingredients as the following recipe, which comes from a Jewish cookery book.

*Take two or three dozen medium-sized cucumbers and lay them in salt water over night. Wipe each one dry, discarding all that are soft and lay them in a wooden vessel (which is better than a stone one) along with grape leaves and green grapes, if you can get them, whole peppers, or one or two green peppers, a few bay leaves, a few pieces of whole ginger, a few cloves and a stick of horseradish sliced up on top of all. Use plenty of dill between each layer. Boil enough water to cover the pickles. Use about one pound of salt to six quarts of water, and one cup of vinegar. If you wish to keep them all winter, have your barrel closed by a cooper [barrel maker].*

## ❧ 166. SPICY RED-CHILE SAUCE ❧

*(Pinedo, 1898)*

Deveining chiles, a step called for in this recipe, greatly lessens the intensity of their heat, much of which is contained in the seeds and inner membrane removed in the process.

*Remove the crowns [stem ends], then flatten and devein ten or twelve chiles; toast them in a warm oven, and when they are quite toasted, take them out and put them in cold water, then hot. Wipe them off and put in a casserole.*

*Bathe the chiles in boiling water; let them soak for one or two hours, or let them simmer.*

*Then take them out of the water in which they have been soaking; add a small amount of fresh water so the sauce will have a uniform consistency.*

*After grinding the chiles well in a mortar, pass the sauce though a heavy strainer.*

## ❧ 167. CUCUMBER SAUCE ❧

*(Corson, 1885)*

Cucumber sauce was often served with fish. The following recipe suggests pairing it with broiled pompano (recipe 162), a prized fish found in the Atlantic and Gulf Coast waters. Victorian cucumbers were more bitter than most modern varieties; some Victorians believed them indigestible while others drank their juice as a diuretic.

*Cucumber sauce is delicious with broiled pompano; it is made by adding a very little juice squeezed from grated cucumber, or the cucumber itself, to a mayonnaise sauce (recipe 189). The cucumber-juice must be used with great caution, because it possesses decided medicinal properties.*

## ❧ 168. HOLLANDAISE SAUCE ❧

*(Rorer, 1898)*

This widely renowned sauce became quite fashionable in the United States at the turn of the century. It is traditionally made with lemon juice in lieu of the vinegar called for here. It can be served with the asparagus found in recipe 173. It also plays an essential role in eggs Benedict, which, according to legend, was first dished and served at a New York City restaurant in the 1890s.

*2 tablespoonfuls of butter*
*1 tablespoonful of flour*
*Yolks of two eggs*
*1/2 teaspoon of salt*
*1 saltspoonful of pepper*
*1 bay leaf*
*2 tablespooonfuls of tarragon vinegar*
*1 tablespoonful chopped onion*
*1/2 pint boiling water*

*Put the bay leaf and onion in the vinegar, bring to the boiling point and cool. Rub the butter and flour together, add gradually the water, stir until boiling, add the vinegar, strained. Take from the fire, stir in gradually the yolks of the eggs. Heat very gently just a moment, add the salt and pepper, and strain at once in the sauce boat. This is one of the most elegant of the fish sauces. Lemon juice may be added in place of the vinegar. If the sauce is to be served with boiled fish, use a half pint of water in which the fish was boiled.*

### ⇥ 169. HORSE RADISH SAUCE ⇤

*(Hearn, 1885)*

Previously called "German mustard" by many Americans, horseradish is a relative of the mustard plant. The grated root is often used to make a pungent condiment that pairs well with seafood such as oysters and shrimp, as well as cold poached fish. Because the root loses its bite when cooked, horseradish is most often used in its raw state. The following sauce can be used in the oyster cocktail recipe 160.

*To a spoonful of mustard add three tablespoonfuls of vinegar and a little salt; if you have it, put in two spoonfuls of cream. Grate into this as much horse radish as will thicken it; then mash a clove of garlic, and your sauce is ready.*

### ⇥ 170. MUSHROOM SAUCE ⇤

*(Shuman, 1893)*

Mushroom sauces pair well with meat and fish. Although it does not specify, the following recipe calls for canned mushrooms, as did many mushroom sauce recipes from the turn of the century. Many authors, however, specified fresh, which can easily be substituted for the canned. The juice released when fresh mushrooms are sautéed precludes any need for canned mushroom juice. The following sauce is required for the beef à la mode recipe 136.

*Melt one tablespoon butter; stir in a tablespoon of flour, and when it is well browned, add, after heating, six tablespoons of stock with half the juice from the can of mushrooms and one-half teaspoonful of lemon juice, seasoned with pepper and salt; add the button mushrooms and let all simmer about ten minutes. Pour over the filet of beef and serve.*

---

### ✦ CANNED GOODS

In 1880, a process for mass producing cans from tin plate was invented, and the use of canned goods became common.

---

### ⤙ 171. TOMATO SAUCE ⤚

*(Rorer, 1898)*

With the growing availability of canned tomatoes, sauces such as the following could be made year-round. This sauce can be served on codfish balls (recipe 156). It can also be served with meat.

*1 tablespoonful of butter*
*1 tablespoonful of flour*
*1/2 pint of strained tomatoes*
*1/2 teaspoonful of salt*
*1 level saltspoonful of pepper*
*1 teaspoonful of onion juice*
*1 bay leaf*

*Strain the tomatoes, add the onion and bay leaf, salt and pepper. Rub the butter and flour together in a saucepan; add the tomato, stir until boiling; stand over hot water for ten minutes, strain and it is ready for use.*

## VEGETABLES, SALADS, AND SALAD DRESSINGS

### Vegetables

### ⤙ 172. ARTICHOKES ⤚

*(Pinedo, 1898)*

Long a vegetable eaten by wealthy Americans, artichokes were slower to make their way onto the average American table, in part because they were not widely available. In the 1890s, however, northern California farmers began to produce sufficient quantities to ship large numbers of the vegetable out of state. Artichokes are often served with hollandaise (recipe 168).

*Remove the [outer] leaves from around the artichokes, then soak them.*

*Simmer the artichokes with the heads down, about one-third covered in the water. Hermetically seal the casserole with a piece of linen and put the cover on this. Put it on the fire, which should be fairly hot. The steam will penetrate the artichokes and preserve their natural flavor.*

*You can use one-half water and one-half olive oil. If you like them cold, serve with oil, vinegar, salt, and pepper.*

### ⇥ 173. ASPARAGUS À LA HOLLANDAISE ⇤

*(Rorer, 1898)*

In addition to being served cold as it is in the following recipe, boiled asparagus was often arranged on top of toast, dressed with butter, and served hot.

*Wash and tie into bundles and boil the asparagus; when done drain, put on a platter and stand aside to cool. Serve very cold and pass with it hot sauce Hollandaise (recipe 168). To eat, lift each piece by the butt, with the fingers, dip the head in the sauce and lift it to the mouth. Eat only the tender portion.*

*Asparagus may also be served plain boiled and cold with French dressing [recipe 188].*

### ⇥ 174. CAULIFLOWER, WITH COOKED MAYONNAISE DRESSING ⇤

*(California Women, 1905)*

In addition to being dressed with cooked mayonnaise, boiled cauliflower was often served with a white sauce made of flour, milk, and butter; it was also commonly pickled.

*Carefully prepare a nice head of cauliflower, boiling in salted water until tender. To make dressing take one tablespoon vinegar, four tablespoons water and put on to boil. Beat together the yolk of one egg and two tablespoons olive oil, adding one saltspoon salt, one saltspoon sugar, dash of cayenne pepper, few drops onion juice, one teaspoon water. Stir the mixture in the boiling vinegar and water, and when it begins to thicken take from fire and stir in the juice of half a lemon. To be served hot on cauliflower at table.*

*Also an excellent dressing to serve with string beans.*

---

### ➔ SUGGESTED VEGETABLE COOKING TIMES

*(Rorer, 1898)*

As typical of most Victorian cookbooks, the suggested cooking times found below far exceed contemporary standards.

Green peas, young and fresh ... ... .... 15 minutes
Green peas, old and not fresh ... ... .... 30 minutes
String beans ... ... .... 45 minutes
Cauliflower and broccoli ... ... .... 30 minutes
Okra ... ... .... 30 minutes
Brussels sprouts, fresh ... ... .... 30 minutes
Kale ... ... .... 45 minutes
Asparagus ... ... .... 45 minutes

## ⇥ 175. TO BOIL GREEN CORN ⇤

*(Tyree, 1879)*

Like most nineteenth-century directions on boiling vegetables, the following recipe calls for a far longer cooking time than recommended today; it specifies an hour to boil corn.

*Strip off the outer shucks, leaving only the thin white ones. Cut off the ends. Throw into boiling water. Boil an hour. Strip off the silk with the shuck. Cut from the cob while hot. Sprinkle over salt, add a tablespoonful of fresh butter and serve hot.*

## 176. CYMLINGS FRIED WITH BACON ⇤

*(Tyree, 1879)*

Cymlings, also called "patty pan" or "scalloped squash," are a summer variety, which were also stewed or made into fritters or puddings.

*Fry some slices of fat bacon in a pan. Remove the bacon when done and keep hot. Fry in the gravy some cymlings that have been boiled tender and cut in slices. While frying, mash fine with a large spoon, and add pepper and salt. Fry brown, and serve with the bacon, if you like.*

## ⇥ 177. BAKED POTATOES ⇤

*(Rorer, 1898)*

Just as they do today, potato recipes proliferated in the nineteenth century. So, too, did directions on how best to bake, boil, and mash them. Some baked potato recipes suggest sending them to the table ready split and buttered; others, such as the following, give explicit instructions to keep their skins intact. The cooking time given in this recipe would be sufficient for a small potato.

*Brush the potatoes until the skin is perfectly clean, rinse them in cold water. Place them in a pan or on the grate in a moderately heated [375°] oven; bake slowly until tender, about three-quarters of an hour. When done take each potato in a towel or napkin in the hand, press it gently without breaking the skin until it is thoroughly mashed within. Never stick a fork in a potato to see it is done; this ruptures the skin, allows the steam to escape, and makes the potato soggy. If the oven is too hot, the skins will become hardened and prevent the evaporation of water; this also makes potatoes heavy, dark and wet.*

*If baked potatoes are mashed according to directions, in the skin, they will keep in good condition, in a warm oven, one hour. To serve, place them on a folded napkin and send to table, uncovered.*

### ᘓ 178. POTATO DUMPLINGS ᘗ

*(Aunt Babette, 1889)*

A staple of German-American cookery, dumplings were served alongside meat dishes and also added to soups and stews. Sweet and sour sauces, like the one given in the recipe here, are also a standard part of German-American meals, which rely heavily on blends of vinegar and sugar to complement foods ranging from beef and vegetables to dumplings.

*Boil as many large potatoes as you wish dumplings (to twelve dumplings, twelve potatoes). It is better to boil the potatoes the day before using. Boil them in their jackets, pare and grate them then add half a loaf of grated stale bread, a tablespoonful of melted butter or suet, a teaspoonful of salt, two tablespoonfuls of flour, half of a grated nutmeg, and part of the grated peel of a lemon, three or four eggs and a saucerful of bread which has been cut in the smallest dice shape possible and browned in butter or fat. Mix all thoroughly and form into round dumplings. Put them into boiling salt water and let them boil until done. As soon as they raise to the top of the water, take up one and try it, if cooked through the center remove them all. Serve with a fruit sauce, or heated fat, with an onion cut up very fine and browned in it. A sweet and sour is also very nice, made as follows: Boil vinegar and water together in equal parts and sweeten to taste. Melt a piece of butter in a spider, throw in a spoonful of flour, mix rapidly, then add a pinch of salt, and also add the boiling vinegar gradually to this, also some ground cinnamon and a pinch of ground cloves.*

### ᘓ 179. SARATOGA POTATOES ᘗ

*(Women of the First Congregational Church, Marysville, Ohio, 1876)*

These thinly sliced deep-fried potatoes are American potato chips. The following recipe calls for a slaw-cutter, which works like a mandoline—a utensil that sits on legs and houses a razor-sharp cutting edge specifically designed to evenly slice or julienne vegetables and hard fruits.

*Pare and cut into thin slices on a slaw-cutter four large potatoes (new are best); let stand in salt water while breakfast is cooking; take a handful of the potatoes, squeeze the water from them and dry in a napkin; separate the slices and drop a handful at a time into a skillet of boiling lard, taking care that they do not strike together, stir with a fork till they are a light brown color, take out with a wire spoon, drain well, and serve in an open dish.*

### ᵈ 180. TO DRESS RAW ONIONS ᵉ

*(Tyree, 1879)*

The following recipe is of particular note because it calls for raw onions. In so doing, it marks an unusual acceptance of the onion in its raw state—albeit tamed by a saltwater bath and a liberal coating of vinegar. In cookbooks up until this time period, onion recipes usually called for extensive boiling, stewing, or frying with the express goal of cooking out the onion's bite and, hence, the odor it imparts to the breath and skin.

*Slice and chop fine, and put in weak salt and water till just before dinner. Then drain off and dress with half a teacup vinegar, two tablespoonfuls pepper vinegar, two tablespoonfuls made mustard, two tablespoonfuls white sugar, one tablespoonful salt.*

*Lay a large lump of ice on top, and garnish with curled parsley; which, eaten after onion, is said to remove the scent from the breath.*

### ᵈ 181. SALSIFY FRITTERS ᵉ

*(Fox, 1904)*

Also known as "oyster plant" or "vegetable oyster," this root vegetable enjoyed a far greater role in the nineteenth century than today. Like other root vegetables, such as carrots and potatoes, salsify is commonly scraped, or peeled.

*Boil the salsify and then scrape it and mash into a batter. Add 2 eggs, pepper, and salt, and thicken with 1 tablespoon of flour. Fry in hot lard.*

### ᵈ 182. TO BROIL TOMATOES ᵉ

*(The Ladies Association of the First Presbyterian Church, Houston, Texas, 1883)*

In addition to being broiled, tomatoes were also baked, fried, scalloped, sliced and served as salads, stewed, and stuffed.

*Take large, round tomatoes, wash and wipe, and put them on a gridiron over live coals, the stem side down. When brown, turn them, and let them cook till quite hot through. Place them on a hot dish and send quickly to the table, when each one may season for himself with pepper[,] salt and butter.*

## Salads

### ❧ 183. ALLIGATOR PEAR SALAD ☙

*(California Women, 1905)*

Indigenous to Central America, the alligator pear, or avocado, was not commercially grown in the United States until the late nineteenth century. Although it had been grown in Florida and California much earlier and had featured in Mexican cookery, its commercial cultivation spurred its availability in the United States. By the turn of the century, it began appearing in salad recipes such as the following.

*Take two large alligator pears, peel and remove the stone; cut in one-half-inch cubes, sprinkle with salt, add two tablespoons or more of the best olive oil, with or without a very small piece of onion minced fine to flavor. Put in a salad dish already prepared with crisp lettuce leaves.*

### ❧ 184. COLD SLAW ☙

*(Curtis, 1903)*

Cole slaw, deriving from the Dutch *koolsla*, is a shredded cabbage salad commonly dressed with sour cream, mayonnaise, or, on occasion, French dressing (recipe 188).

*Chop with one small head of cabbage two hard boiled eggs. Take one-half cup of sour cream, one tablespoonful of sugar, a little salt and pepper, and a teaspoon of celery seed; beat all together, then add one teacup of vinegar, and pour over the cabbage. If this is put in a tight vessel, it will keep several days.*

### ❧ 185. DANDELION SALAD, GERMAN FASHION ☙

*(Rorer, 1898)*

The bacon and vinegar dressing used in this salad is more commonly served today with spinach, as opposed to dandelion. A bitter green, dandelion has long been a feature in spring tonics and soups drunk to purify the body after the winter's dearth of fresh vegetables.

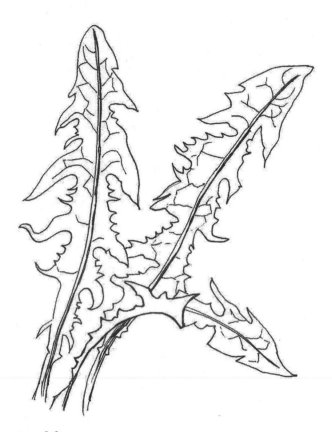

*Dandelion.*

*2 ounces of bacon*
*2 tablespoonfuls of vinegar*
*1 saltspoonful of paprika*
*1 quart of fresh dandelion*
*leaves*
*1 saltspoonful of salt*
*1 tablespoonful of chopped*
*onion or chives*

*Cut the bacon into strips; put it in a frying pan with two tablespoonfuls of water. Let the water evaporate and the bacon fry carefully until crisp, but not dry. Lift, and stand it aside while you shake the dandelions perfectly dry, and cool the bacon fat. Arrange the dandelions in your salad bowl and put over the slices of bacon. Add to the bacon fat the vinegar, salt, pepper and onion or chives; mix and pour over the dandelions and serve at once.*

## ᴥ 186. FRUIT SALAD ᴥ

*(Kander, 1903)*

In the late nineteenth century, fruit finally shed its long association with disease (many previously thought eating fresh fruit caused illness). Intricate fruit salads, often served inside the rind of a larger fruit, became commonplace on the American table. A mania for peeling and seeding grapes continued unabated through the 1950s. The Malaga is a white grape variety.

*3 oranges*
*3 bananas*
*1/2 lb. Malaga grapes*
*Sugar to taste*
*Juice of 1 lemon*
*12 English walnut meats*

*Cut the oranges in two crosswise, reserving the peels as salad cups. Remove orange pulp separately from each section. Remove skins and seeds from grapes. Mix orange pulp and grapes, sprinkle with sugar, add lemon juice, and let stand in cool place several hours. Before serving, add the bananas sliced, and the walnut meats. Fill the orange shells with this mixture. One-fourth cup of wine may be added, if desired.*

### ❧ 187. AMERICAN POTATO SALAD ❧

*(Corson, 1885)*

During the late nineteenth century, potato salad recipes proliferated throughout the United States. The following recipe is a cold mayonnaise-based version. Another version, which was frequently served warm, incorporates bacon, vinegar, and sometimes onion; warm potato salad became widespread after the German immigrant influx of 1870.

*Peel half a dozen cold boiled potatoes, and slice them, not too thin; boil two eggs hard; wash, and chop rather fine, one head of celery; peel one onion, and chop it fine; break the yolks of the hard boiled eggs smooth with the yolk of one raw egg; stir with them a gill [4 oz.] of oil, two tablespoonfuls of vinegar, a level teaspoonful each of salt and dry mustard, and a saltspoonful of pepper; mix this dressing with the potato, celery, and onion, and serve the salad.*

## Salad Dressings

During this era, salad dressings became a cookbook category of their own, apart from sauces and gravies. The following dressings are suitable for salads and for vegetables served cold, such as asparagus, artichokes, or beets.

### ❧ 188. FRENCH DRESSING ❧

*(Shuman, 1893)*

The French dressing referred to here bears little resemblance to the orange commercial French dressing sold in the Unites States. The following version is a blend of oil and vinegar, often called vinaigrette. It can be served in lieu of the hollandaise with the asparagus recipe 173. It can also be tossed with cherries to make a fruit salad that was popular at the turn of the century.

*One tablespoon of vinegar; three tablespoons of olive oil; one saltspoon of pepper, and one saltspoon of salt. (This is half a spoon too much pepper for Americans.) Add a trifle of onion, scraped fine, or rubbed on the salad bowl, if it is desired at all. Pour the oil, mixed with the pepper and salt, over the salad; mix them well together; then add the vinegar, and mix again. Serve on a leaf of crisp lettuce.*

## ⊰ 189. MAYONNAISE DRESSING ⊱

*(Curtis, 1903)*

In addition to dressing cold meat and fish salads as well as entrées with mayonnaise, Victorians also dressed lettuce with a thin version of the condiment.

*One egg yolk, one cup of olive oil, one and one-half teaspoons of salt, one-quarter teaspoon of cayenne, one and one-half teaspoons of mustard, one tablespoon of lemon juice, one tablespoon of vinegar. Mix in a cold bowl mustard, salt, pepper, yolk of egg and lemon juice, stir well, then add oil drop by drop; as mixture thickens thin with vinegar, keep in cold place until ready to serve. If a thinner dressing is liked, add one-half cup of beaten cream to the above mixture. If dressing is to be kept for any length of time use the yolk of a hard-boiled egg in addition to the raw yolk.*

## EGGS, RICE, PASTA, AND SUNDRY OTHER DISHES

## ⊰ 190. CHEESE SOUFFLÉ ⊱

*(Parloa, 1880)*

Soufflés, like pies and pudding, can be savory or sweet. The "escalop dish" called for in the following recipe would be equivalent to a casserole dish. An actual soufflé dish is a glazed, round ceramic dish with straight sides.

*Two table-spoonfuls of butter, one heaping table-spoonful of flour, half a cupful of milk, one cupful of grated cheese, three eggs, half a teaspoonful of salt, a speck of cayenne. Put the butter in a saucepan, and when hot add the flour, and stir until smooth, but not browned. Add the milk and seasoning. Cook two minutes; then add the yolks of the eggs, well beaten, and the cheese. Set away to cool. When cold, add the whites, beaten to a stiff froth. Turn into a buttered dish, and bake from twenty to twenty-five minutes. Serve it the moment it comes from the oven. The dish in which this is baked should hold a quart. An escalop dish is the best.*

## ⊰ 191. ENCHILADAS ⊱

*(California Women, 1905)*

The following recipe for enchiladas is one of three included the *Los Angeles Times Cook Book*, published in 1905; two are made from corn tortillas and one from flour.

*The first thing to do is to prepare the chili sauce by splitting open the chilis, about two dozen; and removing the seeds and the four or five veins that run lengthwise; put to soak in cold water and let remain two hours in order to take out the fire, or as the Spaniards have it, "that they will not ask you to take water." Throw off this water and cover with fresh, and put on the back of the stove, where they will barely simmer for one hour; put forward and boil rapidly for fifteen minutes. Remove from the stove and with a dull knife scrape the pulp from the skins. If you have allowed sufficient time for the soaking, your pulp will be all of a quarter of an inch thick. Now take a large onion, chop fine and fry in butter until a delicate brown; then into the same pan put a couple of spoons of flour, let brown and add the chili pulp, onion and a cup of strained tomato juice and a cup of the water in which the chilis were boiled; let simmer until the consistency of thick cream, season well with salt. While the chilis are soaking you can prepare the tortillas, or pancakes. Take one quart of flour, a large spoonful of lard, teaspoon of salt and moisten with water as for biscuits; take a piece of the dough as large as an egg and roll out to the size of a breakfast plate. When you have a half dozen rolled you may begin to bake, which you can do in either of two ways—by baking on top of the stove (the Spanish way,) or by frying in deep fat in a frying pan (the latter makes a richer tortilla.) Do not fry brown; the fat must not be as hot as for doughnuts. Proceed until all the dough is used, which will make about a dozen tortillas. Now have ready one pound of good eastern [Cheddar] cheese, grated, a quart of olives, some finely chopped onion which you can fry lightly, (if preferred cooked,) one pound of stoned raisins, three hard-boiled eggs chopped fine. Have the chili sauce hot, dip the tortillas in one at a time; place on a large hot platter or on a hot plate in which it is to be served; on one-half place a little of the raisins, olives, cheese, egg; pour a spoonful of the sauce over it and fold over the other half of the tortilla; so proceed until all are filled; pour over what sauce remains and sprinkle a little grated cheese over all. Keep the sauce hot while preparing and serve as soon as possible.*

*When I want the enchiladas extra fine, I have some minced chicken to add to the other filling and then with a cup of good coffee or a glass of claret [red wine] nothing more is necessary for a delicious meal.*

### ❧ 192. DEVILED EGGS FOR LUNCHEON OR PICNICS ☙

*(Shuman, 1893)*

Although deviled dishes are typically so called because they include hot spice such as tabasco, cayenne, or paprika, the following recipe includes no such deviling device. To add a bit of fire to the mix, just toss a dash of cayenne or paprika into the mayonnaise and yolk filling.

*Boil any number of eggs very hard, turning over carefully in the water several times to prevent their being unevenly cooked; put into cold water a few moments and then take off shells; cut in halves carefully and take out the yolks; mash these fine with a silver spoon (use a silver knife for cutting and filling) and add to them as much good mayonnaise dressing [see recipe 189] as may be required to make a smooth paste with which fill the empty halves; put them evenly together, fasten with toothpicks, and wrap each egg in white tissue paper and put in the ice chest until ready to serve.*

### ≈ 193. CURRIED EGGS ≈

*(Rorer, 1898)*

Egg dishes such as the following were often served in chafing dishes for lunch or a light supper. Heated from below by a flame, the chafing dish became quite trendy in the 1890s. Many cookbooks began to devote entire sections to dishes that benefited from such a heat source—in particular, those containing eggs and cheese sauces.

*Peel and cut into very thin slices three large onions. Put them with two tablespoonfuls of butter into a saucepan; stand this in a pan of hot water and cook until the onions are a soft golden yellow. Now add a teaspoonful of curry powder, one clove of garlic mashed, one-fourth teaspoonful of ground ginger, a half teaspoonful of salt, and a tablespoonful of flour. Mix thoroughly and add a half pint of stock or water. Stir until boiling and stand the sauce over hot water while you prepare the eggs. Hard boil six eggs; cut them into thin slices crosswise; arrange them around a mound of rice on a platter, drain over the curry sauce, and send at once to the table [or place in a chafing dish].*

*This dish is made still more attractive by garnishing the edge with carefully cooked sweet peppers.*

### ≈ 194. MIXED EGGS AND BACON ≈

*(Gillette, 1887)*

By the late nineteenth century, eggs and ham or bacon had become a standard breakfast dish, a trend still in full swing at breakfast diners across the nation.

*Take a nice rasher of mild bacon; cut it into squares no larger than dice; fry it quickly until nicely browned, but on no account burn it. Break half a dozen eggs into a basin, strain and season them with pepper, add them to the bacon, stir the whole about, and, when sufficiently firm, turn it out into a dish. Decorate with hot pickles.*

### ≈ 195. JUMBERLIE [JAMBALAYA]—A CREOLE DISH ≈

*(Fisher, 1881)*

More commonly spelled jambalaya, this dish resembles both a Spanish paella and a French pilau in different ways. As a result, its origins are a matter of contention: some believe it originated during the Spanish settlement of Louisiana, others during French control. Jambalaya, like the Spanish paella as well as some African dishes, often contains meat and seafood; like pilau, however, jambalaya calls for long-grained rice.

*Take one chicken and cut it up, separating every joint, and adding to it one pint of cleanly washed rice. Take about half a dozen large tomatoes, scalding them well and taking the skins off with a knife. Cut them in small pieces and put them with the chicken in a pot or large porcelain saucepan. Then cut in small pieces two large pieces of sweet ham and add to the rest, seasoning high with pepper and salt. It will cook in twenty-five minutes. Do not put any water on it.*

### ⇥ 196. LIMA BEANS ⇤

*(Aunt Babette, 1889)*

In addition to serving as a key ingredient in succotash or being boiled on their own, as in the following recipe, lima beans were also fashioned into fried bean cakes or puréed into a cream-based side dish or soup.

*Shell and put into cold water and let them remain in it for half an hour before boiling. Drain and put into boiling water and cook until tender. Pour off the water, add a little cream and butter, and season with pepper and salt. Let them simmer in this dressing for a few minutes before serving. You may boil a few tomatoes with the beans if you like; very nice for a change. Dried Lima beans should be soaked over night and allowed two hours to cook.*

### ⇥ 197. NOODLES ⇤

*(Babette, 1889)*

In German-American cookery, egg noodles, like dumplings, are frequently added to soups (such as the green corn soup recipe 130) and stews.

*How to make. Put a large handful of flour into a bowl, sifted of course. Make a hollow in the center of the flour, break in an egg. Take the handle of a knife and stir the egg slowly, always in the same direction, until the dough is so stiff that you can not stir it anymore with the knife. Flour a baking board and empty your dough upon it, and knead with the hollow of your hand, work with the hands until quite stiff. Flour your board and roll out as thin as possible. Lay on a clean table near the kitchen fire to dry. Cut into halves, double up, and cut as fine as possible; spread lightly to dry. If in a hurry just cut into little squares. Tastes just as nice, the only difference being in looks.*

### ⊰ 198. OATMEAL ⊱

*(Parloa, 1880)*

After a long history of being used as food for livestock in America, oats finally became known as a grain fit for human consumption with the help of Scottish and Dutch immigrants. In 1877, the Quaker Mill Company began selling its rolled oat cereal, helping to make oatmeal a common breakfast dish. Their instant version arrived on the market in 1921. A comparison of this oatmeal recipe with hominy recipe 71 illustrates how much more detailed late nineteenth-century cookbooks were than their predecessors.

*Oatmeal, Indian meal, and hominy all require two things for perfection—plenty of water when put on to boil, and a long time for boiling. Have about two quarts of boiling water in a large stewpan, and into it stir a cupful of oatmeal, which has been wet with cold water. Boil one hour, stirring often, and then add half a spoonful of salt, and boil an hour longer. If it should get too stiff, add more boiling water; or, if too thin, boil a little longer. You cannot boil too much. The only trouble in cooking oatmeal is that it takes a long time, but surely this should not stand in the way when it is so much better for having extra time. If there is not an abundance of water at first, the oatmeal will not be very good, no matter how much may be added during the cooking. Cracked wheat is cooked in the same way.*

### ⊰ 199. CLUB SANDWICH ⊱

*(Curtis, 1903)*

The first recipe for a club sandwich was printed in 1894. Although its exact origins are not known, the sandwich's name indicates that it may have originated in "men's clubs." By the late 1890s, the club had become a popular menu item at New York restaurants.

*Toast a slice of bread evenly and lightly and butter it. On one half put, first, a thin slice of bacon which as been broiled till dry and tender, next a slice of the white meat of either turkey or chicken. Over one half of this place a circle cut from a ripe tomato and over the other half a tender leaf of lettuce. Cover these with a generous layer of mayonnaise, and complete this "whole meal" sandwich with the remaining piece of toast.*

## BREAD AND BISCUITS

### ⊰ 200. POTATO YEAST ⊱

*(Women of the First Congregational Church, Marysville, Ohio, 1876)*

Although commercial yeast cakes went on the market shortly after the Civil War, home cooks still made their own yeast until the turn of the century. Both this recipe and yeast recipe 78 rely on a mixture of hops, potato, and sugar. Potato yeast was often made, however, without the addition of hops and vice versa with hops yeast.

*Take four small Irish (white) potatoes or three large ones, peel and grate raw and place in a procelain [sic] kettle with two quarts water; put one cup hops in a bag [or tie in cheesecloth], drop in the kettle and boil until the water tastes bitter; take out hops and add one cup white sugar and one tablespoon salt; keep constantly boiling, and stir continually; cook from five to ten minutes, and when done it will boil up thick like starch; turn into a jar, and when just tepid, in summer, or quite warm in winter, add one-half pint good yeast (always save some to start with.) Set jar in a large tin pan, and as often as it rises stir down until fermentation ceases; (it will then be quite thin;) tie up, and set away in a cool place and it will keep two weeks. When yeast smells sour but does not taste sour it is good; if it has no smell it is dead. One cup will make six good sized loaves, and if properly made you need never have sour bread. I have used it four years, and always with success.*

### ﹊ 201. BUCKEYE BROWN BREAD ﹉

*(Women of the First Congregational Church, Marysville, Ohio, 1876)*

The following recipe is a version of thirded bread, so-called because it is made from one-third corn, one-third rye, and one-third wheat flours.

*One cup each of corn, rye and Graham [whole wheat] meal. The rye meal should be as fine as the Graham. Use a coffee cup for measuring. Heap the cup before sifting, then sift all together, (the three kinds), as closely as possible. Two cups Porto Rico [Puerto Rican] molasses, two cups sweet milk, one cup sour milk, one dessert spoon soda, one teaspoon salt; beat all together thoroughly, pour into a tin form and place in a kettle of boiling water and steam four hours. Boil as soon as mixed. It may appear to be too thin, but it is not, as this recipe has never been known to fail. Serve warm, with your Thanksgiving turkey. The bread should not quite fill the form, (or tin pail with cover will answer,) as it must have room to swell. See that the water does not boil up to the top of the form; also take care it does not boil entirely away or stop boiling. To serve it remove the lid and set it a few moments into the open oven, so as to dry the top of the loaf; then it will turn out in perfect shape. This bread can be used as a pudding, and served with a sauce made of thick sour cream, well sweetened and seasoned with nutmeg; or, it is good toasted the next day.*

### ﹊ 202. MARYLAND BEAT BISCUIT ﹉

*(Fisher, 1881)*

These biscuits, which are popular throughout the South, were traditionally beaten for up to an hour with a heavy object, such as a mallet or rolling pin. The heavy beating makes for a denser, crisper biscuit. They became so popular that a beaten biscuit machine was invented; it often took the form of a marble slab fitted with metal rollers through which the biscuit dough was fed enough times to form a smooth, tight, elastic dough. Today's food processor does a nice enough job.

*Take one quart of flour, add one teaspoonful of salt, one tablespoonful of lard, half tablespoonful of butter. Dry rub the lard and butter into the flour until well creamed; add your water gradually in mixing so as to make dough stiff, then put the dough on pastry board and beat until perfectly moist and light. Roll out the dough to thickness of third of an inch. Have your stove hot and bake quickly. To make more add twice the quantity.*

## ⊰ 203. RAISED POTATO-CAKE ⊱

*(Gillette, 1887)*

This bread recipe, which calls for two leavening agents (fresh yeast and soda), would be well suited as an accompaniment to the roast lamb (recipe 142), roast beef (recipe 139), country fried chicken (recipe 152), or the fricasseed chicken (recipe 36).

*Potato-cakes, to be served with roast lamb or with game, are made of equal quantities of mashed potatoes and of flour, say one quart of each, two tablespoonfuls of butter, a little salt, and milk enough to make a batter as for griddlecakes; to this allow half a teacupful of fresh yeast; let it rise till it is light and bubbles of air form; then dissolve half a teaspoonful of soda in a spoonful of warm water and add to the batter; bake in muffin tins. These are good also with fricasseed chicken; take them from the tins and drip in the gravy just before sending to the table.*

## ⊰ 204. KENTUCKY CORN DODGERS ⊱

*(Fox, 1904)*

A "favorite dinner bread" according to the recipe author, corn dodgers (also known as pone) are an eggless cornbread that can be fried or baked.

*Sift the best meal made from the white corn, any quantity desired. Salt to taste. Mix with cold water into stiff dough and form into round, long dodgers with the hands. Take the soft dough and form into shape by rolling between the hands, making the dodgers about 4 or 5 inches long and 1 1/2 inches in diameter. Have a griddle hot, grease a little with lard, and put the dodgers on as you roll them. Put in oven and bake thoroughly, when they will be crisp and a rich brown.*

*This bread does not rise.*

## ❧ 205. RYE MUFFINS ❧

*(Farmer, 1896)*

The following muffins were served with breakfast. Because rye does not contain enough gluten, or protein, on its own to rise substantially, rye flour is usually combined with another more glutenous grain; the following muffins are made with a half-and-half blend of rye meal and flour.

*1 cup rye meal*
*1 cup flour*
*1/4 cup sugar*
*1 teaspoon salt*
*1 cup milk*
*1 egg*
*1 tablespoon melted butter*
*3 1/2 teaspoons baking powder*

*Mix and sift dry ingredients; add milk gradually, egg well beaten, and melted butter; bake in hot oven in buttered gem pans twenty-five minutes.*

## ❧ 206. WATER TORTILLAS ❧

*(Pinedo, 1898)*

The recipe author calls these tortillas "water" tortillas to differentiate them from what she calls "Spanish flour tortillas," which are made with milk instead of water.

*Make a dough with two pounds of sifted flour, a half ounce of salt, and an ounce of lard.*

*Knead with warm water, being careful not to make it tough.*

*Knead it loosely, leaving it tender. Let it rest for a bit. Form into small balls, and rest on a napkin sprinkled with flour. Then make the tortillas. [Roll into thin circles and place on a hot, dry skillet. When bubbles appear on the surface, flip and cook for another 5 to 10 seconds.]*

## PIES AND PUDDINGS

## ❧ 207. RHUBARB CUSTARD PIE ❧

*(Aunt Babette, 1889)*

Although botanically a vegetable, rhubarb has been so frequently used by Americans as a fruit that in 1947 the U.S. Customs Court at Buffalo, New

*Rhubarb.*

York, ruled it a fruit. In addition to its inclusion in pies, cobblers, and preserves, it was also used as a digestive aid. Custard and cheese pies were common in the Midwest, where dairy production flourished.

*Strip the skin carefully from the stalk of the pie-plant [rhubarb] and cut it into small pieces. Scald with boiling water, then drain and press out every drop of water with your hands. Now set over the fire to stew, with as little water as possible. When done, press through a collander [sic] or wire sieve, sweeten to taste and flavor with grated nutmeg or lemon. Bake with strips of dough put across the top. I forgot to add: Beat up two eggs for each pie, after mixing the sugar. You may put in the yelks [var. yolks] alone and use the whites for a meringue. If you do this, bake the paste first, then the custard.*

### ❧ 208. COUNTRY BATTER PUDDING WITH FRUIT, CHEAP AND NICE ☙

*(Hearn, 1885)*

As the title indicates, the following recipe, like most puddings, makes an economical dish.

*This is a pudding which requires no paste and is a nice way to use fruit, such as pie-plant [rhubarb], berries, strawberries, peaches, etc. To a quart of buttermilk add one egg, a large teaspoonful of soda, a little salt, and flour enough to make a thick batter. Pour it over a quart of chopped fruit, such as mentioned, beat it a little, tie it tightly in a bag, drop it in a kettle of hot water, and let boil two hours. Serve with sugar and cream. This pudding may be poured into a cake pan and baked, if not convenient to boil it. Put in plenty of fruit.*

### ❧ 209. PEACH COBBLER ☙

*(Fisher, 1881)*

A cobbler, also called a slump or grunt, is usually made with sweetened fruit topped with pastry and sugar.

*Peel the peaches (freestones) and make a pastry the same way as for pie, and roll out the dough as thin as for pie crust. Put one layer at the bottom of the dish, and cut the peaches into pieces the size of a plum and fill the dish with them, sprinkling them freely with fine sugar. Cover them over with another layer of pastry, cut with a knife two or three air-holes on the top and put to bake. Let it bake brown. It makes a delicious luncheon or dessert. Season the peaches with powdered cinnamon to taste.*

### ᲄᲞ 210. LEMON PIE ᲼

*(Shuman, 1893)*

Lemon pie was a much-prepared dessert in the late nineteenth century. The following version, topped with meringue, remains a perennial favorite. In the Midwest and Great Plains, where lemons were harder to come by, vinegar was often used in lieu of lemon juice.

*Two cups of sugar; one cup of boiling water; four eggs; two lemons; one and one-half tablespoon flour. Stir the sugar and flour well together; add the juice and grated rind of the lemons; to this add the well beaten yolks; after stirring well, add the boiling water; put over a clear fire and stir constantly until it boils, then pour into the shells. Spread over the top a meringue made of the whites of the four eggs and one tablespoon of sugar; place in the oven and brown slightly. This is sufficient for two pies. The shells should be made of ordinary pie pastry and baked before being filled with the mixture.*

### ᲄᲞ 211. PUMPKIN PIE ᲼

*(Fox, 1904)*

Often made with molasses instead of sugar, pumpkin pie has been a nationally renowned Thanksgiving treat since the early nineteenth century. Printed pumpkin pie recipes date back much further—at least to the seventeenth century. In addition to its use in pies, pumpkin meat was mashed, boiled, roasted, and fried.

*Cut the pumpkin in small pieces and stew in a little water. Strain, and to 1 quart of the pumpkin add 1/2 pint of sugar, 1 cup of cream, cinnamon, and allspice to taste, 3 eggs, and 3 tablespoons butter. Beat it well. Line a pie-plate and pour the custard over it. Make a top with strips of pastry and bake till a rich brown.*

## CAKES, COOKIES, CUSTARDS, AND CREAMS

With the advent of the stove, cake baking became a national obsession as less time-consuming and more economical recipes flourished. Americans began using fewer eggs and more flour as chemical leavening became common place after the Civil War. Cooks also relied increasingly on cup

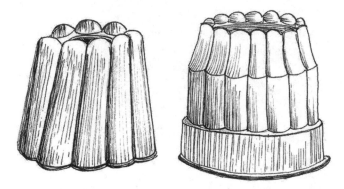

*Food molds for forming creams, ice creams, and cakes.*

measurements rather than weight in making cakes, greatly simplifying preparation.

## Cakes and Cookies

### ❧ 212. BROWNIES ☙

*(Farmer, 1896)*

The following recipe is the first brownie recipe in print. Molasses, rather than chocolate, provides its rich color.

*1/3 cup butter*
*1/3 cup powdered sugar*
*1/3 cup Porto Rico [Puerto Rican] molasses*
*1 egg well beaten*
*7/8 cup bread flour*
*1 cup pecan meat cut in pieces*

*Mix ingredients in order given. Bake in small, shallow fancy cake tins, garnishing top of each cake with one-half pecan.*

---

### ➔ ADULTERATED SUGAR

(Ellett, 1871)

After the Civil War, the adulteration of food became a national problem, as the following excerpt from a late nineteenth-century cookbook attests. The easy introduction of adulterants into sugar and flour, in part, spurred the national craving for white sugar and flour, although both products are better digested in their less processed brown and whole grain forms. In response to growing public protest, the Pure Food and Drug Act was passed in 1906, making it illegal to sell adulterated or mislabeled food products interstate.

*The sugar, if it be brown, without taking note of such items as a little lead, a good deal of sand, some clay and flour is pretty nearly as thick as it can hold of chips of cane and swarms of mites…. For sugar, the best advice is—if you like to pay for dirt, and to mix it with your preserves, pudding, and pastry, and choose to believe that sugar which moistens even the thick paper they place it in, and which looks dark, smells strong, and sticks to your fingers, is richer in sweetening than clear sparkling white sugar, out of which none of the sweetening but all of the dirt has been washed—then buy brown sugar.*

## ❧ 213. COFFEE CAKE ❧

*(Gillette, 1887)*

German and Scandinavian immigrants helped popularize the coffee break in America. A more casual mid-morning or mid-afternoon gathering than the British-inherited tea, these informal social hours paired coffee with an array of pastries and cakes.

*One cup of brown sugar, one cup of butter, two eggs, one-half cup of molasses, one cup of strong, cold coffee, one teaspoonful of soda, two teaspoonfuls of cinnamon, one teaspoonful of cloves, one cup of raisins or currants, and five cups of sifted flour. Add the fruit last, rubbed in a little of the flour. Bake about one hour.*

## ❧ 214. JELLY CAKE ❧

*(Fisher, 1881)*

Jelly cakes were a familiar treat at the Victorian table. Layered versions of the jelly cake are an American invention and first appeared in cookbooks after the Civil War. Another form, the jelly roll also became popular during this time. Although the recipe does not specify the number of layers to be baked in pans, the following portions can make two to three layers depending on the size of the cake pans. See recipe 225 for directions on making orange marmalade.

*For this cake make an orange marmalade and use in the place of jelly, as it makes a more delicious cake.... For making the cake, one teacup of butter to two of sugar, three of flour and half a dozen eggs. Beat the whites and yelks [var. yolks] of eggs separate, very light. Cream butter and sugar together, add the yelks of eggs to creamed sugar and butter, then add the whites, and add flour and stir till light. Sift two teaspoonfuls of best yeast powder with the flour. With the above directions the cake is made. Place it in the pans and put to bake; fifteen minutes will bake it. Spread marmalade over the cake after it is baked. Icing for the cake: Take the whites of four eggs and beat them very light indeed. Add three tablespoonfuls of powdered sugar, beat sugar and eggs together light, and spread on cake while cake is warm. Take one teacup of fine grated cocoanut [sic] and sprinkle over cake while icing is soft.*

## ❧ 215. MARBLE CAKE ❧

*(Burr, c. 1886)*

The following cake recipe incorporates two popular cake varieties—gold and silver cakes. A gold cake, as is the "dark" cake here, is made from egg yolks. The molasses is added in the following version to transform the gold cake into a darker, and hence more dramatic, color. The light cake is a standard silver cake, which only calls for egg whites to maintain its light color.

*FOR THE DARK—Yolks of seven eggs, one cup molasses, one teaspoonful cloves, five cups flour, one teaspoonful allspice, two cups brown sugar, one teaspoonful soda, one cup sour cream, two teaspoonfuls cinnamon, one cup butter, and one nutmeg.*

*FOR THE LIGHT—Whites of seven eggs, one cup of butter, two of white sugar, three of flour, one-half cup of sweet milk, one teaspoonful cream of tartar, half a teaspoonful of soda. Always cream butter and sugar together and beat eggs separately.*

## ⇥ 216. PEANUT COOKIES ⇤

*(Kander, 1903)*

Peanuts did not play a major role in the American diet until after the Civil War. By the 1890s, roasted and salted peanuts were sold on street corners and recipes for peanut butter began appearing in cookbooks. By the early twentieth century, peanuts had made an indelible mark on the nation's culinary landscape, thanks in large part to George Washington Carver. A tireless promoter of peanut farming, Carver distributed hundreds of recipes featuring the legume. Just a few such dishes Carter promoted include peanut sausage, peanut bread, peanut macaroni, peanut salad, and peanut ice cream.

*2 tablespoons butter*
*1/4 cup sugar*
*1 egg*
*1/2 cup flour*
*1 teaspoon baking powder*
*1/4 teaspoon salt*
*2 tablespoons milk*
*1/2 cup finely rolled peanuts*
*1/2 teaspoon lemon juice*

*Cream the butter, add sugar and egg, well beaten. Sift and mix flour, salt and baking powder, and add to first mixture; then add milk, peanuts and lemon juice. Drop from a teaspoon on an unbuttered sheet one inch apart. Bake in moderate oven twelve to fifteen minutes. Makes twenty-four cookies.*

## ⇥ 217. DOUGHNUTS ⇤

*(Burr, c. 1886)*

Early recipes for these deep-fried cakes describe them as "oil cakes" or "fried cakes," after the Dutch term *oliekoecken*. First introduced to America by Dutch immigrants, these deep-fried cakes had become a regular part of the American diet by the mid-nineteenth century. The following recipe calls for the removal of the dough-nut's center, the form so famil-iar today, but they were origi-nally shaped as rounded balls Although the earlier doughnuts were breadlike, the introduction of chemical leavening (included in this recipe) transformed them into the more cakelike consis-tency so well known today.

*One cup of sweet milk, one half cup of sweet cream, one and one-half cups of sugar, three eggs, well beaten with Dover egg beater [a popular commercial brand], one half nutmeg, one teaspoonful salt, two teaspoonfuls cream of tartar, one teaspoonful soda, flour enough to roll out, though not very stiff. Cut round, with hole in centre, and fry in hot lard.*

*Dover egg beater.*

## Custards and Creams

### ❦ 218. BAVARIAN CREAM ❧

*(Burr, c. 1886)*

Introduced in the late nineteenth century, commercial gelatin was soon added to creams, making them sturdy enough to mold and cut.

*Let one quart of milk come to a boil. Beat the yolks of two eggs and two large tablespoonfuls of sugar to a froth; to this add one-third of a box of gelatine [sic] dissolved. Stir in the boiling milk and cook a few minutes, and when half cool strain into the dish to be used on the table. Beat the whites of the eggs and add to them two tablespoonfuls of powdered sugar as in frosting. Stir through the milk, set it on ice and let it stand from twelve to twenty hours. Serve with cream and a little jelly or preserve.*

### ❦ 219. CREAM PUFFS ❧

*(California Women, 1905)*

The following cream puffs would have been served as a relatively light luncheon dessert.

*Puffs: Boil 1 cupful hot water and 1/2 cupful of butter together, and while boiling stir in 1 cup of dry sifted flour. Take from the fire and stir to a thin paste, and after this cools stir in 3 eggs. Stir 5 minutes. Drop in tablespoonfuls on a buttered tin, and bake in a quick oven 25 minutes.*

*Cream: One cup milk, 1 cup sugar, 1 egg, 3 tablespoonfuls flour, vanilla to flavor; stir the flour in a little of the milk; boil the rest; stir this in, and stir until the whole thickens; when both this and the puffs are cool, open the puffs with a sharp knife, and fill them with the cream.*

### ᨑ 220. PINEAPPLE ICE CREAM ᨑ

*(Parloa, 1880)*

By the end of the century, the number of ice cream flavors soared. Just a few popular flavors include tutti-frutti [recipe 222], caramel, coffee, fig, pineapple, pistachio [recipe 221], coconut, ginger, brown bread, and macaroon.

*Pare a pineapple and cut it fine. Put it in a saucepan with one pint of water and a scant pint of sugar. Simmer gently for thirty minutes. Rub through a sieve, add the cream, gradually, and freeze.*

### ᨑ 221. PISTACHE [PISTACHIO] ICE-CREAM ᨑ

*(Corson, 1885)*

Because pistachio trees did not begin to flourish in American, specifically Californian, soil until the 1930s, recipes such as the following would have been made from imported nuts.

*Pistache ice-cream is made by adding about two ounces of blanched [skins removed] pistache nuts to a quart of any good ice-cream; the nuts are shelled, boiling water is poured over the kernels, and the skin rubbed off with a wet towel; the nuts are then pounded to a smooth paste in a mortar, a few drops of rosewater being added to prevent oiling, and colored with spinach green, a harmless vegetable coloring sold by dealers in confectioners' supplies.*

### ᨑ 222. TUTTI-FRUTTI ICE CREAM ᨑ

*(Fox, 1904)*

This version of tutti frutti is adapted from the fruit dessert known by the same name, which consists of fresh fruits, sugar, and brandy. Like the fruit dish after which it was named, the ice cream was popular in the late nineteenth-century South.

*1 quart cream*
*1 pint milk*
*Yolks of 5 eggs*
*3 cups sugar*
*1 lemon*
*1 glass whisky*
*Crystallized fruit or candied fruit of any kind, cherries, raisins, currants, citrons, peaches, etc.*

*Beat sugar and eggs together and add to the milk, which must be at boiling point. Boil 10 minutes. When cold, add the cream and freeze. When half frozen, add 1 pound fruit, which has been mixed with the lemon and whiskey. Cover and freeze well.*

### ₃ 223. WATER MELON ICE ₰

*(The Ladies Association of the First Presbyterian Church, Houston, Texas, 1883)*

Although the habit of eating flavored ices has been around for millennia, ice cream and ices became a popular part of the American home cook's repertoire during the late nineteenth century, when ice boxes and ice chests became widely available.

*Select a very ripe and red melon. Scrape some of the pulp and use all the water. A few of the seeds interspersed will add greatly to its appearance. Sweeten to taste and freeze. If wished very light, add the whites of three eggs, thoroughly whipped to one gallon of the mixture just as it begins to congeal. Beat it very hard.*

## PRESERVES

### ₃ 224. CRAB APPLE JELLY ₰

*(Fisher, 1881)*

The tart crabapple is often made into jellies and jams to be served with meat or poultry. The following jelly is a suggested accompaniment for broiled squab (recipe 154). The brandy-dipped paper used to seal the jelly was commonly used to prevent bacteria from growing.

*Put the apples to boil; one quart of water to one quart of apples and let them boil till soft; then mash the apples and put the apples and the water they were boiled in a linen rag, and let all the juice drip into a vessel; measure the juice and take one quart of the dripped juice to one quart of sugar, and put* on to boil for jelly. Boil thirty minutes and then dip some into a saucer and set in the air to cool; if it is congealed when cool, it is done. Put up in glasses, first dipping the glasses in boiling hot water and letting them drain; put the jelly into the glasses hot, and then set to cool. Paper the same way as you do currant jelly [have good brandy; cut some thin paper for the inside of the glass and wet it in the brandy, then lay it on the jelly inside of the glass], and put away in a dark place. Use a porcelain kettle and granulated sugar.

## ⇥ 225. ORANGE MARMALADE ⇤

*(Hearn, 1885)*

This orange marmalade can be used between the layers of jelly cake (recipe 214).

*Quarter the oranges and take out the seeds and white strings. To every pound of pulp, add a cup of cold water, and let it stand thus for twenty-four hours. Boil some of the peel in several waters until quite tender, then to each pound of pulp, add one-quarter of a pound of boiled peel, and one and a quarter pound of white sugar. Boil this slowly until it jellies, and the bits of peel are quite transparent.*

## ⇥ 226. DAMSONS ⇤

*(Aunt Babette, c. 1889)*

Damsons, like greengages, are a type of plum included in many late nineteenth-century preserve recipes. Preserved whole plums are frequently paired with pork dishes such as the baked fresh pork recipe 146.

*Make a syrup of three-quarters of a pound of sugar to every pound of fruit and allow about a pint of water to every three pounds of fruit. Prick the damsons with a needle to prevent bursting. When the syrup is clear, put in your damsons, a quart at a time. Boil each quart five minutes, not fast, or they will burst badly. Fill up jars with the fruit, pour in the syrup until it is overflowing and seal immediately as you do other fruit.*

## ⇥ 227. CHERRY PRESERVES ⇤

*(Tyree, 1879)*

In addition to being made into preserves and baked into pies, cherries were also fashioned into soups and wine, deep fried in fritters, and topped with French dressing and served as salad.

*Wash, pick and stone the cherries, saving the juice. Allow one pound sugar to each pound fruit. Boil the juice and sugar to a thick syrup, then put in half the cherries and stew till nearly done. Take them out with a perforated spoon and lay on dishes. Put in the other half, let them stew as long as the first; then take out and lay in dishes. Meantime boil the syrup gently. When the cherries are cool, put them again in the syrup and boil a short time. Pour in a large bowl and cool, then put in glass jars and cover tightly.*

*Scarlet short stems and large wax cherries are best for preserving.*

## ◂§ 228. TOMATO PRESERVES §▸

*(Kander, 1903)*

Technically a fruit, tomato was often paired with ginger, as it is in the following recipe, to make preserves. By the turn of the century, Americans had begun to take full advantage of the tomato's versatility. Just a few of the myriad dishes made from the fruit include tomato soup (recipe 134); tomato sauce for use on meats or pasta; tomato salad; tomatoes broiled, baked, or stewed and served as a vegetable; tomato fritters; fried green tomatoes; tomato pickle; and tomato catsup.

*1 lb. yellow pear tomatoes, or, the red ones, slices*
*1 lb. sugar*
*2 oz. Canton [common] ginger, or a few pieces of ginger root*
*1 lemon*

*Scald the tomatoes to peel. Cover with the sugar, and let stand over night. Pour off the syrup and boil until clear and quite thick. Skim, add tomatoes, ginger and lemon sliced and seeded. Cook until the fruit is clear. Pour into jars or crocks.*

# 3
# 🌿 1911–1945

## Major Foodstuffs

- Meat: beef and veal; pork; mutton and lamb
- Game: rabbit, squirrel, venison
- Poultry and Fowl: chicken, duck, goose, quail, turkey
- Fish: bass, catfish, cod, flounder, haddock, halibut, herring, perch, pompano, salmon, shad, snapper, trout, tuna, whitefish
- Shellfish: clam, crab, lobster, oyster, shrimp
- Vegetables: asparagus, beans, beets, cabbage, carrots, celery, corn, cucumbers, artichokes, lettuce, okra, parsnips, peas, potatoes, radishes, spinach, squash, tomatoes, turnips
- Fruits: apples, bananas, cherries, grapefruit, grapes, melons, oranges, peaches, pineapples, pears, plums, strawberries
- Grains: corn, rice, wheat flour
- Dairy: cow's milk, cream, and cheese grew in popularity as commercially produced varieties became available at lower prices

## Cooking Methods

### Heat Sources

- Gas and electric cookstoves

*1930s electric stove.*

### Preservation

- Well-insulated iceboxes
- Refrigerators
- Wartime "liberty gardens" spurred home canning

### Preparation

- Electric gadgets
- Pressure cookers
- Out-of-a-can cookery
- Biscuit and cake mixes

## PREVALENT CULTURAL INFLUENCES

- British
- French
- Spanish
- African American
- Eastern European
- Central European
- Mexican
- Italian
- Greek
- Chinese

## BASIC COOKING EQUIPMENT

Kitchen ranges that required building and maintaining an actual fire for a day's cooking were replaced by gas stoves, which rose in popularity during the 1920s. Cheap lightweight pots and pans of aluminum or enameled steel began to replace the heavy iron cooking equipment necessary for hearth cooking. Better insulated iceboxes and refrigerators (which became popular during the 1930s) regulated cooling temperatures, thereby extending the shelf life of perishable foods. By the late 1930s, home freezers began to rise in popularity, extending storage time and space for fruits, vegetables, meat, and even fish. Electricity began to appear in kitchens; from 1907 to 1941 the number of homes wired with electricity rose from 8 to 80 percent. Once wired, kitchens began to accrue many of the gadgets still in use today. By the 1930s, electric stoves had begun to rival gas stoves in popularity.

## SPECIAL GADGETS

Between the World Wars many kitchens acquired electric toasters, waffle irons, and coffee percolators. Ovenproof glass baking dishes were introduced before the 1920s; pressure cookers became widespread after the 1930s.

## FOOD PRESERVATION

During World War I, housewives began to heed governmental advice to plant "liberty gardens" where they grew vegetables for immediate consumption and home canning. Such gardens became even more important during the Great Depression when store-bought items became a luxury for many as the nation's unemployment rate soared. Nonetheless, the use of canned and frozen foods continued to skyrocket.

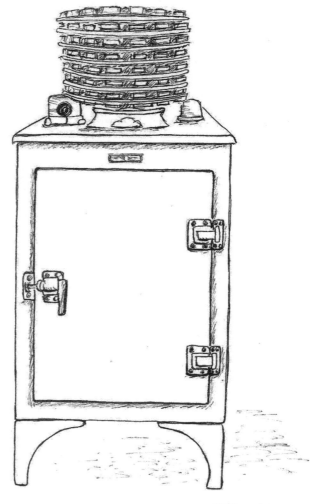

*1930s refrigerator.*

## COOKING METHODS

Two World Wars and the Great Depression required that cooks work diligently to conserve cooking fuel and concoct economical dishes. Although such conservation methods as growing and preserving vegetables had long been a part of American cookery, the common hiring of cooks among the middle classes followed by the advent of packaged foods had left many housewives unfamiliar with more than basic cooking techniques. With the onset of World War I, many servants left domestic jobs to work in factories, leaving middle-class housewives to fend for themselves. Many relied heavily on commercially produced canned and bottled sauces, soups, and vegetables to produce family meals.

## DINING

Eating out became an activity enjoyed by all classes, as opposed to just the wealthy. Coffee shops, drugstore lunch counters, luncheonettes,

*Toaster.*

cafeterias, diners, inexpensive Chinese or Italian eateries, tea shops, hamburger joints, soda fountains, pushcarts, and candy stores proliferated. Except in large cities, the only upscale restaurant choice was likely to be a hotel dining room. When eating at home, Americans opted for simpler meals than ever before; all but the wealthy had lost the cooks and other house servants that housewives had previously relied on to prepare and serve elaborate dinner parties.

## MEALS

Encouraged by heavy advertising, Americans began to eat vast amounts of packaged cereals, a trend that transformed the nation's breakfast table. As more and more women entered the workforce, lower- and middle-class Americans began to rely heavily on public eating houses for their lunches. Americans could also buy popular dinner entrées, such as lobster Newburg, and desserts, such as plum pudding, in a can. In the 1930s, frozen dinners went on sale along with biscuit and cake mixes; commercial pickles began to usurp the homemade variety.

## POPULAR RECIPES

Packaged gelatin spurred the popularity of congealed salads, often made with canned fruits and vegetables and the number of lettuce salads rose, in part, because of the introduction of iceberg lettuce to the American table. An economical dish, the casserole was popularized by immigrants hailing from Italy, Greece, and Hungary. Marshmallows and waffles began appearing in courses other than dessert, and meringue desserts grew fashionable. The southwestern influence began to take hold in the form of Spanish rice and tamale pie. Chinese-American dishes such as chop suey and chow mein, which were regularly featured on Chinese-American restaurant menus, began to turn up at the occasional home dinner. Women's cookbooks began to devote sections to luncheon fare, which often consisted of molded salads, crustless sandwiches, cottage cheese, and fish or chicken salads.

Male-authored cookbooks that eschewed ladies' luncheon fare in favor of heartier and more game-centered dishes began to appear.

---

### ✦ THE HOMEMAKER

(Allen, 1924)

During the late 1800s and early 1900s, women worked hard to raise the level of appreciation for domestic work by presenting it as crucial to the development of the nation or, as here, the world.

*Home-making is the biggest job in the world; it bosses them all. It hangs over the others like a storm cloud or a ray of light, as the case may be. It is the gigantic hub of the wheel of life, with its radiating spokes of lesser positions on which the world rides to its destiny....*

*No matter whether [a homemaker] is working in her own kitchen, or whether she is at the head of an institution, or conducting a tea room or cafeteria, her opportunity is there. And by making possible perfectly cooked, well-combined, digestible meals, she is literally contributing to the welfare of humanity and conducting one of the biggest jobs in the world.*

---

## SOUPS, CHOWDERS, AND STEWS

Soup continued as a widely popular dish, largely because many varieties were canned. The soup pot also provided an economical way of using leftovers during a time when the American budget suffered from hardship.

### ❧ 229. BORSCHT ☙

*(Moody, 1931)*

Popularized in the United States by Jewish immigrants who arrived during the late-nineteenth and early-twentieth centuries, borscht can be served either hot or cold. It is often accompanied by potato pancakes (see recipe 275).

*12 crisp fresh beets*
*2 cups of vinegar, one cider and one tarragon*
*1 pt. of sour cream*
*2 tablespoons of butter*
*2 sweet onions*
*2 leeks*
*2 young carrots*
*Parsley*
*Bay leaves*
*2 tablespoons of flour*

*1 tablespoon of salt*
*1/2 teaspoonful of black pepper*
*2 quarts of beef broth*
*2 more young tender beets*

*The recipes for Polish or Russian borscht are almost as various as the books that include them.*

*They pass from a recipe that includes 2 ducks and 4 lbs. of soup meat, to a recipe that has no meat of any kind in it. In our kitchen it is made this way.*

*Take 12 young, crisp, fresh beets. Wash them and scrape them, and pass them through a vegetable grinder. Cover them with the 2 cups of good vinegar.*

*Melt 2 large tablespoonfuls of butter in a frying pan, and in it braise 2 sweet onions which have been passed through a fine vegetable grinder, the white part of 2 leeks sliced thin, 2 young carrots—scraped and sliced, a sprig of parsley, a bay leaf, and 1/2 tablespoon of flour. All these are fried in the pan until the vegetables are a rich brown. Add to them the rest of the flour, and stir it carefully into the browning vegetables, being careful not to let it burn.*

*Drain the vinegar from the ground beets. Dry them, and add them to the cooking vegetables. Put in a tablespoonful of salt and 1/2 teaspoonful of black pepper, and a bay leaf.*

*Cover all with 2 qts. of good strong consommé [or beef broth].*

*Let all this simmer on the back of the stove until the vegetables are tender....*

*Grate 2 more young tender beets, which you have washed and scraped, and add them, with a tablespoonful of vinegar, to the cooking vegetables. The color should be a bright red beet color. The mixture is delicious.*

*It is nice to serve this with potato pancakes on the side [recipe 275], and together they constitute a meal.*

*Sour cream is passed as a garnish to the borscht.*

---

## ✢ SOUPS FROM CANS

(Ellsworth, 1939)

*Somewhere you have a shelf for rows of cans. These may contain almost any article of human food—fruits, nuts, meats, vegetables, bread, ice cream, special dishes all prepared, or raw materials ready to finish with a minimum effort. But of all the canned things on your shelves, probably the most versatile are the soups, for they represent both raw material and finished product in one can.*

## ⋈ 230. CHICKEN MUSHROOM SOUP ⋈

*(Platt, 1941)*

Recipes such as the following one, which combines different canned foods, were abundant. Such dishes provided welcome shortcuts for women who worked full time and cooked dinner every night for the family, as well as for those housewives who did not enjoy spending all day at the stove.

*2 cans of Campbell's condensed cream of mushroom soup*
*2 cans of condensed chicken soup*
*3 cups of rich milk*
*Salt and freshly ground black pepper*
*3 tablespoons of sherry*
*Whipped cream*

*This easy-to-prepare soup is quite worthy of being served with pride and confidence. Open 2 cans of condensed cream of mushroom soup and place the contents in a large saucepan. Add slowly, stirring constantly, 2 cans of condensed chicken soup. Also stir in about 3 cups of rich milk. Heat gradually to boiling point, stirring constantly, then add fresh ground black pepper, salt to taste, and 2 to 3 tablespoons of good sherry. Serve it at table from a hot soup tureen, adding a tablespoon of whipped cream to each plate, as you serve it.*

## ⋈ 231. CIOPPINO ⋈

*(Callahan, 1933)*

A variant of an Italian fish stew, cioppino is said to have been invented by Italian immigrants living in the rich fishing region of San Francisco. The following version is baked in the oven; the dish, however, is more typically stewed on top of the stove.

*6 pounds of striped bass*
*2 small red codfish*
*6 pounds of cockles*
*10 pounds of mussels (if obtainable)*
*4 large cooked crabs*
*1 pound of picked shrimps*
*4 dozen clams—opened and cleaned*

*Clean bass and codfish and cut into pieces for serving. Allow cockles and mussels to stand in fresh cold water for 1 hour to remove sand, and scrub thoroughly. Cut crabs in serving pieces and crack legs with a mallet. Place fish in layers in a large covered roasting pan. First some pieces of fish, then a few cockles and mussels in their shells, a few pieces of crab in the shells, some shrimps, some clams with the juice, then another layer of bass, and so on. Cover with the prepared sauce [the Cioppino Sauce recipe 266], put the lid on and bake for 1 hour in a moderate oven (350°).*

## ᴥ 232. CREAM OF MUSHROOM SOUP ᴥ

*(Council of Jewish Women, Portland, Oregon, 1914)*

The following recipe calls for the mushrooms to be passed through a sieve, a step that effectively reduces them to a purée. A food processor, a common feature of today's well-equipped kitchen, makes light work of this tedious step; the processor was first introduced to American kitchens in the 1970s. In addition to mushrooms, "creamed" soups were (and still are) often made from artichokes, asparagus, tomatoes, or spinach.

*Peel, rinse and cut fine one pound fresh mushrooms; put them to boil with one quart of either chicken or veal stock; cook until tender; press through a sieve and return to kettle; add four tablespoons sago [starch thickener]; cook twenty minutes longer; season with salt and paprika; add one quart scalded milk; simmer for five minutes longer. Take out about one cup of the broth; stir slowly into the well-stirred yolks of four eggs. Pour slowly into the soup and serve at once.*

## ᴥ 233. MINESTRONE ᴥ

*(Shay, 1941)*

This Italian soup appeared regularly at American tables during this period, although less often during World War II; some people eschewed dishes hailing from those countries with which the United States was at war. Marrow beans are the largest of the white beans. Yellow-eye beans are a variety of cowpea. By the turn of the century, "portable soup" recipes (see recipe 10) had disappeared from cookbooks. Now instead of making a beef stock reduction to have on hand for flavoring soups and sauces, home cooks simply bought canned consommé or packets of dried bouillon cubes from the local grocery store.

*1 cup dried white marrowfat beans or yellow-eye beans*
*4 ounces salt pork, diced*
*6 cups soup stock, or 3 cans concentrated consommé or 6 bouillon*
*cubes in 6 cups of boiling water*
*1 clove garlic, minced*
*2 carrots, sliced*
*1 onion, sliced*
*2 tablespoons chopped parsley*

1 cup chopped cabbage
1 cup cooked spaghetti, chopped
1 stalk celery, sliced
1 cup canned Italian tomatoes
1/2 teaspoon salt
1/4 teaspoon pepper
Grated Parmesan cheese

Soak beans overnight. Drain, cover with cold water, and bring to a boil, then simmer for 2 hours. Drain again, Place the soup stock in a large kettle and bring to a boil. Add diced pork, carrots, onion, garlic, parsley, celery, cabbage, salt, pepper, and beans, and simmer until all vegetables are tender. Add tomatoes and spaghetti, and cook 10 minutes more. Just before serving add grated cheese.

### ⊰ 234. ONION SOUP ⊱

*(Moody, 1931)*

Recipes for onion soup appear in the earliest American cookbooks, often with a reference to the soup's restorative function and its popularity in France. These earlier "restorative" versions usually include the egg yolk whisked into the broth at the last minute, which, once dished, is topped with a slice of bread. This recipe, which omits the egg yolk and calls for grated cheese on top of the bread, is similar to versions found in cookbooks today.

4 medium-sized onions
2 tablespoonfuls of flour
2 qts. of bouillon or chicken consommé
Slices of thin rye bread
Grated parmesan or some snappy American cheese
4 tablespoonfuls of butter

Take 4 medium-sized sweet onions. Slice them, and fry them in 4 tablespoonfuls of butter until they are a golden brown. This should be done in an aluminum pan with an asbestos plate under it for slower cooking. Sprinkle over the onions 2 tablespoonfuls of flour. Let them simmer for 10 minutes, stirring to keep the flour from burning.

Add 2 qts. of bouillon or consommé. Let the kettle boil slowly for 20 or 30 minutes.

Toast slightly the requisite number of slices of rye bread cut thin. Draw these from the oven, and cover each slice with a thick layer of grated cheese, either Parmesan, Romano, or some snappy American variety. Set them back into the oven long enough for the cheese to melt partly, and serve a slice of this toast on the top portion of soup, in cups or plates.

*Instead of melting cheese on your rye bread, it is especially acceptable to spread the rye toast with Welsh rarebit made as follows:*

*Melt in a chafing dish or a sauté pan 1 oz. of sweet butter. Add to it 4 ozs. of Gruyère, Romano or any snappy cheese, half a teaspoonful of French mustard, a pinch of cayenne, and half a cup of ale or beer. Heat it rapidly, stirring all the time, till it is creamy. Do not let it stand to string; spread it on the toast, and float a slice on top of each portion of soup.*

## ☙ 235. OYSTER BISQUE ❧

*(Mosser, 1939)*

Unlike a cream-based shellfish chowder, which calls for ingredients similar to those listed here, a bisque contains ground or finely minced oysters, clams, crawfish, or lobster to form a dish with a smoother consistency than most chowders. The following recipe includes egg yolks, which provide a rich texture and flavor. Like the aforementioned shellfish varieties, tomato and corn bisques remain popular throughout the United States and have long been available in canned form.

*1 pint oysters*
*1 1/2 tablespoons butter*
*1 1/2 tablespoons flour*
*2 cups milk*
*1 cup cream*
*1 teaspoon salt*
*1/4 teaspoon pepper*
*2 egg yolks*
*2 tablespoons cold water*
*1 dozen powdered oyster crackers*

*Bring oysters to the boiling point in their liquor. Drain, reserving the liquor. Chop and mash the oysters. Melt butter, add flour, then milk and cream, and cook until smooth. Add oysters with their liquor, salt and pepper. Beat egg yolks with water and stir into the bisque. Add powdered oyster crackers, simmer 2 minutes and serve.*

## ☙ 236. PURÉE MONGOLE ❧

*(Ellsworth, 1939)*

Although virtually unheard of today, Mongole soup enjoyed wide celebrity in the 1930s. Most commonly a blend of canned split-pea and tomato soups, Mongole became so hip that it was served at the New York City restaurant "21," from which the following version comes.

*Cook a cup of carrots cut in shoestrings and a cup of fresh peas. Mix and heat a can of Campbell's tomato soup and one of Campbell's split pea; add the carrots, peas, and half a teaspoonful of onion juice and serve from a tureen, with bread sticks. Sherry, a scant tablespoonful to a serving, adds the final touch.*

### ⌁ 237. U.S. NAVY BEAN SOUP ⌁

*(Smith, 1938)*

Like the following dish, many economical recipes that had a patriotic edge grew in popularity during and between the wars. An economical dish to prepare en masse, Navy bean soup was frequently served to the military.

*One gallon of good ham stock*
*3/4 pound [dried] white navy beans*
*1 onion*
*Ground cloves*
*Cayenne pepper*
*Salt*

*Wash the beans thoroughly with fresh water, and soak them overnight. Bring them to a boil, in water to cover, and let simmer for an hour. Now add the ham stock, the onion (chopped), a pinch of ground cloves, and let simmer for two hours. Season to taste with salt and cayenne pepper. Serve piping hot with croutons.*

## MEAT

Because of the Great Depression and war rationing, many recipes from this time period use "meat extenders" such as bread crumbs or meat substitutes such as nuts and beans. The variety of meats available shrank during this time, and game, much of it having been hunted close to extinction, featured infrequently at the average American table; exceptions would include such widely available meat as rabbit, squirrel, and possum.

### ⌁ 238. CHOP SUEY ⌁

*(Bosse, 1914)*

This Chinese-American dish is thought to have been invented in the West by Chinese immigrants who worked for the Pacific railroad in the mid-nineteenth century. By the early 1900s it was served in most Chinese-American restaurants and at lunch counters around the United States.

*One and one half pounds of pork; one and one half pounds of veal; two onions; one dozen water chestnuts; one half can of bamboo shoots; two pounds of*

*sliced or quartered tomatoes, crushing with a spoon to extract the juice. Cook for about 10 minutes, seasoning with salt, pepper and a dash of cayenne. Cut the steak into 4 inch squares, beat well and season with salt and pepper. Add them to the tomatoes and onions, dilute the sauce with a little hot stock or water, as it should not be too thick, cover the pan with a dish and simmer for about 30 minutes till the meat is tender, adding a little more stock or water if the sauce thickens, and turning the meat occasionally. To serve, put the grillades on a hot dish and pour the sauce over them.*

*Grillades can also be made with slices of veal and slices of gammon [meat from the hindquarters of a pig], cut just under 1/2 an inch thick; and they can be made with left-over cold meat, in which case the sauce is simmered for 30 to 35 minutes and the cooked meat added to it 10 minutes before serving.*

## ⇥ 242. POT ROAST ⇤

*(Smith, 1938)*

Tougher, less expensive cuts of meat (such as round or chuck cuts) are well suited for pot roast, which calls for an extended cooking time. Like many dishes in which meat is braised, or browned, before being slow-cooked in liquid, the meat in the pot roast is browned during the initial stage of preparation. The casserole dish called for in this recipe refers to a deep container with a tight-fitting lid that can be used on the stovetop and in the oven. Countless variations of this dish continue to proliferate. This particular version hails from the Midwest, where the pervasive use of sour cream attests to the region's Germanic heritage.

*6 lb. pot roast (top round beef, or an inexpensive cut such as rump or chuck)*
*1/2 cup butter*
*1 cup thick sour cream*
*2 teaspoons salt*
*Dash pepper*
*2 tablespoons flour, 4 cups water*
*2 bay leaves*
*2 small onions*
*Garlic*
*Small tomato*

*Rub casserole with garlic, and brown butter over heat. Rub salt and pepper into meat, dredge [lightly coat] with flour, and brown in butter being careful not to burn it. Add cream, turn the meat until the cream is thoroughly browned. Then add bay leaves, onions diced, tomato, and water. Cover and cook in moderate oven for three hours. Remove meat and bay leaves, and make gravy of liquid in pan, adding water if you wish more gravy.*

### ⊰ 243. SWISS STEAK ⊱

*(MacPherson, 1935)*

Swiss Steak can be made from an inexpensive cut of meat; recipes for the dish often call for pounding the meat to tenderize it. The meat in the following version is tenderized by slow cooking and by the addition of tomatoes to the sauce. Recipes for Swiss steak began to appear in American cookbooks in the early twentieth century. By the 1940s, Swiss steak had become a widely popular dinner dish.

*2 lbs. round or flank steak*
*1 small can tomatoes*
*3 tablespoons drippings or shortening*
*1 medium sized onion, chopped fine*
*1 cup water*
*1/4 teaspoon pepper*
*1 teaspoon salt*
*1/2 cup sifted flour*

*Sprinkle a little water over steak. Sift flour into large bowl or onto large plate, then put steak into flour and press as much flour into the steak as you can.*

*Put drippings or shortening into a large frying pan and when sizzling hot put the floured steak in. Brown the steak thoroughly on both sides. The steak can either be cooked on top of the stove or in the oven; whichever way you cook it the pot or baking pan should have a lid. Grease the pot or baking pan with a little dripping and transfer the browned steak to it. Now put the cup of water into the frying pan the steak was browned in, and let the water boil while you run a fork over the pan to loosen up any of the steak juices and flour that may be sticking to the pan. Then pour the boiling water from the frying pan over the steak, add 1 medium sized onion, finely chopped, and add a small can of tomatoes; add salt and pepper. Bring to a boil, then turn flame down and cover the pan or pot with a lid, and allow to simmer for 2 hours. If cooked in the oven, cover the baking pan and bake in a slow [300–325°] oven for 2 hours. Serve with mashed potatoes.*

### ⊰ 244. WIENER SCHNITZEL ⊱

*(Shay, 1941)*

A standard dish in German-American cookery, wiener schnitzel consists of scalloped (thinly sliced) veal, which has been breaded and fried. Masculine wording, such as this recipe's opening word, "manhandle," typified many male-authored cookbooks of this era.

*Manhandle 4 thinly cut slices of veal steak, pounding them with a wooden potato masher after sprinkling with salt and pepper. Dip into 2 well-beaten eggs, then into flour. Melt 1/2 cup butter in frying pan and cook steaks until lightly browned on both sides; sprinkle with juice of 1/2 lemon while cooking. Reduce heat and continue cooking slowly until tender; remove to a warm oven. Add a scant cup of water, salt, pepper, and 1 heaping teaspoon capers to the drippings in the pan, and let simmer while you fry 4 eggs. Pour the sauce over the steaks, place a fried egg on top of each, and garnish with lemon slices.*

## Lamb and Mutton

### ⇥ 245. CROWN ROAST OF LAMB ⇤

*(Allen, 1924)*

Crown roast was fashionable in the 1920s, 1930s, and early 1940s, when it was served at formal dinners. Although made frequently from lamb, it can also be made from pork, in which case it pairs well with apple sauce (recipe 54) in lieu of the mint.

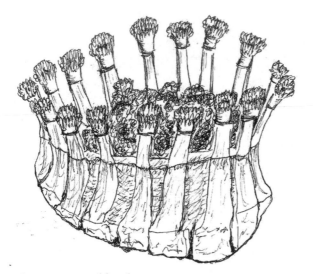

Crown roast of lamb.

*2 racks of lamb*
*Salt pork*
*Salt and pepper*
*Flour*

*The rack of lamb consists of the undivided neck chops, and in preparing a crown roast these are Frenched. The chine bone, that is, the flat backbone which runs along the thick end of the chops, is cut off and the two racks thus trimmed are put together and tied with string to form a circle or "crown" with the meat inside.*

*Place in a roasting pan. Put a small thick piece of salt pork on top of each exposed bone to protect it from charring and to baste the meat. To do this cut a gash in each piece of pork with a sharp knife so that it can easily be slipped over the bone. Allow twenty minutes to each pound of meat and have the oven heat at first 400–425 degrees F., reducing after twenty minutes to 350 degrees, that the lamb may cook thoroughly yet not be dry. Baste with the fat in the pan, adding a little more if necessary. Dust the roast with salt, pepper, and flour when half done. Serve with brown gravy, potatoes, peas, or any preferred green vegetable, and with mint sauce [recipe 56] or currant jelly [recipe 121].*

*After the meat is cooked remove the pieces of pork and replace them with cutlet frills.*

### ◈ 246. LAMB AND ARTICHOKES ◈

*(Mosser, 1939)*

Artichokes enjoyed a boost in popularity in the 1930s when they were sautéed, stuffed and baked, creamed, turned into omelettes and soufflés, fashioned into salads, and stewed. They appeared equally at home as the starring ingredient or as a flavor-enhancing addition.

*2 pounds lamb*
*1/2 cup butter*
*1 onion, finely chopped*
*Salt and pepper*
*3 pints water*
*8 artichokes*
*3 eggs*
*Juice of 1 lemon*

*Cut lamb in small pieces and sauté in butter. Add onion, salt and pepper. When brown add water and boil 1/2 hour. Discard dried [outer] artichoke leaves. Cut tips from tender leaves, remove chokes, halve and add to meat. Boil 1 hour. Beat eggs, add lemon juice and 1 cup of meat broth. Heat—don't boil—till thick, stirring constantly. Pour over meat and serve at once.*

### ◈ 247. MINCED MUTTON ◈

*(Estes, 1911)*

The following recipe, like a hash, is made from leftovers. Such dishes were often prepared for lunch when a roast had been served for dinner the preceding night. The roux called for here is a mixture of flour and fat used to thicken soups and sauces. The flour is slow cooked in butter or lard to make a white, a blond, or a brown roux. The cooking length determines the color; brown roux features in many Creole dishes.

*Mince the meat from a cold roast of mutton, put into a saucepan. Make a rous [roux], moisten with a little stock and season with salt and pepper, adding butter and some gherkins. Put the minced meat in the sauce and let it cook without boiling. Serve with thin slices of bread around the plate.*

## Pork

### ◈ 248. BAKED VIRGINIA HAM ◈

*(Sedlak, 1939)*[1]

That the following recipe relies on store-bought ham grounds it firmly in the twentieth century, as does the addition of pineapple for a finishing touch. Although pineapple had appeared in the nation's cookbooks since the early nineteenth century, they were not available to most Americans until the 1920s. During this decade, the canned variety became inexpensive enough that pineapple began to appear in countless meat dishes, fruit and vegetable salads, and cakes.

*Get precooked smoked ham or Swift's [brand] tenderized ham. Leave inside wrapping paper on. Set in roaster and bake required time according to size. Then take out of oven and remove paper and all of rind off ham. Sprinkle generously with brown sugar. Add sliced pineapple and cherries on top and return to oven until fruit is cooked a little or if desired put only brown sugar on and decorate with cloves (whole).*

### ⊰ 249. FRIED HAM ⊱

*(Estes, 1911)*

As they remain today, ham and eggs were a popular breakfast combination. They could also be served for lunch or an informal dinner.

*Cut off a thick slice of ham. Place in a saucepan over the fire, with sufficient water to cover and let come to a boil. Pour off the water, and fry the ham slowly until it is brown on both sides. Season with pepper and serve. Eggs are usually served with fried ham. They may be fried in the same pan or separately, in sufficient grease to prevent burning. Season with salt and pepper. Place around the ham.*

### ⊰ 250. PORK TENDERLOIN ⊱

*(Moody, 1931)*

Pork featured prominently in nineteenth-century cookbooks, but it received less attention in early twentieth-century cookbooks. Those recipes included typically tend toward the most basic preparation methods such as pan-fried pork chops and baked pork tenderloin.

*Pork tenderloin*
*1 cup of stale bread crumbs*
*3 onions*
*2 stalks of celery*
*Butter*
*Water*
*Salt, pepper, nutmeg*

*Soak the bread crumbs in water for a few minutes. Mince the onions and celery. Froth some butter in a sauté pan. Add the celery and onions, and cook on a slow fire about 10 minutes being very careful not to burn.*

*Squeeze all the liquid out of the bread. Add salt, pepper, and nutmeg, then the celery and onion.*

*Take the tenderloin. Cut it lengthwise about three-quarters of the way. Fold the top back. Slip in the filling. Bring the top over the filling. Twist the ends slightly. Roll the tenderloin in flour. Brown it in butter and baste it in the oven until it is done. Serve with apple sauce (recipe 54).*

### ⇥ 251. PORK ROAST WITH SAUERKRAUT AND DUMPLINGS

*(St. Andrews Guild, Spokane, Washington, c. 1944)*

This is a quintessential German-American dish common throughout the Midwest. Potatoes might be substituted for the dumplings to make another popular trio.

*1 to 4 lb. pork roast*
*1 qt. sauerkraut*
*1 tsp. caraway seed*
*3 Tbsp. sugar*

*Brown roast in large heavy roaster. Then put in sauerkraut, adding water to cover. Add sugar and caraway seed, and finish cooking in oven at 325 degrees about 2 hours.*

**Dumplings**

*2 c. flour*
*2 tsp. Calumet [brand] baking powder*
*2 eggs*
*3/4 c. water*
*1/2 tsp. salt*

*Sift dry ingredients into bowl add eggs and water. Beat with heavy spoon until smooth and springy.*

*Remove roast from kraut. If juice has cooked down add enough water to generously cover kraut and bring to a rolling boil. Drip big spoonfuls of dough in. Cover tightly and cook 12 minutes. (Do not lift cover before done.) Arrange dumplings around roast leaving enough room for kraut between roast and dumplings.*

## Game

### ⇥ 252. GUNNERS' LUCK STEW ⇤

*(Shay, 1941)*

Although game dishes dwindled during the twentieth century, recipes for venison, hare, rabbit, squirrel, duck, turkey, and quail were still included in

---

### → MEN IN KITCHENS

(Shay 1941)[1]

As the following quotation attests, some men were entering the home kitchen, although typically only on occasion. They were also writing cookbooks, which centered around "hearty" fare such as game and meat dishes; they also omitted the "Preserves" section.

*In the sacred white-tiled precincts of women, wherein no man was admitted unless he was delivering something or had been summoned to mend a leak, there are heard the tread of heavy feet, the clash of pot against pan, muttered exclamations of delight, and from under the door emanate savory and palate-exciting aromas. Men have invaded the kitchen in a really big way, easing the little women to chairs on the sidelines, sending them off to the movies, even home to mother in tears.*

---

cookbooks that wished to aid the recreational hunter. Many of these game-friendly cookbooks were penned by men, such as the author of the following recipe.

*To give the ingredients for this number with any degree of exactness is to lean on the side of prophecy. What goes into it is what the gunner has gunned; and it may, with a slight twist of fate, become a fisherman's chowder or a plain, everyday mulligan [stew]. The advantage of the following recipe is that in it may be combined miscellaneous game, and it may be cooked in camp or at home. It was excellent once when the combined bag of gunners comprised 2 squirrels, 1 rabbit, and 1 quail. A near-by farmer provided the vegetables.*

*2 pounds of game (after cleaning)*
*1/4 cup lard or bacon fat*
*1 pint dried lima beans*
*2 onions, chopped*
*4 potatoes, diced*
*1 cup carrots, diced*
*1 cup turnips, diced*
*4 cups water*
*Pepper*
*Salt*
*Flour*

*It is not absolutely necessary to soak dried lima beans overnight. Instead, wash them thoroughly, cover with hot water, and cook quietly for 1 hour.*

*Wash game and cut in pieces for serving, sauté in lard until nicely browned on all sides, and place with beans in a deep kettle, cover with boiling water, and cook uncovered for 1 hour, adding more boiling water as needed; add vegetables and seasonings and cook for another half-hour. Mix 2 or 3 tablespoons flour with a little cold water, add to the stew, and cook until slightly thickened.*

### ⇥ 253. POSSUM AND 'TATERS ⇥

*(Colquitt, 1933)*

As the following recipe indicates, possum was not a highly prized meat source. However, for those living in the country who were undergoing economic hardship or for those city-dwellers who enjoyed hunting on occasion, possum proved a respectable catch.

*While it is generally conceded that the fun lies more in the chase of the elusive coon than in the eating, there are those who hold that possum and 'taters is a most delectable diet, so here is the prescription for cooking your game after you have bagged it.*

*Before you go to bed that night scald the possum with lye and scrape off the hair. (Or have it done, which would be altogether more pleasant all around.) Dress whole, leaving on head and tail. Rub well with salt and put in a cool place overnight.*

*When ready to cook, put in a deep pan with one quart of water, place three or four slices of breakfast bacon reverently across the breast, and put in oven. When half done, remove from oven and stuff with a dressing made of bread crumbs, a little onion, salt and pepper and possum juice taken from the pan in which he has been reposing. Return him to pan, and place around him some small peeled sweet potatoes, and bake all until a light brown, basting frequently with the gravy.*

## Poultry and Fowl

### ⇥ 254. ARROZ CON POLLO [CHICKEN WITH RICE] ⇥

*(MacPherson, 1935)*

This dish took hold in Spanish-influenced parts of the country, such as Florida and the Southwest, and slowly spread across the nation. By the 1930s, it appeared in some of the nation's best-selling cookbooks. Unlike many "foreign" dishes served in the early twentieth century, this version resembles the recipe as it would be cooked in Spain with chicken, saffron, rice, and peas as the main ingredients. Mexican-inspired versions of the dish often include a healthy dose of chiles in lieu of peas.

*1 roasting chicken or capon [a castrated, fattened, young rooster], cut up*

*1/4 cup olive oil*
*1 1/2 tablespoon salt*
*1 teaspoon good imported paprika*
*1/3 saltspoon saffron powder*
*1/2 teaspoon pepper*
*1 clove of garlic, finely chopped and mashed with the flat of a knife*
*1 tablespoon parsley, finely chopped*
*2 bay leaves*
*1 large onion, chopped fairly small*
*2 cups rice*
*6 cups boiling water*
*3 pimientoes, cut up*
*1 cup peas (fresh or canned) if desired*

*Use a large pot with a lid. Place over moderate fire and put in the olive oil; when hot, add the chopped onion and the garlic. When a golden color, add the cut up chicken, salt, pepper, paprika, and finely chopped parsley. Cook 15 minutes without a cover, turning the pieces occasionally. Then add 6 cups of boiling water (3 cups of water to each cup of rice used; you can thus use more or less rice as desired); when the water is boiling, add the saffron powder and then the rice. Sprinkle the rice in gradually in order not to stop the boiling. When the rice is all in, reduce the heat under the pot and put the lid on. Allow to slowly boil for about 45 minutes, stirring every 10 minutes, or oftener, to prevent rice from sticking to the pot. Add the cut up pimiento during the last 15 minutes of cooking.*

*Some people like green peas mixed with the rice. These should be cooked separately and then mixed in during the last few minutes of cooking. Canned peas can be used.*

### ⇥ 255. CHICKEN CHOW MEIN ⇤

*(Home Institute of The New York Herald Tribune, 1938)*

This dish was first introduced to the United States by Chinese immigrants and had become a feature in many "all-American" cookbooks by the 1930s. Although its ingredients vary considerably, American chow mein usually consists of stewed meat or shrimp with vegetables served over fried noodles.

*1 cup celery strips*
*1 small onion, sliced*
*1 green pepper, finely sliced*
*2 cups chicken stock or bouillon*
*1 teaspoon salt*
*2 teaspoons soy sauce*
*1/2 cup sliced mushrooms*
*2 cups shredded cooked chicken*

*1 teaspoon cornstarch*
*2 tablespoons water*
*1 can (No. 2 1/2) [29 oz] Chinese noodles [crisp noodles]*

*Cook celery, onion and green pepper in stock 20 minutes; add salt, soy sauce, mushrooms, chicken and cornstarch mixed with water, and cook 10 minutes, stirring until thickened. Serve on crisp noodles; garnish top with slices of breast meat if desired.*

### ⊰ 256. CHICKEN SAUTÉ À LA CRÉOLE ⊱

*(Morphy, c. 1936)*

Also made with shrimp in lieu of chicken, this dish remains a favorite among Louisianians. Like most other creole dishes, chicken creole arises from a blend of French and Spanish culinary techniques and ingredients, which have been interpreted and prepared by African American cooks. Although the following recipe does not include piquant ingredients, many cooks often add paprika or cayenne to spice up the dish.

*Ingredients: 2 spring chickens, 6 large tomatoes, 2 large onions, 2 cloves of garlic, 6 fresh sweet green peppers or pimientos, 2 or 3 sprigs of thyme and parsley, 1 bayleaf, 2 tablespoons of butter, 2 of flour, 1 pint of stock or water, salt and pepper.*

*Method: Divide the chickens into joints, and season well with salt and pepper. Melt the butter in a saucepan and, when hot, put in the pieces of chicken and cook till a golden brown on all sides. Slice the onions, add to the chicken and brown lightly. Then sprinkle with the flour, mix well and cook till the flour browns. Now put in the sliced tomatoes, the chopped garlic and herbs, and the sliced pimientos, and simmer gently with the lid on for 20 minutes. Then add the hot stock or water, season highly with salt and pepper, and simmer gently for 45 minutes. To serve, put the pieces of chicken on a hot dish and pour the sauce over them. Boiled rice is served with this.*

### ⊰ 257. CREAMED CHICKEN ⊱

*(Home Institute of The New York Herald Tribune, 1938)*

Creamed dishes can feature vegetables, seafood, beef, eggs, or fowl that have been cooked in a sauce made from flour, milk, and butter. The à la king version typically calls for diced chicken, pimientos, mushrooms, green pepper, and an optional dash of sherry to be added to the base white sauce. The following recipe calls for the chicken to be served over bread, but it can also be served over waffles (recipe 301).

*2 cups Medium White Sauce (recipe 268)*
*2 cups diced cooked chicken*

*Buttered hot toast, croustades, or patty shells*
*Paprika or minced parsley*

*Prepare white sauce with rich milk, substituting 1 cup chicken stock for 1 cup milk; add chicken, diced or cut in strips, and heat thoroughly. Serve on toast and sprinkle lightly with paprika or parsley.*

### ᘓ 258. FRIED CHICKEN ᘔ

*(Dull, 1928)*

The following fried chicken recipe contains far more detail than the battered chicken (recipe 33). The author assumes a reader who can "dress and disjoint" chicken but who may not know the subtleties of frying. The following dish might be served with hot biscuits, rice, stewed corn, string beans, and sliced tomatoes for an all-American summer dinner.

*Select a young chicken weighing from 1 1/2 to 2 lbs. Dress and disjoint, chill. When ready, have a deep fry pan with grease at least two inches deep.*

*Sift enough flour in which to roll the chicken pieces (a cup and a half or two cups). Add salt and pepper to the flour, roll each piece in flour and place in the hot grease. Put the largest pieces in first and on the hottest part of the pan. When all is in, cover for 5 minutes. Remove top and turn when the underside is well browned. Replace top for another 5 minutes, remove and cook in open pan until the bottom side is browned. About 30 minutes in all will be required for cooking chicken if it is not too large. Do not turn chicken but once; too much turning and too long cooking will destroy the fine flavor which is there when well cooked.*

*The fat should be deep enough to cover the pieces when it boils up.*

*To make cream gravy:*

*Pour off the grease, leaving 2 to 3 tablespoons in the pan with the browned crumbs. Add 2 tablespoons butter, 4 tablespoons flour, blend and cook until a golden brown; add 1 cup milk and 1 cup hot water. Stir until smooth and the right thickness and add salt and black pepper. Pour into a gravy boat and serve with hot biscuit or dry rice. Never pour gravy over chicken if you wish Georgia fried gravy.*

### ᘓ 259. ROAST WILD DUCK ᘔ

*(Shay, 1941)*

As with other game, wild fowl recipes began to disappear from cookbooks in the twentieth century. However, duck, like venison, remains popular among hunters.

*Clean and wash thoroughly and remove all pin feathers by singeing or with tweezers. Then let the birds soak for 2 hours in heavily salted cold water.*

*Dry thoroughly, inside and out, and put a piece of celery, an apple, and a small onion inside each duck, but do not sew it up. Dust with salt, pepper, and flour. Lay strips of bacon across the breast, fastening them in place with toothpicks.*

*Place ducks, breast-side down, on a rack in an uncovered roasting pan and roast in a very hot oven (500° F.), basting every 5 minutes with the fat in the pan. As with hanging [an aging method used to tenderize meat], how long you roast wild ducks is a moot point. Some sportsmen remove them from the oven at the end of 15 or 20 minutes, when blood still follows the knife; others cook them upwards of half an hour. Remove apple, celery, and onion, and serve the ducks with wild rice and gravy made from pan drippings and chopped giblets. A tart jelly makes a fine accompaniment.*

## SEAFOOD

### 260. CLAMS CASINO

*(Ellsworth, 1939)*

The following recipe is a simplified version of the original one, which was created in 1917. It is named after the Casino restaurant in New York City.

*Fill with crushed rock salt as many shallow earthenware soup plates as you have portions to prepare, and heat them in the oven. Place on each six opened clams, sprinkle with lemon juice, finely chopped chives and fresh-ground pepper. Put a square of raw bacon on top of each clam and set them in a hot oven (400°) for ten minutes. When the bacon is done and edges are curled on the clams they are ready. Serve melted butter, lemon, and cucumbers in sour cream with them.*

### 261. LOBSTER NEWBURG

*(Allen, 1924)*

The following rich, expensive dish became so fashionable that a canned variety appeared on the market. The recipe calls for top milk—the cream that floats to the top of unhomogenized milk. Homogenization, which became a widespread practice within the dairy industry in the 1960s, breaks down the fat particles so that they no longer clump together and rise to the surface. Printed in 1924, this recipe calls for "sherry flavouring" rather than the traditional sherry, a nod to Prohibition, which outlawed the production, sale, or transportation of alcoholic beverages from 1920–1933.

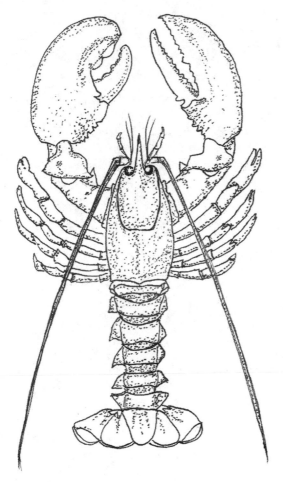

American lobster.

*1/4 cupful butter*
*3 cupfuls cooked lobster meat*
*1 tablespoonful cornstarch*
*1 1/2 cupfuls top milk or part milk and part cream*
*Yolks of 3 eggs*
*1 teaspoon salt*
*1/8 teaspoonful cayenne*
*1 teaspoonful lemon juice*
*Sherry flavouring to taste according to the kind used*

*Melt the butter, cut the lobster into large dice and cook the two together for five minutes, stirring continuously. Add the cornstarch and cook a moment longer. Next add one cupful of the milk, or milk and cream, bring to boiling point, place over hot water (double boiler or chafing dish), add the yolks of the eggs slightly beaten with the remaining milk, and stir constantly until thickened. Add the seasonings, lemon juice, and sherry flavouring. Serve on toast or crackers.*

### ⇥ 262. POMPANO [EN] PAPILLOTE ⇤

*(Federal Writers' Project, 1944)*

This dish was invented at Antoine's restaurant in New Orleans in 1901 to honor the French air balloonist Alberto Santos-Dumont. Cooked en papillote, the fish is wrapped in parchment paper, which, when baked, puffs like a balloon.

*5 fresh mushrooms*
*1 medium onion*
*2 tbsp. butter*
*2 tbsp. flour*
*1/2 pint fish stock*
*1 cup cream*
*1 cup crab meat*
*1 dozen cooked shrimp*
*1 2 lb. pompano*

*Stuffing:*

*Chop mushrooms and onion. Fry in butter until brown. Add flour and mix well. Add fish stock and cream and boil 2 minutes. Add crab meat, shrimp, and sherry. Remove from heat.*

*To Bake Fish:*

*Roll pompano in flour. Fry lightly in butter. Fill with stuffing. Lay on oil parchment [buttered parchment paper]. Fold diagonally and twist edges together to make air tight. Bake at 375 degrees for 15 minutes. Serve in paper.*

### ≈ 263. A MOLD OF SALMON ≈

*(Estes, 1911)*

Molded fish, vegetable, and meat dishes proliferated. Some, such as the following, were bound with egg and cooked in order to set their shape. Others were set in gelatin and chilled to accomplish the same.

*If [one lives] where one cannot get fresh fish, the canned salmon makes a delicious mold. Serve very cold on a bed of crisp lettuce or cress. Drain off the juice from a can of salmon, and flake, picking out every fragment of bone and skin. Mix with the fish one egg lightly beaten, the juice of half lemon, a cup fine dry bread crumbs, and salt and pepper to season. Pack in a buttered mold which has a tight-fitting tin cover, steam for two hours, and cool. After it gets quite cold set on the ice until ready to carve.*

### ≈ 264. PLANKED FISH ≈

*(Council of Jewish Women, Portland, Oregon, 1914)*

Planked dinners experienced a vogue in the 1930s. Each diner's meal could be cooked, warmed, and served on an individual plank. Cold or tepid dishes would naturally be placed on the plank after the cooking of the hot dishes had been completed.

*A white fish weighing between three and four pounds is the most satisfactory to plank. If your plank is new, oil all over very well, put it into a warm oven and gradually increase the heat until the oven is very hot, to prevent warping. Have cracker crumbs, finely chopped greens, such as parsley, onion and green peppers, at hand, and all kinds of vegetables, shrimps, mushrooms, etc. Clean and season the fish well, inside and out, and on the plank put small pieces of butter, scattering cracker crumbs and chopped greens over. On this place the fish, and after flaking with butter, scatter more greens; add seasoning, such as tomato catsup, Worcestershire sauce, one-quarter cup of sherry and strained tomato juice, keeping some of the latter for basting later on. Prepare some creamed potatoes and just before putting the fish into the oven place them around the edge of the plank in tablespoonfuls, using a fork to fashion them like roses, and flaking same with small pieces of butter. Have the oven very hot, and allow the fish to bake from one-half to three-quarters of an hour, according to the size of the fish. While the fish is baking prepare the vegetables, slicing cucumbers, peppers, tomatoes, etc. Watch the fish, occasionally basting with the tomato juice. Ten minutes before removing the fish from the oven garnish with the vegetables, boiled peas (if you have some on hand), shrimps, mushrooms, truffles, etc. Do not disturb the fish or garnishings, but put the plank on a large tray and serve. It is a most attractive dish.*

## GRAVIES, SAUCES, CATSUPS, AND PICKLES

### 265. CHILI SAUCE

*(Wright, 1912)*

The following "sauce" is a form of pickle used frequently as a condiment. Mixed with French dressing and mayonnaise, it dresses the Crab Louis salad (recipe 279).

*Eighteen ripe tomatoes, 6 onions, 3 green pepper, 1 cup sugar, 2 1/2 cups vinegar, 2 teaspoonfuls salt, 1 teaspoonful each of cinnamon, allspice, and nutmeg, and 1/2 teaspoonful of cloves. Scald and peel the tomatoes, and cook with onions and peppers until tender; then add sugar, vinegar and spices, and cook 10 minutes.*

### 266. CIOPPINO SAUCE

*(Callahan, 1933)*

This sauce should be poured over the layered fish dish (Cioppino recipe 231) before it is baked. It would also serve well as a sauce for pan sautéed fish accompanied by rice or potatoes.

*2 large onions*
*1 small clove of garlic*
*1 small head of celery*
*1/2 cupful of olive oil*
*1/4 pound of dried mushrooms*
*3 No. 2 1/2 [29 oz] cans of tomatoes*
*Parsley, minced*
*Bay leaf*
*A few pepper corns*
*Sherry wine seasoning to taste*
*Salt and pepper*

Cut onions, garlic, and celery in small pieces and brown slowly in the oil in a large skillet, stirring continuously. Pour hot water to cover over the dried mushrooms and let stand 1/2 hour. Add the tomatoes to the onions, with the chopped parsley, bay leaf, and a few pepper corns. Remove the mushrooms from the water and add them, allowing any sediment to settle in the cup, after which carefully add the water to the sauce. Cook slowly for 2 or 3 hours, adding water when necessary, and stirring frequently. Some of the sherry seasoning is salted so care must be used in adding that to taste. Season well with salt and pepper.

### ❧ 267. CORN RELISH ❧

*(Moody, 1931)*

A type of pickle, relishes are mixed into, served alongside, or spooned on top of other foods to add flavor. Although corn has been used for centuries in countless forms and fashions, it did not begin to appear regularly in published relish recipes until the twentieth century.

*10 ears of fresh, young, sweet corn*
*2 cups of sugar—Reserve 1/4 of this to put in at the end*
*1/4 cup of salt*
*1/4 cup of flour*
*2 onions*
*1 green pepper*
*1/4 of a small cabbage*
*1 oz. of mustard*
*3 cups of vinegar*
*1/2 teaspoonful of turmeric*
*1/2 tablespoonful of celery seed*

Cut off the top of the kernels of corn, and scrape out the milk from the hulls left on the cob. Chop the onions, cabbage, and pepper very fine.

Put the corn, the corn milk, 1 1/2 cups of the sugar, the salt, onion, pepper, cabbage, mustard, and celery seed into a kettle, with half the vinegar. Let them boil 5 or 6 minutes. Then add the rest of the vinegar, and boil 30 minutes.

About 10 minutes before the cooking is finished, mix the remaining 1/2 cup of sugar with the flour and turmeric. Dip out a little of the hot liquid, and wet this mixture. Then stir it into the kettle, and cook 10 minutes longer.

Put in glass jars and seal. This is excellent.

Be very careful in choosing your vinegars to get those of excellent flavor. There is a most important choice to be shown there. Cider vinegar is perhaps best; but it is well to replace 1/2 cup of this with the best tarragon vinegar. Vinegar stimulates the appetite, and contributes to bodily nourishment, if not taken in excess.

### ❦ 268. MEDIUM WHITE SAUCE ❦

*(Home Institute of The New York Herald Tribune, 1938)*

White sauces form the base of countless dishes, ranging from soups to soufflés. The medium white sauce that follows provides the base for creamed and scalloped dishes, such as the creamed chicken (recipe 257), which calls for a doubled portion of this recipe.

*2 tablespoons butter*
*2 tablespoons flour*
*1 cup milk, rich milk or light cream*
*1/2 teaspoon salt*
*1/8 teaspoon pepper*

*Melt butter and stir in flour; gradually stir in milk and stir until mixture boils and thickens, then cook about 3 minutes longer, stirring occasionally; add seasonings. Place over hot water to keep hot and cover tightly to prevent crust from forming on top.*

### ❦ 269. WATERMELON RIND PICKLE ❦

*(Colquitt, 1933)*

Although they originated in the South, watermelon rind pickle and watermelon preserves became popular throughout the country. The pickle section of cookbooks shrunk exponentially during the first half of the twentieth century; however, watermelon remained one of the few fruit varieties commonly listed.

*Select watermelon with thick rind. Cut rind into small pieces and weigh. One melon usually makes about five pounds of rind, and this receipt is for that amount.*

*Make syrup of five pounds of sugar, two and one-half pints of vinegar, one ounce of root ginger, broken up, one-half ounce of cloves, one ounce stick of cinnamon, and let come to boil. Cover fruit with hot water and boil until you can pierce it with a straw. Then drain off the water and put the fruit into syrup and let boil up once. Put in stone crock and let stay covered for three days. Then pour off syrup, and boil and pour over fruit in jars.*

## VEGETABLES, SALADS, AND SALAD DRESSINGS

The consumption of vegetables, including salads, increased during this time. And because the government encouraged housewives to plant their own gardens to allay food shortages, home canning of vegetables made a comeback during both World Wars.

## Vegetables

### ❧ 270. BAKED BROCCOLI ☙

*(Callahan, 1933)*

Broccoli, which was grown in America as early as the 1700s, did not enjoy widespread popularity until the 1930s.

*Broccoli for six servings (2 to 3 pounds)*
*2 tablespoons of butter*
*2 tablespoons of flour*
*1 teaspoonful of salt*
*Pepper*
*1 cupful of evaporated milk diluted with*
*1 cupful of water or meat broth*
*1/2 cupful of buttered crumbs*
*1/4 cupful of grated cheese*

*Soak broccoli, heads down, in cold water. Cook, heads up, in boiling salted water in uncovered kettle until barely tender—about 7 minutes. Prepare white sauce of butter, flour, salt, pepper, and diluted evaporated milk. Put broccoli in a buttered baking dish, cover with white sauce and sprinkle with crumbs mixed with cheese. Bake in moderate oven (325°) until crumbs are brown. Sprinkle top with chopped parsley and pimiento before serving. Yield: 6 servings.*

### ❧ 271. GLAZED CARROTS ☙

*(Shay, 1941)*

In the 1930s, cooks began to treat carrots much as they did sweet potatoes, which were often dressed with butter and brown sugar. The following dish can still be found on many restaurant menus and remains a popular recipe with many home cooks.

*Use the small young carrots or slice mature carrots in julienne strips. Make a dressing of 2 parts brown sugar, 1 part butter, and 1 part hot water, cooked together for 10 minutes. Brush carrots liberally with sauce and bake in a moderately hot oven (350° F.) for 10 to 15 minutes, basting frequently with remaining sauce.*

### ❧ 272. STEWED CORN ☙

*(Dull, 1928)*

The following detailed recipe calls for half the cooking time recommended in some nineteenth-century recipes, which designate up to an hour to boil corn. This considerably shortened length of time reflects a widespread trend toward less exhaustive cooking of vegetables.

*6 ears corn*
*3/4 cup water*
*1/2 cup sweet milk or cream*
*3 tablespoons butter or bacon drippings*

*Select full tender corn. Shuck and remove silks. With a knife split each row of grains. Cut off about one-third of the grain all around.*

*This gives a fine cut corn.*

*Add water. Put grease into a saucepan and make hot.*

*Pour in the corn and stir constantly until hot. Lower the fire and cook slowly for 30 minutes. Heat and add milk, salt and pepper. Mix well and it is ready to serve. Sometimes there is more starch in the corn and it thickens more or less. Add more or less water to suit. [Should h]ave the consistency to eat with a fork.*

*Corn should be cooked from twenty to forty minutes. That depends on the age and quantity. Too much and too long heat will toughen corn.*

*Usually the can vegetables require very little cooking.*

### ᥍ 273. FRENCH FRIED ONIONS ᥞ

*(MacPherson, 1935)*

Versions of this American classic comfort food have been appearing in cookbooks since the turn of the century. By mid-century French fried onions, or onion rings as they are more commonly called today, had become an indelible part of the American public's love affair with fast food thanks to the proliferation of roadside diners and drive-ins.

*2 large Spanish onions*
*1/2 pint milk*
*1/2 cup flour, or [a] little more*
*1/3 teaspoon salt*

*Peel onions and sift flour and salt into a bowl. Cut onions into slices about 1/4 inch thick. Separate the rings and soak in milk; then lift and drop into flour and salt. When floured, drop into deep fat, heated to temperature of 380° F. If you do not have a thermometer, test heat of fat with a cube of bread. When it browns in 60 seconds, the fat is the right temperature. When the onions are cooked to a golden brown, remove and drain on unglazed paper to absorb fat; then serve. This is a delicious way of frying onions.*

### ↭ 274. MASHED POTATOES ↫

*(Platt, 1941)*

The following recipe, which suggests an electric egg beater to whip the potatoes, speaks to the growing availability of electric kitchen gadgets. It also requires a ricer, a large metal gadget that forces the potato through tiny holes so that it comes out the other side in a form resembling rice. Like a food mill, it produces a smoother end product than a fork or a potato masher, although either of these instruments will do.

*12 potatoes*
*1/2 lemon*
*Salt*
*Lump of butter*
*Cup or so of hot cream*

*Peel, wash, and quarter 12 potatoes. Place them in an enamel pan with 1/2 lemon. Cover well with water, salt lightly, and boil until tender, but not falling apart. Drain well, remove lemon, and put potatoes through a ricer. Add a lump of butter and a little salt, and place pan on low fire. Beat well until perfectly smooth, then add, little by little, a cup or so of hot cream, beating furiously meanwhile, with a wire or wooden masher or electric beater, until light and fluffy.*

---

### ✦ ELECTRICITY

In 1936, the Rural Electrification Act was passed, helping to bring electricity to the entire nation.

---

### ↭ 275. POTATO PANCAKES ↫

*(Shay, 1941)*

The following pancakes might accompany Borscht (recipe 229) or pot roast at dinner, or be served along with bacon or ham and eggs for breakfast.

*1 1/2 cups sifted white flour*
*2 eggs, well beaten*
*2 cups grated raw potatoes*
*2 cups milk*
*1/2 teaspoon salt*
*1/2 tablespoon shortening*
*1/4 teaspoon baking powder*

*Beat eggs into the milk. Sift flour, salt, and baking powder together and add slowly to the eggs and milk; when well-mixed add grated potatoes. Bake immediately on hot well-greased griddle. Serve with meat dishes.*

### ⋙ 276. SPINACH ⋘

*(Council of Jewish Women, Portland, Oregon, 1914)*

The following recipe, published in 1914, gives a thirty-minute cooking time for spinach after it has been boiled until tender, quite a long time by contemporary standards. The trend toward shorter cooking times slowly began to take root in the first half of the century, spurred, in part, by the discovery of vitamins and the subsequent realization that nutritional content is compromised by excessive exposure to heat.

*Pick and clean thoroughly two pounds of spinach; cover with boiling water, and let cook until tender. Pour off water and drain in colander. Chop very fine. Heat two tablespoons of fat or butter in a pan; add chopped spinach, two cloves of garlic or a little finely chopped onion, salt, pepper and water or soup enough to moisten. Let cook about half an hour. Chop a hard boiled egg and sprinkle over the top when ready to serve.*

---

### ✦ VITAMINS

Scientists began discovering a range of vitamins in 1912. With this knowledge came an increasing concern for a "balanced" diet along with the awareness that fresh fruits and vegetables provided crucial nutrients. Soon after the discovery of vitamin C, orange juice became a ubiquitous part of the American breakfast.

---

### ⋙ 277. BAKED ZUCCHINI ⋘

*(Weingart, 1930s)[2]*

In the 1920s, California farmers began growing and distributing large volumes of vegetables that were popular among Italian Americans. As a result, ingredients such as zucchini began to feature regularly in American cookbooks.

*3 zucchini (cut in 1/4 inch slices)*
*3 tomatoes*
*1 cup bread crumbs*
*3 tablespoons grated parmesan*
*3 cloves garlic, finely minced*
*Butter*

*Heat butter and sauté garlic for about 30 seconds. Add zucchini rounds and cook, turning once, for 3 to 5 minutes. Butter a baking dish, and layer one-third of the zucchini rounds on the bottom. Follow with one-third of the tomatoes and the same proportion of bread crumbs and parmesan. Pile the same layers twice more and top with 1 tablespoon butter. Bake at 350° until zucchini is just tender.*

## Salads

> → **SALADS**
>
> (Moody, 1931)
>
> *The salad affords the host or hostess a delightful opportunity for displaying originality and delicacy of taste, and for evoking the sensitive appreciation of friends; for the combining of a salad is really as delicate and as aesthetic a performance as the grouping of flowers. The salad indeed constitutes the bouquet of the dinner, though not in the sense of being a garniture for the table. It is to the dinner itself what flowers are to the setting.*

### ⊰ 278. BOSTON SALAD ⊱

*(Wright, 1912)*

Although iceberg featured regularly in green salads, endive, watercress, and romaine starred occasionally. Recipe 188 provides directions for making French dressing.

*Place 2 tablespoonfuls of endive in a salad bowl, add 2 sliced cucumbers, 1 shredded green pepper, and 1/2 cup of chopped filberts [hazelnuts]; add highly-seasoned French dressing and garnish bowl with cress.*

### ⊰ 279. CRAB LOUIS ⊱

*(Callahan, 1933)*

Crab salad has long been among the American repertoire of fish dishes. This particular version dates from the early twentieth century. Some say it originated in San Francisco; others say it hails from Seattle.

*This West Coast specialty is justly famous the country over. To make it, arrange lettuce leaves around the inside of a salad bowl, with a few shredded leaves at the bottom. Put crab meat on top of the shredded lettuce and a few sliced hard-cooked eggs and chopped chives on top of the crab meat. In another bowl mix*

*1/2 cupful of French dressing [recipe 188]*
*1/2 cupful of chili sauce [recipe 265]*

*2 tablespoonfuls of mayonnaise [recipe 189]*
*1 teaspoonful of Worcestershire sauce*
*Salt and pepper to taste*
*Pour over the salad, and serve very cold.*

## ≈ 280. PERFECTION SALAD ≈

*(Dull, 1928)*

Molded salads such as the following were fashionable at ladies' luncheons. They usually contain a variety of diced, shredded, or crushed vegetables and fruits, encased in gelatin. Jell-O, the presweetened, colored commercial gelatin dessert, became popular in the early twentieth century and often served as the jelling agent for molded salads. One popular version, the Golden Glow or Sunshine salad, was made with yellow Jell-O.

*1/2 cup vinegar*
*2 teaspoons salt*
*Red pepper to taste*
*3 pimentoes [sic] or sweet fresh green pepper chopped fine*
*3 cups shredded cabbage*
*1 box gelatine [sic] dissolved in 1/2 cup cold water*
*1 cup boiling water*
*1 cup cold water*

*Soak gelatine [sic] in the cold water for 5 to 10 minutes. Add cup of boiling water to dissolve gelatine well. Add the cup of cold water to hasten the cooling. Add all seasoning, set aside to jell. When it begins to thicken stir in the cabbage and peppers, and let stand until firm. Unmold and serve with mayonnaise. Have the cabbage crisp, a bit of sugar may be added if a sweet flavor is liked. Any kind of vegetable may be added that will blend with cabbage.*

## ≈ 281. TOMATO ASPIC ≈

*(Home Institute of The New York Herald Tribune, 1938)*

The term *aspic* refers to a dish of sliced, diced, or crushed poultry, meat, game, fruit, or vegetables molded in a savory jelly. A classic version of the molded salad, tomato aspic appears on occasion in turn-of-the-century American cookbooks. With the rise of packaged gelatin, however, tomato aspic enjoyed a sharp rise in popularity.

*2 cups canned tomatoes*
*3/4 cup water*
*1 stalk celery, chopped*
*2 carrots, sliced*
*1/2 small onion, chopped*
*1/2 small green pepper, chopped*

*2 whole cloves*
*1/4 teaspoon peppercorns*
*blade of mace*
*1/4 teaspoon salt*
*Dash of pepper*
*1 1/2 tablespoons gelatin*
*1 tablespoon lemon juice*
*4 hard-cooked eggs*

*Put tomatoes and 1/2 cup water in saucepan and add prepared vegetables and seasonings; bring to boiling point and simmer 15 minutes; strain. Soften gelatin in remaining 1/4 cup cold water about 5 minutes; add hot tomato juice, stirring until gelatin is dissolved; add lemon juice. Pour into individual molds; chill until firm. Unmold on crisp lettuce and garnish with mayonnaise. One to 2 cups mixed cooked vegetables or diced hard-cooked egg may be added if desired, or plain aspic may be molded in 1 large or 6 small ring molds and served with chicken, fish or vegetable salad heaped in center. Approximate yield: 6 to 8 salads.*

## ⸷ 282. WALDORF SALAD ⸶

*(Robinson, 1913)*

The original salad, invented at New York's City's Waldorf-Astoria hotel in the 1890s, called for diced apple and celery to be tossed in mayonnaise; the following version also includes walnuts, which remain a standard addition in most versions served today.

*Select even-sized, well-colored, red Jonathan apples. Cut a slice from the stem end thick enough to include the stem which will serve for a handle. Scoop out the center of the apple, being careful to keep the pieces large enough for the salad, leaving a perfect shell.*

*Mix the apple with an equal quantity of celery, 1/2 c. Malaga grapes, halved and seeded, and 1/2 c. English walnuts. Mix with [Lemon] Cream sauce [recipe 283].... Fill the apple shells with the salad and cover with the tops. Serve on lettuce leaves on salad plates. If there is too much to fill the apples put into a bowl and cover tightly with a wet cloth.*

## Salad Dressings

### ⸷ 283. LEMON CREAM SAUCE ⸶

*(Robinson, 1913)*

Such cream-based dressings were wildly popular throughout the late nineteenth and early twentieth centuries. They were served on top of plain lettuce or used to dress fruit-based salads, such as the Waldorf, recipe 282.

*To 1/2 cream, whipped, add 4 T sugar and 3 T lemon juice. Pour over the salad.*

### ⊰ 284. ROQUEFORT DRESSING ⊱

*(Harris, 1918)*

The following dressing was often slathered over a quartered head of iceberg lettuce to make a quick salad dish still served in homes and restaurants today.

*French dressing [recipe 188] with Roquefort cheese mashed smoothly into it.*

### ⊰ 285. THOUSAND ISLAND DRESSING ⊱

*(Dull, 1928)*

This American invention began appearing in print during the early twentieth century and is supposedly named after the Thousand Islands in New York. In addition to its widely popular use as a salad dressing, it is also spread on sandwiches as a condiment.

*1 cup homemade mayonnaise [recipe 189]*
*1/4 cup chili sauce [recipe 265]*
*1 tablespoon chopped onion*
*1 tablespoon chopped pickles*
*1 tablespoon Worcestershire sauce*
*1 teaspoon paprika*

*Make mayonnaise as usual, add all ingredients, mix well and it is ready to use. A hard-boiled egg is sometimes added. Cucumbers may be used, too, if served with fish.*

## EGGS, RICE, PASTA, AND SUNDRY OTHER DISHES

### ⊰ 286. BEAN LOAF ⊱

*(Winn-Smith, 1942)*

The following recipe provides an alternative to meat loaf during times of scarcity. (See the meat loaf recipe 240 to compare ingredients.) The beans and peanut butter pack the protein that could be hard to come by during meat shortages.

*2 c. dried beans (lima or navy)*
*4 tbsp. peanut butter*
*1 c. fine breadcrumbs*
*1 tsp. salt*
*1/4 tsp. pepper*

*3 tbsp. minced onion*
*1 tsp. sage*
*1 tbsp. bacon or sausage drippings or salad oil*
*1 c. milk*

*Wash the beans and soak them overnight in plenty of water. Next day, drain and cover with boiling water; boil about 45 minutes or until soft. Drain, cook, and run through a coarse sieve or colander. Mix crumbs with the seasonings, peanut butter[,] drippings, and milk; add the beans, and mix well. Place in a well-greased loaf tin and bake in a moderately hot oven, 375°–400° F, for 30–35 minutes. Serve with broiled tomatoes or tomato sauce [recipe 171].*

## ❧ 287. GRITS ☙

*(Morphy, c. 1936)*

Grits have long been a regular breakfast or side dish in the South. Grillades (recipe 241), a traditional Louisiana dish of diced, braised meat, is typically served over grits.

*Ingredients: For 2 cups of grits allow 2 quarts of water and 2 teaspoons of salt. The grits should be well washed in cold water. Put them in a saucepan of cold salted water, bring to the boil and simmer for 1 hour, stirring occasionally. The mixture should be of the consistency of thick starch, or even drier, according to taste. It is served hot, with meat, with gravy, or as a breakfast dish with milk and sugar in the same way as porridge, or it is eaten with butter. It is a delicious and wholesome dish.*

## ❧ 288. FLUFFY OMELET ☙

*(Home Institute of The New York Herald Tribune, 1938)*

An outgrowth of the domestic science movement, the minute detail that appears in the following recipe is typical of this time period, during which cookbook authors assumed little cookery knowledge among their readers.

*4 eggs, separated*
*1/2 teaspoon salt*
*Dash of pepper*
*1/4 cup milk*
*1 tablespoon butter*
*Parsley*

*Beat egg yolks until thick and light; add seasonings and milk; fold into stiffly beaten egg whites. Turn into buttered, hot 9-inch frying or omelet pan and cook over low heat for 3 to 5 minutes, or until omelet puffs up and is browned* on bottom. *(Test by raising edge of omelet with spatula.) Place in moderate oven (350° F.) for 10 to 15 minutes, or until top springs back when pressed with finger. Cut about 1-inch incisions at opposite sides and crease down through center in line with cuts; then fold carefully on crease by slipping spatula under half of omelet to fold over. Slip on to hot platter and garnish with parsley; if an omelet pan is used, merely fold over; omelet will shrink slightly when removed from pan. Serve at once. Approximate yield: 6 portions.*

### ◄ 289. BANANA SANDWICHES ►

*(Estes, 1911)*

One of the least expensive fruits sold in stores, imported bananas have been a part of the mainstream American diet for close to a century. In addition to being mashed and spread on bread, they are also sliced and served with cereal, tossed into fruit salads, turned into banana cream pies, and flambéed or fried for dessert.

*Remove the skin and fibers from four bananas, cut them in quarters and force through a ricer [or mash well with a fork]. Mix with the pulp the juice of half a lemon, a dash of salt and nutmeg and set it away to become very cold while you prepare the bread. This should be cut in very thin slices, freed from crusts and trimmed into any preferred shape. Slightly sweeten some thick cream and add a speck of salt. Spread the bread with a thin layer of the cream, then with the banana pulp put together and wrap each in waxed paper, twist the ends and keep very cold until serving time.*

### ◄ 290. PIMIENTO SANDWICHES ►

*(Allen, 1924)*

Just as the variety of sandwiches proliferated during this time, the role they played expanded as well. Light sandwiches such as the following were served at afternoon teas. More substantial sandwiches, often filled with meat or fish and fried, were served for lunch or light supper. Heavy toasted sandwiches (such as the club) or sandwiches with heated fillings (such as what was then called Hamburg steak) were eaten as a main course at lunch or supper.

*These may be varied according to individual taste—for instance—either rye bread, white bread, whole-wheat, nut bread, or Boston brown bread [recipe 81] may be used. The pimientos (trimmings left from garnishing may be used) are to be finely chopped, seasoned with a little salt and used plain as a filling; or they may be minced and flavoured with two tablespoonfuls of mayonnaise to a half cupful of pimientos, or worked with equal quantity of cream cheese if a more substantial sandwich is desired. The cream cheese and pimiento filling is particularly good for service with buttered Boston brown bread.*

## ᕯ 291. QUICHE LORRAINE ᕤ

*(Platt, 1941)*

Although savory pies suffered a sharp decline in popularity by the turn of the century, this rich French dish would prove a twentieth-century exception. Unlike many of the pies imported from the British, which included pastry on both the top and the bottom, quiche Lorraine remains uncovered.

*1 1/2 cups of pastry flour*
*1/2 teaspoon of salt*
*1 bar [stick] of salt butter (1/4 pound)*
*4 tablespoons of ice water*
*1 cup of grated Swiss cheese*
*1 1/2 dozen strips of bacon*
*4 eggs*
*2 cups of cream*
*Pinch of nutmeg*
*Pinch of sugar*
*3/4 teaspoon of salt*
*Pinch of cayenne*
*Freshly ground black pepper*

*First make a paste in the following manner: Sift 1 1/2 cups of pastry flour with 1/2 teaspoon of salt. Work into it with finger-tips 1 bar of salt butter (1/4 pound). Moisten with just enough ice water to make it hold together (about 4 tablespoons). Make a smooth ball of it, wrap in waxed paper and place in refrigerator for 1/2 hour or so, before rolling it out thin on a lightly floured board. Line a very large tart or pie pan with it, trim the edges and crimp them. Prick the surface with a fork and place in refrigerator while you prepare the following ingredients. But first set your oven to 450° F. and light it. Grate Swiss cheese until you have a cup of it. Fry or grill about 1 1/2 dozen strips of bacon until crisp, but don't overcook it. Break or cut into small pieces. Break 4 whole eggs into a bowl and add to them 2 cups of thick or thin cream, a pinch of nutmeg, a pinch of sugar, 3/4 teaspoon of salt, a big pinch of cayenne, and plenty of freshly ground black pepper. Beat with rotary beater just long enough to mix thoroughly. Now rub a little soft butter over the surface of the pastry and sprinkle the bacon over the bottom, sprinkle the cheese over the bacon, and pour the egg mixture over all. Place in preheated hot oven, and bake 10 to 15 minutes, then reduce the temperature to 325° F., and continue cooking until an inserted knife comes out clean, showing the custard has set (about 25 to 30 minutes). If not a light golden brown on top, place under a hot grill for a second before serving piping hot.*

*Note: Variations of this pie may be made by substituting thinly sliced ham, sizzled in butter, for the bacon; or parboiled salt pork, cut in tiny squares and fried until a golden brown, may be used; also sizzled chipped beef may be used. The cheese may be omitted, too, if you like, or thinly sliced onions browned slowly in butter may be added.*

### ⊰ 292. SPAGHETTI ITALIAN ⊱

*(Callahan, 1933)*

By the 1930s, many Americans had finally begun to differentiate between the myriad pastas (such as spaghetti, fettuccine, and vermicelli) and to make variations of sauce that bore some resemblance to what one might find in Italy. The large number of Italian-Americans and their prominent role in the food industry as restaurant owners, cooks, and grocers helped integrate pasta into the American diet. The following recipe is typical for the time, except that most authors would have recommended cooking the pasta when the sauce was a few minutes away from completion.

*1 8 ounce package spaghetti*
*1/2 pound chopped meat*
*1/2 pound fresh mushrooms*
*1 clove garlic*
*1 No. 2 [20 oz] can tomatoes*
*1/2 chopped green pepper*
*4 tablespoons butter or olive oil*
*1 tablespoon chopped parsley*
*Salt and pepper*

*Cook spaghetti in salted boiling water and drain. Sauté sliced garlic in olive oil, add meat and green pepper, seasoning with salt and pepper to taste, and cook slowly until meat is browned. Add sliced mushrooms, tomatoes, and parsley, and cook slowly for 1 1/2 hours, covered. Stir frequently.*

*Pour meat sauce over the spaghetti and serve with grated Parmesan cheese.*

### ⊰ 293. TAMALES ⊱

*(Edwords, 1914)*

Long served at Mexican festivals and eaten by many in the Southwest on New Year's Eve, the tamale dates back to pre-Colombian times. The following recipe calls for butter; the traditional Mexican tamale calls for lard. The masa, or cornmeal dough, can be stuffed with sweet or savory filling. Tamales are often steamed, a method that helps keep the masa from escaping the corn husk wrapper. Tamales wrapped in corn husks are still eaten primarily in the Southwest where they have been served at roadside stands, and more recently restaurants, since the early days of Texas. Tamale pie, a casserole form of the dish, was popularized throughout the United States during the

1920s. It dispenses with the husk in lieu of a casserole dish and is baked in the oven rather than boiled or steamed.

*Boil one chicken until the meat comes from the bones. Chop the meat fine and moisten it with the liquor in which it was boiled. Boil six large chili peppers in a little water until cooked so that they can be strained through a fine strainer, and add to this the chopped chicken, with salt to taste and a little chopped parsley. Take corn meal and work into it a lump of butter the size of an egg, adding boiling water and working constantly until it makes a paste the consistency of biscuit dough. Have ready a pile of the soft inner husks of green corn and on each husk spread a lump of dough, the size of a walnut, into flat cake covering the husk. In the center of the dough put a teaspoonful of the chopped meat with minced olive. On a large husk put several tablespoonfuls of chopped meat with olives. Roll this together and lay on them other husks until the tamale is of the size desired. Tie the ends together with strips of fine husk and put in boiling water for twenty minutes. Either veal or pork may be used instead of chicken.*

### ⊰ 294. WELSH RAREBIT [RABBIT] ⊱

*(Moody, 1931)*

This British import was frequently served as an inexpensive main course for lunch or a light supper. It became especially handy when meat was rationed, as it was during World War II. Most American cookbooks of the 1930s and 1940s, use the "rarebit" spelling, but many authorities hold that "rabbit," which is the first known printed spelling, is correct. As indicated in the following recipe, cheddar is commonly used; in the 1930 and 1940s, American cheese was also often specified. Rather than the usual ale, this recipe calls for "near beer," an ingredient that dates the cookbook from which it came to the Prohibition Era; "near beer" contains no alcohol.

*To make a Welsh rarebit it is best to use a chafing dish. The rarebit should be made in the presence of those who are going to eat it, for it sustains delay worse than most things. Use a chafing dish, and be seated at the table with those with whom you are going to serve; and if you are not very expert, use a chafing dish with a water bath. But if you are quick of motion, and have a heavy-plated chafing dish, it is better to work without the water bath, because it is more rapid.*

*The rarebit is not what it used to be when there was real imported English ale to put into it. Many authorities on this subject substitute sauces or milk or cream to replace it; but I prefer to take a chance with "near beer." The selection of your cheese is an all-important point in making Welsh rarebit. Get one-half pound of rich dry cheese and grate it. The old imported Cheddar was excellent for it. There are Herkimer County [New York] cheeses that are very good. Be sure to have something snappy.*

*Before you begin, take slices of fine fresh white bread. With half a pound of cheese you will make four ample servings. Cut off the crust of the bread; toast it rapidly on both sides. Butter each slice well and cut it diagonally into four triangles. Put each group on a separate hot serving plate, to be ready for immediate use when the rarebit is done.*

*Put a tablespoonful of butter into the chafing dish. When it is melted, put in the grated cheese, a small pinch of cayenne, and, if you wish, 1/2 teaspoonful of mustard. While the cheese is melting, add 1/2 cup of "near beer"; and when the mixture is creamy, dish it out onto the toast on the various plates. You may, if you like, substitute cream for the beer, but I do not recommend it.*

*The Welsh rarebit becomes a golden buck when you stir in one or two egg yolks as the cheese turns liquid.*

*It is really much better to grate your cheese than to add it in lumps, because the success of Welsh rarebit depends upon rapid melting and rapid serving.*

### 295. WESTERN SANDWICH

*(Allen, 1924)*

This egg and onion sandwich, which dates back to the frontier days, may have been invented by pioneer women or by chuckwagon cooks. Contemporary versions usually include red and green bell pepper. In the 1920s, when this recipe appeared, the Western would have been served as the main dish for luncheon or for late supper. It is also known as the Denver sandwich; without bread it becomes a Western or Denver omelette.

*For these the bread should be either cut in large rounds or cut from a round loaf and lightly buttered. For each sandwich allow a beaten egg, a tablespoonful of scraped or minced onion, and three tablespoonfuls of minced ham, cooked in butter in small frying pan until firm like a pancake.*

## BREAD AND BISCUITS

### 296. CHEESE BISCUITS

*(Colquitt, 1933)*

Although simple to prepare, biscuits were made even easier in the 1930s when General Mills began selling its packaged biscuit mix Bisquick. As the following recipe indicates, some biscuit recipes take little time to prepare from scratch. Nonetheless, General Mills's product was a huge success, as it eliminated the need to measure out ingredients.

*1/4 pound flour*
*1/4 pound grated cheese*

*1/4 pound butter*
*Salt to taste*

*Mix quickly with as little handling as possible. Roll thin and bake in a quick oven.*

### ⇥ 297. FIVE O'CLOCK TEA BISCUITS ⇤

*(Council of Jewish Women, Portland, Oregon, 1914)*

In America, the term *biscuit*, which means cracker or cookie in England, refers to a small, quick bread. Biscuits and dainty sandwiches often accompanied the afternoon tea. In the 1920s, tea service began to move out of the house and into public tea rooms, which proliferated in larger cities.

*Mix one-fourth of a pound of flour and one teaspoon Crescent [brand] baking powder, one cup of sugar, the rind and juice of two lemons with one-half pound of butter, which has been worked into a smooth paste, add to this the whites of two eggs and a little milk. Roll this and cut into biscuits, and brush them over with the yolks of the eggs. Sprinkle with a little sifted, pulverized sugar and bake in buttered tins.*

### ⇥ 298. BLINTZES ⇤

*(Weiss, 1920s)*[3]

Brought to the United States by Jewish immigrants from Russia and Poland, blintzes can be served with a wide array of savory or sweet fillings and are often topped with sour cream.

#### Dough

*5 eggs*
*2 1/2 cups milk*
*2 1/2 to 3 cups flour, sifted*

#### Filling

*1 1/4 lb. farmer's cheese*
*1 lb. cottage cheese*
*3 tablespoons sour cream*
*A little sugar if too sour*
*A little cinnamon*

*Prepare the filling by mixing the ingredients. For the dough, beat the eggs and add a little milk at a time. Add flour slowly and stir until smooth. The batter should be thin enough to coat a hot skillet before it begins to solidify. Add more milk or more flour as needed to thin or thicken the dough. Pour a thin layer of the batter onto a well greased skillet, which has previously been heated to medium. Maneuvre skillet quickly until entire base is covered with the batter. Cook until solid, and place on a plate with the cooked side up. Continue until the batter is used up. Place a large spoonful of filling on the cooked side of each pancake and fold so that the batter is securely encased. Fry or bake the blintzes until golden brown on both sides.*

### ➽ 299. HASTY BRAN BREAD ❧

*(Winn-Smith, 1942)*

Quick, or here hasty, bread typically incorporates baking soda or baking powder as a leavening agent rather than yeast. As a result, it does not require kneading or rising time.

*1 1/2 c. flour*
*1/2 tsp. salt*
*3 tsp. baking powder*
*1 1/2 c. bran*
*1 egg*
*1 c. milk*
*2 tbsp. melted shortening*
*1 tbsp. honey, molasses, or sugar*

*Sift the flour, salt, and baking powder together, add the bran. Beat the egg, add the milk, shortening, and sweetening, and stir into the flour mixture. Bake 1 hour in a moderate oven, 375 degrees F. Makes two small loaves or one large loaf.*

### ➽ 300. PARKER HOUSE ROLLS ❧

*(Moody, 1931)*

These light, fluffy yeast rolls were first prepared at Boston's Parker House Hotel in the 1850s and were well integrated into home cooking by the turn of the century.

*1 pt. of warm milk*
*1 1/2 tablespoonfuls of lard*
*1 1/2 tablespoonfuls of butter*
*2 tablespoonfuls of sugar*
*1 teaspoonful of salt*
*6 cups of flour a little more or less, but keep your dough as slack as possible*
*1 yeast cake*
*1/4 cup of tepid water*

*Mix the lard, butter, and sugar together, and add the warm milk. Let the mixture stand till it is tepid. Dissolve the yeast in the tepid water, and add it* to the mixture. Stir in 2 cups of the flour. Beat this thoroughly and set it in a warm place to rise for at least 2 hours.

When it has risen, knead in the rest of the flour, with which the salt has been sifted. Put this dough in a buttered bowl in a warm place, and let it rise till it doubles in bulk.

When it has risen, take it out on a lightly floured board. Knead it, and roll it out about 1/4 of an inch thick. Lift it from the board to let it shrink, so that the rolls can be made uniform. Cut it with a round cutter, about 2 1/2 inches in diameter. Dip the cutter in flour before using it. Brush one-half of each round of dough with melted butter. Fold the other half over it, so that the edges are even. Press down lightly. Put the rolls in a pan, and let them rise 1/2 hour in a warm place. Bake them 15 or 20 minutes in a hot oven. Wash them lightly with melted butter after baking.

### ❦ 301. WAFFLES ❦

*(Allen, 1924)*

Waffles have been a part of the American diet since soon after the Pilgrims landed. By the late nineteenth century, they had become a regular feature of the American breakfast, and many home kitchens housed waffle irons specifically designed to make them. They were frequently eaten with maple syrup just as they are today. They were also eaten as a savory dish; in the 1930s, they were often topped with creamed chicken (recipe 257) and served for lunch or a light supper.

*1 1/2 cupfuls bread flour*
*2 teaspoonfuls baking powder*
*2 eggs*
*1 cupful of milk*
*2 tablespoonfuls melted shortening*
*1/2 teaspoon salt*

Sift together the flour and salt; beat the egg yolks; pour the milk into them and add the melted shortening. Stir this into the dry ingredients, then fold in the egg whites, beaten stiff. At this point, beat the mixture with a spoon or wire whisk until it is full of bubbles; then cook as directed [below].

The waffle iron should be heated until smoking hot, when it should be oiled, unless an aluminum waffle iron is being used.... The waffle mixture should be put in a pitcher and sufficient poured into each compartment of the waffle iron barely to fill it (a tablespoonful is usually enough). The top should then be lowered, and when the waffle is brown on one side, which should take about three minutes, the iron should be turned to brown the other side; this will take about five minutes longer. Waffles should be turned but once in the baking.

## Pies, Puddings, and Fruit Desserts

### ⇥ 302. APPLE CRISP ⇤

*(Weingart, 1930s)[4]*

This one-crust apple pie is a variation of the American classic. The use of margarine instead of butter dates this recipe to the 1930s and 1940s, when food shortages gave the butter substitute a boost in sales. Although margarine had been sold in the United States since the late nineteenth century, it suffered a complicated reception, largely as a result of state dairy interests.

*6 to 8 apples (or 1 quart) sliced*
*1 teaspoon cinnamon*
*1/2 cup water*
*3/4 cup flour*
*1 cup sugar*
*7 tablespoons margarine melted*
*Bake 1/2 hour 350°*

*Put apples in greased casserole and cover with the cinnamon and water. Mix the flour and sugar. Add the melted margarine and mix until it forms fine crumbs. Pour over the apples and pack down. Bake 1/2 hour at 350°.*

### ⇥ 303. BAKED CANNED PEACHES ⇤

*(Platt, 1941)*

The rise in recipes that rely on canned fruits and vegetables rather than fresh enabled Americans to eat a given dish throughout the year rather than seasonally, as had previously been the case. Many argue that this change initiated a decline in the quality of American food; canned may be more convenient and often cheaper than fresh, but flavor and texture can be compromised in the commercial canning process.

*1 can of tree-ripened peaches*
*2 dozen blanched almonds*
*1 cup of light brown sugar*
*1/8 pound butter*

*Open and drain, but save, the juice from 1 large can of tree-ripened peaches. Lay the peaches, cut side up, on a flat round buttered Pyrex dish. Pour enough juice on them to cover the bottom of the dish well. Sprinkle with 1 cup of light brown sugar, dot with 1/8 pound of sweet butter. Place in preheated (500° F.) oven and bake until well heated through and until syrup has boiled down a bit. Remove from the oven, and place in each center 2 or 3 blanched almonds, soaked in cold water as per [following] directions. [Heat some water to boiling point, pour over 2 dozen shelled almonds, and let them soak 3 minutes, then pinch off skins, cover the almonds with cold water, and put in refrigerator to chill]. Serve hot, accompanied by a pitcher of thin cream.*

### ◈ 304. PECAN PIE ◈

*(Colquitt, 1933)*

Because pecan trees prefer milder climates, their nuts are eaten more frequently in the southern states such as Georgia, Louisiana, and Texas, where pecan pie has long been a favored dessert available in homes and public eateries alike. Although a variation of pecan pie may have existed before the twentieth century, historians have not been able to trace a recipe for the dish that predates 1925. The following recipe, which dates from 1933, calls for Karo syrup; so, too, do most pecan pie recipes, a fact that has led at least one historian to conjecture that the Karo company's home economists might have invented the dish to promote their product.

*4 eggs*
*1 cup sugar*
*1 tablespoon butter*
*1 1/2 cups Karo syrup (red label)*
*1/2 cup shelled pecans*
*Pinch of salt*
*1 teaspoonful vanilla*

*Beat eggs and mix with all ingredients. Line pan with pastry, pour in the mixture and bake one hour.*

### ◈ 305. SHOO-FLY PIE ◈

*(Smith, 1938)*

An invention of the Pennsylvania Dutch, shoo-fly pie is a molasses and brown sugar concoction. The pie can take three forms: dry, wet, or cake-like. The dry version, which follows, uses less liquid in the base and is topped with crumbs. The wet version is so called because it uses more water than molasses. Like the dry, it is topped with crumbs. The cakelike version, often called shoo-fly cake, uses alternate layers of crumbs and molasses mixture.

*Ingredients for crumbs: 1 1/2 cups flour, 1 cup brown sugar, 1/4 cup butter*

*Molasses Mixture: 1/2 cup New Orleans molasses, 1/2 cup hot water, 1/2 tsp. baking soda, 1/4 tsp. cream of tartar.*

*Line three small pie tins (four inches in diameter at the bottom) with uncooked pastry. Dissolve soda and cream of tartar in hot water and mix with molasses.*

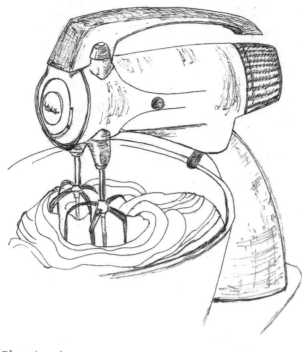

*Electric mixer.*

*Make crumbs of flour, sugar and butter. Divide molasses mixture in pastry crusts, and top with crumbs. Bake in hot oven until crust edges start to brown (about ten minutes). Reduce heat and bake twenty minutes.*

## CAKES, COOKIES, CUSTARDS, AND CREAMS

### ❧ 306. ANGEL CAKE ☙

*(Council of Jewish Women, Portland, Oregon, 1914)*

Often made to use up leftover egg whites, angel cake makes a light dessert. One legend of its birth in the United States comes from a cookbook published in 1931. According to the author, the recipe for angel cake came to the United States from India, where it was introduced to a woman from Atlantic City. On her arrival home, the woman began to reproduce the cake for sale. Hence its fame spread. As with the origins of many recipes, several other legends exist.

*One and one-half tumblers granulated sugar sifted seven times, one tumbler flour sifted with one level teaspoon cream tartar, four or five times, whites of twelve eggs, one teaspoon vanilla. Beat the whites to a stiff froth in a large mixing bowl; add the sugar gradually, beating constantly, then fold in the flour and add vanilla. Pour into pan at once and bake in a slow oven [325°] fifty or sixty minutes. Cover while baking with brown paper. See that your cream of tartar and eggs are fresh. Do not grease pan. Invert to cool.*

### ❧ 307. ICE-BOX CAKE ☙

*(Colquitt, 1933)*

Frequently made from lemon, chocolate, or crushed pineapple, ice-box cakes (along with ice-box pies and ice-box cookies) became trendy in the 1920s when refrigerators began to enter American home kitchens. Although custards and creams had long been chilled in old-fashioned ice-boxes and ice-cream makers, the refrigerator simplified the process.

*Melt three squares of Baker's [brand] chocolate. Beat the yolks of nine eggs until creamy, add one cup of sugar, and pour the hot chocolate into this. Then add the well-beaten whites of the eggs, and one-half cup of powdered sugar and a teaspoon of vanilla.*

*Line a mold with lady fingers, pour this mixture and let stand [in refrigerator] several hours. Serve with whipped cream.*

## ❧ 308. LADY BALTIMORE CAKE ❦

*(Allen, 1924)*

This lady cake spiked in popularity after the 1906 publication of Owen Wister's novel Lady Baltimore, which was named for the confection that the story's narrator eats in a Charleston tea room. Taking its name after the type of person to whom it could be served, the term *lady* designates a less expensive and elaborate cake than a "king" or "queen" cake. The candied sugar icing earns it the Baltimore part of its name; Baltimore was a revered candy-making center during this time. The original version called for both egg yolks and whites; the following version calls for just the whites.

### *Cake*

*1 cupful butter*
*2 cupfuls sugar*
*1 cupful milk*
*1 teaspoonful rose water*
*3 cupfuls pastry flour*
*3 teaspoonfuls baking powder*
*Whites of 5 eggs*
*1/4 teaspoonful salt*

*Cream the shortening and sugar until very light, add the milk and rose water, then the flour, baking powder, and salt sifted together, and last of all fold in the whites of the eggs beaten until stiff. Bake in three oiled layer-cake pans in a moderate oven—350 degrees F.—about twenty-five minutes. Fill and cover with Lady Baltimore filling and frosting.*

### *Filling and Frosting*

*3 cupfuls granulated sugar*
*1 cupful boiling water*
*Whites of 3 eggs*
*1 1/2 cupfuls quartered raisins*
*1/2 cupful chopped figs*
*1/2 cupful chopped nut meats*

*Boil the sugar and water together until they thread—if using a candy thermometer cook to 230 degrees. Pour over the whites of eggs, which have been beaten until stiff, and beat until cool. Add the raisins, figs, and nut meats and use both as filling and frosting.*

### ⌘ 309. MARSHMALLOW MOULD ⌘

*(Morphy, c. 1936)*

Marshmallows featured in numerous recipes during the 1920s and 1930s. They were served in molded salads, on top of sweet potato casserole, or in desserts such as the following.

*This is made with half a pint of stiff whipped cream, flavoured with vanilla, sugar and a little fruit syrup, to which is added 6 ozs. of chopped marshmallows, 12 chopped walnuts, a few cherries in brandy or in maraschino [a liqueur made from marasca cherries], and the whole is put into a mould and well iced. When turned out, it can be decorated with more cherries and chopped marshmallows.*

### ⌘ 310. MERINGUES ⌘

*(Mosser, 1939)*

Meringues became trendy in the 1920s, when they were baked as small cookies, placed on top of pies, and set drifting as floating islands in a sea of cream sauce.

*4 egg whites*
*1 1/2 cups sugar*
*1/2 teaspoon cream of tartar*
*3/4 teaspoon vanilla*

*Beat egg whites until dry [stiff]; gradually beat in sugar, cream of tartar and vanilla. With a spoon shape in mounds on ungreased [parchment] paper-covered baking sheet. Bake in a slow oven about 60 minutes. Remove from paper with spatula while still warm.*

### ⌘ 311. SNAP-DOODLE CAKES ⌘

*(Weingart, 1930s)*[5]

The following recipe is likely a cake variation of the snickerdoodle, a cookie that was wildly popular in nineteenth-century New England. Like the snickerdoodle, the snap-doodle is topped with cinnamon.

*1/4 cup butter*
*1 egg, beaten*

*1/2 cup milk*
*2 1/2 teaspoons baking powder*
*1/2 cup sugar*
*1/4 teaspoon salt*
*1 1/2 cups flour*
*1/2 teaspoon vanilla*
*2/3 cup brown sugar*

*Cream butter and add half the sugar gradually. Add remaining sugar to egg. Combine mixtures. Mix and sift flour, baking powder and salt. Add alternately with milk to first mixture; add vanilla.*

*Pour into greased pie plate and sprinkle 2/3 cup of brown sugar over top. See that it is well covered. Dash cinnamon lightly over the brown sugar, using not more than one-half teaspoonful. Bake thirty minutes at 350° F.*

## PRESERVES

### ◄ 312. GRAPE JELLY ►

*(Dull, 1928)*

Although grape is one of the most popular jelly varieties on the market today, it did not become a common item in the American kitchen until the early twentieth century.

*Select grapes that are not too ripe, part green ones are preferable. Wash before pulling from stem. Place in porcelain kettle, just cover with water, boil until tender and broken which allows juices to flow. Drain juice and boil to reduce one-third or one-half. Measure using 1 cup juice to 1 cup sugar. Bring juice to hard boil, add sugar and cook until it jellies or flakes. Pour into hot, sterilized glasses. When cool cover with paraffin.*

*If grapes have many green ones, one-third reduction of juice will be sufficient.*

### ◄ 313. SCUPPERNONG JAM ►

*(Colquitt, 1933)*

Native to the southeastern United States, the thick-skinned scuppernong is a variety of the muscadine grape. In addition to being made into jam, it is also turned into wine.

*Pop the pulp out of the skins, says the very descriptive old receipt—and, in case you don't know just what that means, try squeezing a scuppernong and you will soon find out. Place skins in a vessel and cover with water, and let simmer until tender. Put pulps in another vessel and cook slowly until seeds separate, then put through colander to remove seeds. Put skins and pulp together, and allow three-quarters pound of sugar to one pound of fruit, and cook until thick. A most excellent accompaniment for meats, and a grand substitute for mince pie!*

### ❧ 314. PEAR AND BLUEBERRY PRESERVES ☙

*(Estes, 1911)*

Native to America, blueberries did not become widely available until the early twentieth century, when they were domesticated. Although native to Asia, pears have played a larger role in the history of American cookery. They have long been dried, made into preserves, baked in pies, and even turned into pear cider, or perry.

*Pick over and wash two quarts of blueberries, add water to nearly cover and stew them half hour. Mash them well, when all are broken turn into a bowl covered with cheese cloth. Drain well and when cool squeeze out all the juice. Put the blueberry juice on to boil, add one pint of sugar to each pint of juice and remove all scum. Allow one quart of sliced pears to one pint of juice. Use hard pears not suitable for canning. Cook them in the syrup, turning over often and when soft and transparent skim them out into the jars. Boil down the syrup and strain over the fruit. Fill to overflowing and seal.*

❧ ☙

# ☙ SUGGESTED MENUS

1. 1840–1875
   ### Modest Breakfast

   Hash (recipe 14)
   Coffee

   ### Moderate Breakfast

   Fish Cakes (recipe 41), Baked Beans (recipe 69)
   Omelette (recipe 74), Buckwheat Cakes (recipe 85)
   Coffee

   ### Economical Dinner

   Baked Beans (recipe 69)
   Baked Indian Pudding (recipe 101)

   ### Moderate Dinner

   Ox-Tail Soup (recipe 8)
   Roast Goose (recipe 38), Apple Sauce (recipe 54), Potatoes (recipe 63),
   Sweet Potatoes (recipe 65), Lamb Fry (recipe 20), Onions (recipe 60)
   Brandy Peaches (recipe 123), Floating Island (recipe 114)

## Dinner Party

Green Pea Soup (recipe 9), Boiled Rockfish (recipe 45) with Egg Sauce (recipe 55), Fried Parsley (recipe 61), Stewed Tomatoes (recipe 67)
Shoulder of Mutton (recipe 23), Roast Duck (recipe 38), Greens (recipe 58), Turnips (recipe 68), Macaroni (recipe 73)
Peach Pie (recipe 95), Charlotte Russe (recipe 113), Lady Cake (recipe 111), Vanilla Ice Cream (recipe 118)
Coffee, Stilton, and Cheddar Cheese

## Modest Supper

Irish Stew (recipe 7) or Dried Bean Soup (recipe 1); Potato Bread (recipe 83)

## Light Moderate Supper

Omelette (recipe 74) or Ham Sandwich (recipe 77) or Beef Olives (recipe 15)
Fruit Fritters (recipe 105) or Apple Dumplings (recipe 102) or Bread Pudding (recipe 99)

## 2. 1876–1910

### Economical Breakfast

Oatmeal (recipe 198)
Rye Muffins (recipe 205)
Coffee

### Hearty Winter Breakfast

Beefsteak (recipe 137), Sausage (recipe 147)
Saratoga Potatoes (recipe 179), Kentucky Corn Dodgers (recipe 204)
Coffee, tea, chocolate

### Picnic Fruit Lunch

Deviled Eggs (recipe 192)
Club Sandwiches (recipe 199), Saratoga Potatoes (recipe 179)
Cream Puffs (recipe 219), Fruit

### Economical Lunch

Cold Meat (recipe 135) or Irish Potato Soup (recipe 133), Buckeye Brown Bread (recipe 201)

## Moderate Lunch

Curried Eggs (recipe 193), Maryland Beat Biscuits (recipe 202), Broiled
Tomatoes (recipe 182)
Raspberries and Cream
Tea

## Economical Dinner

Codfish Balls (recipe 156)
Buckeye Brown Bread (recipe 201)
Tea

## Moderate Dinner

Grapefruit
Roasted Lamb (recipe 142), Baked Potatoes (recipe 177), Broiled Toma-
toes (recipe 182), Asparagus à la Hollandaise (recipes 173 and 168)
Camembert, Water Crackers
Coffee

3. 1911–1945

### Modest Breakfast

Hasty Bran Bread (recipe 299), Grape Jelly (recipe 312)
Tea

### Moderate Breakfast

Orange Juice
Fried Ham (recipe 249), Grits (recipe 287)
Coffee

### Modest Lunch

Western Sandwich (recipe 295) or Chop Suey (recipe 238)
Tea

### Light Lunch

Welsh Rarebit (recipe 294), Parker House Rolls (recipe 300)
Meringues (recipe 310)
Cocoa

### Moderate Lunch

Purée Mongole (recipe 236)

---

### → THE WORKER'S LUNCH BOX (ROBINSON, 1913)

*[A lunch provided for] the out-of-door or manual worker [should consist of] heavier, bulkier and more nutritious food, such as baked bean sandwiches, meats of all kinds, cheese, raw and in the form of rarebits, and fondue for sandwich filling; eggs, hard cooked, fried or salad; small cans of sardines, doughnuts; cookies, especially oatmeal; gingerbread, cinnamon rolls, etc.... For one of sedentary occupation a light and digestible but very nutritious lunch should be provided. Among these may be mentioned meat sandwiches in which the meat is ground, mixed with light relishes and salad dressing; egg sandwiches or salad or hard cooked eggs, cream cheese mixed with chopped olives and pimentoes [sic], chopped fruit and nut sandwiches, light cookies and sweets, with nuts and fruit.*

---

Lobster Newburg (recipe 261), Glazed Carrots (recipe 271)
Angel Cake (recipe 306)

## Economical Dinner

Bean Loaf (recipe 286)
Baked Canned Peaches (recipe 303)
Tea

## Moderate Year-Round Dinner

Chicken Mushroom Soup (recipe 230)
Meat Loaf (recipe 240), Mashed Potatoes (recipe 274), Spinach
(recipe 276)
Baked Canned Peaches (recipe 303), Marshmallow Mould (recipe 309)

## Moderate Summer Dinner

Cantaloupe
Fried Chicken (recipe 258), Cheese Biscuits (recipe 296), Stewed Corn
(recipe 272), Mashed Potatoes (recipe 274), Sliced Tomatoes
Pecan Pie (recipe 304)
Iced Tea

# ⟡ NOTES

## 1. 1840–1875

1. Ketchup appears variably as catsup and catchup in the following recipes, which maintain the original spelling, grammar, and punctuation. Catsup was the preferred spelling in nineteenth-century American cookbooks, although ketchup (today's preferred spelling) and catchup are used on occasion.

## 3. 1911–1945

A handful of the recipes included in this chapter have been selected from family recipe files rather than published cookbooks. Each of the recipes chosen was passed down matrilineally, as are most family recipes. The lineage of each of these recipes is listed in the following notes.

1. The lineage of the Virginia ham recipe: Sedlak, recipe from Marie Sedlak, born Hudak. Passed down through granddaughters, Alena Sedlak Lynch and Andrea Sedlak to greatgranddaughter Cheryl Marie Sedlak Seaver.
2. The lineage of the baked zucchini recipe: Weingart, recipe from Ivy Weingart, born Jensen. Passed down through daughter Ellen Weiss Weingart to granddaughter Margot Weiss.
3. The lineage of the blintz recipe: Weiss, recipe from Rose Weiss, born Grebler. Passed down through daughter-in-law Sara Weiss, born Schneiweis, to granddaughter-in-law Ellen Weiss to greatgranddaughter Margot Weiss.

4. The lineage of the apple crisp recipe: Weingart, recipe from Ivy Weingart, born Jensen. Passed down through daughter Ellen Weiss Weingart to granddaughter Margot Weiss.
5 The lineage of the snap-doodle cake recipe: see previous note.

# ✒ BIBLIOGRAPHY

## Cookbooks

In the nineteenth century, numerous editions of a cookbook were often printed at breakneck speed. Because many of the cookbooks included in this list were national bestsellers, the particular edition listed is typically one of many. For example, more than 40 editions of Eliza Leslie's *Directions for Cookery* were published within 14 years of its original publication in 1837. Because first editions tend to be the rarest, those listed here are not necessarily from the first printing. Versions of many of the following nineteenth-century cookbooks can be viewed online at the Feeding America website listed in the Select Websites section.

Allen, Ann. *The Housekeeper's Assistant.* Boston: J. Munroe, 1845.

Allen, Ida Bailey. *Ida Bailey Allen's Modern Cook Book.* Garden City, New York: Doubleday, 1924.

An American Lady. *The American Home Cook Book.* New York: Dick and Fitzgerald, 1854.

"Aunt Babette." *"Aunt Babette's" Cook Book.* Cincinnati: Bloch Publishing and Printing Co., c. 1889.

Beecher, Catharine E. *Miss Beecher's Domestic Receipt-Book.* New York: Harper & Brothers, 1858.

"Mrs. Bliss." *Practical Cook Book.* Philadelphia, Lippincott, Grambo, & Co., 1864.

Bosse, Sara. *Chinese—Japanese Cook Book*. Chicago: Rand McNally, c. 1914.

Bryan, Lettice. *Kentucky Housewife*. Cincinnati: Shepard & Stearns, 1839.

Burr, Hattie A. *The Woman Suffrage Cook Book*. Boston: Hattie A. Burr, c. 1886.

California Women. *Los Angeles Times. The Times Cook Book, No. 2*. Los Angeles: Times-Mirror Co., 1905.

Callahan, Genevieve. *Sunset All-Western Cook Book*. Stanford: Stanford University Press, 1933.

Campbell, Tunis Gulic. *Hotel Keepers, Head Waiters, and Housekeepers' Guide*. Boston: Coolidge and Wiley, 1848.

Child, Lydia Maria. *The American Frugal Housewife*. Boston: Carter, Hendee, and Co., 1833.

Collins, Angelina Maria. *The Great Western Cook Book*. New York: A. S. Barnes & Company, 1857.

Colquitt, Harriet Ross. *The Savannah Cook Book*. New York: J. J. Little, 1933.

Corson, Juliet. *Practical American Cookery and Household Management*. New Orleans: F. F. Hansell & Bro., Ltd., 1885.

Curtis, Isabel Gordon. *Good Housekeeping Everyday Cook Book*. New York: Phelps Publishing Co., 1903.

Dull, S. R. *Southern Cooking*. Atlanta: Ruralist Press, 1928.

Edwords, Clarence E. *Bohemian San Francisco*. San Francisco: Paul Elder & Co, 1914.

Ellet, Elizabeth Fries. *New Cyclopaedia of Domestic Economy, and Practical Housekeeper*. Norwich: Henry Bill, 1871.

Ellsworth, Mary Grosvenor. *Much Depends on Dinner*. New York: Knopf, 1939.

Estes, Rufus. *Good Things to Eat As Suggested by Rufus*. Chicago: Rufus Estes, 1911.

Farmer, Fannie. *The Boston Cooking-School Cook Book*. Boston: Little, Brown and Company, 1896.

Federal Writers' Project. *Florida Seafood Cookery*. Tallahassee: State of Florida Department of Agriculture, Bulletin No. 119, February 1944.

Fisher, Abby. *What Mrs. Fisher Knows About Old Southern Cooking*. San Francisco: Women's Co-Operative Printing Office, 1881.

Fox, Minerva Carr. *The Blue Grass Cook Book*. New York: Fox, Duffield & Company, 1904.

Gillette, F. L. *White House Cook Book*. Chicago: R. S. Peale & Co., 1887.

Hale, Sarah Josepha Buell. *The Ladies' New Book of Cookery*. New York: H. Long & Brother, 1852.

———. *The Good Housekeeper*. Boston: Otis, Broaders, & Co. 1841.

Hall, Elizabeth M. *Practical American Cookery and Domestic Economy.* New York: Saxton, Barker, & Co., 1855.

Harland, Marion (Mary Virginia Terhune). *Common Sense in the Household.* New York: C. Scribner & Co., 1871.

Harris, Frances, Barber. *Florida Salads.* Jacksonville: Jacksonville Printing Co., 1918.

Hearn, Lafcadio. *La Cuisine Creole: A Collection of Culinary Recipes from Leading Chefs and Noted Creole Housewives.* New Orleans: F. F. Hansell & Bro., Ltd., c. 1885.

Hill, Anabella P. *Mrs. Hill's New Cook Book.* New York: Carleton, 1867.

Home Institute of *The New York Herald Tribune. America's Cook Book.* New York: Charles Scribner's Sons, 1938.

Howland, Esther Allen. *The New England Economical Housekeeper.* Cincinnati: H. W. Derby, 1845.

Kander, Lizzie Black, and Fannie Greenbaum Schoenfeld. *The Settlement Cook Book.* Milwaukee: Milwaukee Settlement House, 1903.

Ladies Association of the First Presbyterian Church. *The First Texas Cook Book.* Houston: Ladies Association of the First Presbyterian Church, 1883.

Ladies of the First Presbyterian Church. *The Presbyterian Cook Book.* Dayton: Crooke & Co., 1873.

Lea, Elizabeth E. *Domestic Cookery.* Baltimore: Cushings and Bailey, 1873.

LeClercq, Ann Sinkler Whaley. *An Antebellum Plantation Household Including the South Carolina and Low Country Receipts and Remedies of Emily Wharton Sinkler.* Columbia: University of South Carolina Press, 1996.

Leslie, Eliza. *Miss Leslie's Directions for Cookery.* Philadelphia: Henry Carey Baird, 1851.

Levy, Esther. *Jewish Cookery Book.* Philadelphia: W. S. Turner, 1871.

MacPherson, John. *The Mystery Chef's Own Cook Book.* New York: Longmans, 1935.

Moody, William Vaughn. *Mrs. William Vaughn Moody's Cook-Book.* New York: Scribner's Sons. 1931.

Morphy, Countess Marcella. *Recipes of All Nations.* Rochester, Kent: Herbert-Joseph, c. 1936.

Mosser, Marjorie. *Good Maine Food.* New York: Doubleday, 1939.

Parkinson, Eleanor. *Complete Confectioner.* Philadelphia: J. B. Lippincott, 1864.

Parloa, Maria. *Mrs. Parloa's New Cook Book.* Boston: Estes and Lauriat, 1880.

Pinedo, Encarnación. *Encarnación's Kitchen.* Selections from Encarnación Pinedo's 1898 *El Cocinero Español.* (Tr.) Dan Strehl. Berkeley: University of California Press, 2003.

Platt, June. *June Platt's Plain and Fancy Cookbook*. Boston: Houghton Mifflin, 1941.

Portland, Oregon Council Of Jewish Women. *The Neighborhood Cook Book*. Portland: Press of Bushong & Co., 1914.

Randolph, Mary. *The Virginia Housewife*. Philadelphia: E. H. Butler & Co., 1860.

Robinson, Eva Roberta and Helen Gunn Hammell. *Lessons in Home Cooking Through Preparation of Meals*. Chicago: American School of Home Economics, 1913.

Rorer, Sarah Tyson. *Mrs. Rorer's New Cook Book*. Philadelphia: Arnold & Co, 1898.

Rutledge, Sarah. *Carolina Housewife*. Charleston. W. R. Babcock & Co., 1847.

St. Andrews Guild, Spokane, Washington. *Favorite Recipes: St. Andrews Episcopal Church*. Kansas City: North American Press, c. 1944.

Sanderson, J. M. *Complete Cook*. Philadelphia: J. B. Lippincott, 1864.

Shay, Frank. *The Best Men Are Cooks*. New York: Coward-McCann, 1941.

Shuman, Carrie V. *Favorite Dishes*. Chicago: R. R. Donnelley & Sons Co., Printers, 1893.

Smith, Grace and Beverly and Charles Morrow Wilson. *Through the Kitchen Door*. Harrisburg: Telegraph Press, 1938.

Spaulding, Lily May, and John Spaulding, eds. *Civil War Recipes: Receipts from the Pages of Godey's Lady's Book*. Lexington: University Press of Kentucky, 1999.

Tyree, Marion Fontaine Cabell. *Housekeeping in Old Virginia: Containing Contributions From Two Hundred and Fifty of Virginia's Noted Housewives*. Louisville: John P. Morton & Co., 1879.

Webster, A. L. *The Improved Housewife*. Hartford: Ira Webster, 1853.

Winn-Smith, Alice. *Thrifty Cooking for Wartime*. New York: Macmillan, 1942.

Women of the First Congregational Church, Marysville, Ohio. *Buckeye Cookbook*. (Comp.) Estelle Woods Wilcox. Marysville: J. H. Shearer and Son, 1876.

Wright, Helen S. *The New England Cook Book*. New York: Duffield, 1912.

## Select Historical Resources

Anderson, Jean. *The American Century Cookbook: The Most Popular Recipes of the 20th Century*. New York: Random House, 1997.

DuSablon, Mary Anna. *America's Collectible Cookbooks: The History, the Politics, the Recipes*. Athens: Ohio University Press, 1994.

Haber, Barbara. *From Hardtack to Home Fries: An Uncommon History of American Cooks and Meals*. New York: Free Press, 2002.

Hess, John and Karen. *The Taste of America*. Chicago: Illinois University Press, 2000.

Hooker, Richard J. A *History of Food and Drink in America*. Indianapolis: Bobs-Merrill, 1981.

Jones, Evan. *American Food: The Gastronomic Story*. New York: Vintage, 1981.

Levenstein, Harvey. *Paradox of Plenty: A Social History of Eating in America*. New York: Oxford University Press, 1993.

Levenstein, Harvey. *Revolution at the Table: The Transformation of the American Diet*. Berkeley: University of California Press, 2003.

Lovegren, Sylvia. *Fashionable Food: Seven Decades of Food Fads*. New York: MacMillan, 1995.

McFeely, Mary Drake. *Can She Bake a Cherry Pie? American Women and the Kitchen in the Twentieth Century*. Amherst: University of Massachusetts Press, 2000.

Plante, Ellen M. *The American Kitchen 1700 to the Present*. New York: Facts on File, 1995.

Schenone, Laura. *A Thousand Years Over a Hot Stove: A History of American Women Told Through Food, Recipes, and Remembrances*. New York: W. W. Norton, 2003.

Shapiro, Laura. *Perfection Salad: Women and Cooking at the Turn of the Century*. New York: North Point. 1995.

Smith Andrew, ed. *Oxford Encyclopedia of American Food and Drink*. New York: Oxford University Press, 2004.

Williams, Susan. *Savory Suppers and Fashionable Feasts: Dining in Victorian America*. New York: Pantheon, 1985.

## Select Web Sites

Culinary History: Research Guides. Contains a menu collection along with selective lists of dictionaries, encyclopedias, sources on the history of food, and historical editions of texts. http://www.nypl.org/research/chss/grd/resguides/culinary/.

Feeding America: The Historic American Cookbook Project. Contains a digital library of historic cookbooks. http://digital.lib.msu.edu/projects/cookbooks/html.

*Food History News.* Contains links to food history resources, a guide to food and drink museums, a calendar of upcoming events, a selection of historic recipes, and several other food-related items of interest. http://foodhistorynews.com/.

History and Legends of America's Favorite Foods. http://www.whatscooking america.net/History.

# ⚓ INDEX

**About the Author**

ALICE L. McLEAN is Honors Postdoctoral Fellow at Sweet Briar College.